The Unfortunate Colonel Despard, And Other Studies

BURT FRANKLIN RESEARCH & SOURCE WORKS SERIES #142
(Selected Essays in History & Social Science Series #5)

THE UNFORTUNATE COLONEL DESPARD AND OTHER STUDIES

THE UNFORTUNATE COLONEL DESPARD

AND OTHER STUDIES

BY

SIR CHARLES OMAN

BURT FRANKLIN RESEARCH & SOURCE WORKS SERIES #142
(Selected Essays in History & Social Science Series #5)

BURT FRANKLIN
NEW YORK

Published By
BURT FRANKLIN
235 East 44th St.
New York, N.Y. 10017

ORIGINALLY PUBLISHED
LONDON: 1922

Printed in U.S.A.

PREFACE

I have from time to time been asked by friends to make more accessible one or other of the eleven essays, or studies, which have now been collected into this volume. I may mention that six of them have appeared as articles in various magazines or reviews, three were addresses given to the Royal Historical Society, one was a lecture given at Cologne to classes from the Rhineland Army of Occupation, the eleventh is an unpublished study written last summer.

I have to make grateful acknowledgement of the courtesy of the proprietors of *Blackwood's Magazine*, *The Edinburgh Review*, *The Nineteenth Century and After*, and *The Economic Review*, all of whom have permitted me to reprint certain papers which I contributed to their periodicals. From *Blackwood* come the essays on Colonel Despard, Arthur Thistlewood, and the Earthly Paradise; from *The Edinburgh Review*, the study of Lord Carteret; from *The Nineteenth Century*, the article on the Trials of the Historian; and from *The Economic Review*, the note on the Debasement of the English Currency by the Tudors. The Council of the Royal Historical Society also permit me to reproduce the three Presidential Addresses which I made to them in 1918–20 on Rumour in Time of War, the Historical Outlook of the Middle Ages, and the Drawing of Boundaries.

Those of the essays which appeared some years back have had to suffer a certain amount of alteration; the Great War caused much change of historical perspective; and the article on Henry VIII and his strange dealings with the currency had to be rewritten, in view of the fact that the Chancellor of the Exchequer of the late Coalition Ministry—first of all modern English statesmen—dared to follow in the steps of the Tudor king, and to present us with shillings exactly like those of 1545 in being composed of 50 per cent. silver and 50 per cent. base metal.

C. OMAN.

OXFORD,
    November, 1922.

CONTENTS

THE UNFORTUNATE COLONEL DESPARD

I was one of the very few non-official spectators at the trial
of Roger Casement. For long hours I watched the swarthy,
sinister, yet not ill-favoured man in the dock, in his neat grey
morning suit, following every word of the pleadings with an
intent ear and a keen eye.

Here, on trial for his life, was a man who had for a quarter
of a century been in the service of the sovereign of Great
Britain, who had been given high official posts, trusted with
grave international inquiries, and honoured with the knight-
hood of St. Michael and St. George. Yet he had bitten the
hand that had fed him, betrayed the King whose honours he had
accepted but two years back, continued to draw his pension
when he was already intriguing with the public enemy, and
stooped to endeavours to seduce poor half-starved soldiers in
German prison-camps to break their military oath. It was a
vile record, and only explicable to those who have heard his
full tale, of which I say nothing. Surely this traitor's case is
unparalleled—I found myself thinking—at least since the
old Jacobite days, when allegiance sat light on unscrupulous
men. For the Irish treason trials from 1797 onwards have
nothing like it ; the United Irishmen and the Fenians were not
led by renegade British officials of high rank, but by adventurers like Wolfe Tone, Jacobin enthusiasts like Edward Fitz-
gerald, idealists and dreamers like Robert Emmet, village
priests and town tradesmen, with a sprinkling of small squireens.
And the Dublin rebel chiefs of 1916, who faced the firing party
before Casement went to the gallows, were men of the same
type as their predecessors. None of them had eaten the King's
bread for half a lifetime, or accepted a title and a pension from
his hand.

And then there came to me in the court, while the defendant's

counsel droned on with his unconvincing arguments, the memory
of the one modern case of a man whose record was almost
parallel to that of Casement, yet whose story is utterly forgotten. Histories of the great French War barely mention it,
or mention it not at all. I allude to the traitor whom his
contemporaries sometimes called "the unfortunate Colonel
Despard." A moment's reflection showed the most extraordinary similarity between the external aspects of his tale
and that of Casement. Both were Irishmen of good family ;
both entered the King's service early, and won rank and distinction therein. Both were trusted with high and responsible
posts—and both held those posts in the Tropics. Does twenty
years in authority spent in Jamaica and British Honduras, or
in the Cameroons and Brazil, lead to megalomania, or merely
to relaxation of the moral fibre, with men of a certain type ?
This much is certain, that both Despard, the petty despot of
Belize, and Casement, Consul-General at Rio de Janeiro, came
back when their colonial career was over, to engage in wild
treason in Europe. Despard, as we shall see, had far more
open provocation for his misdoings. But he ended, like
Casement, in being convicted for seducing British soldiers from
their allegiance, and went to the gallows with some of his dupes.

So it may be worth while to tell the tale of Colonel Edward
Marcus Despard and his treasons. He was born in Queen's
County in 1751, one of the many sons of a typical Irish soldier-
family of the old sort. All his five brothers, save the eldest, to
whom fell the family estate, held commissions in the army ; and
one of them, General John Despard, was a man of mark, who
commanded in Cape Breton for eight years, and died honorary
colonel of a West India Regiment in 1829. Edward, like most
lads destined for the army in those days, started on his military
career very early, obtaining an ensigncy in the 50th Regiment
in 1766, when he was only fifteen. He served with the 50th
for seven years, and got his lieutenancy in 1772, when the corps
was stationed in Jamaica. Here they were found at the outbreak of the War of American Independence in 1775 ; but the
50th was so much under strength, after three years of tropical
diseases, that it could not be sent as a unit to join the army of
Howe. The serviceable men were drafted into battalions

ordered to the front, and a skeleton cadre only was sent
back to England to recruit. With it Despard did not sail.
He had been seconded for special duty as an assistant engineer
on the staff of the Governor of Jamaica.   There can have
been few British officers who did such a continuous term of
service in the Caribbean Sea as Edward Despard, for between
1772 and 1790 he seems to have been in England only for
one visit. Another point to realize, when we try to fix his
mentality, is that from the age of twenty-two onward he
never served with his battalion. As a junior staff officer he
was employed on all manner of small independent jobs, far
from any supervising and immediate authority. Entrusted
from the age of thirty onward with command, first on a small,
and then on a larger scale, where no one could appeal to
authority against his arbitrary rule without intolerable delays,
he lost any idea of obedience that he may have imbibed
during his years of service as a very young ensign and lieutenant.

Though stationed in the West Indies during the whole
of the Great War with France and America, Despard only
saw service against the brown militia of the Spanish Main.
In 1779 he smelt powder for the first time in one of those
nightmare expeditions to which British statesmen, who used
small-scale maps of America, frequently condemned a handful
of British soldiers. This was the absolutely insane San
Juan raid, which would be completely forgotten but for
the fact that one of the very few officers who returned from
it alive was Captain Horatio Nelson of H.M.S. *Hinchinbrooke*,
later of the Nile and Trafalgar. Lord George Germaine, the
Secretary for War, of evil Minden memory, concluded that
as Central America was an isthmus, the strip of land, which
looked narrow enough on the map of the world, between the
mouth of the San Juan river on the Atlantic side and the
town of Leon on the Pacific, might be seized and held, and
the Spanish empire in America cut in twain. The distance
from ocean to ocean was 150 miles as the crow flies, much
more by the route which Nelson's expedition was to take.
The force employed was absurdly small—400 regular troops,
white and black, from Jamaica, any seamen that could be
spared from the crew of Nelson's frigate, a few scores of boatmen

from the small British settlement on the Honduras coast. It was vaguely hoped that a multitude of savage auxiliaries could be enlisted from the Mosquito Indians of the Nicaraguan shore. Everything, of course, went wrong; only a handful of Indians could be collected, the boats and boatmen from the Honduras settlement were three weeks late. The soldiers were beginning to sicken before the flotilla started; no single soul on the expedition knew how far the San Juan river was navigable. But Nelson's will was there to drive. The little force started up-stream. Ten days they laboured in the sweltering heat, and then found that the river would serve them no more. Many men could no longer march, but the survivors pressed through the jungle for two days, and discovered the fort of San Juan, the central guard-post of the isthmus, which lay some miles below the great lake of Nicaragua. The Spanish governor shut himself up and offered a passive resistance only; the fort on its rock seemed impregnable. Nelson's men were dying like flies, but he persisted; a gun or two was dragged up from the portage where the boats had been left, and a feeble cannonade opened. Nelson himself and Despard were almost the only officers left fit for service by this time; "almost every gun that was fired was laid by one or other of them." Twenty-three years later, when the former commander of the *Hinchinbrooke* appeared to give evidence at his sometime comrade's trial, he spoke up most vehemently as to Despard's gallantry and exertions. "We went to the Spanish Main together; we slept many nights together in our clothes upon the ground; we measured the height of the enemies' wall together; in all that period no man could have shown more zealous attachment to his Sovereign and his country than he did."

After six days' ineffective bombardment the garrison of San Juan capitulated; not from the results of Nelson's gunnery, but because their water supply had been cut off. The capture of the fort did not help the expedition to any further advance—there was nobody left fit to march, and the situation was not helped by the arrival of a few hundred reinforcements sent by the Governor of Jamaica. The rainy season was now come, and men sickened as soon as they

arrived. Finally the fever conquered : the relics of the
expeditionary force returned to Jamaica.

Nelson came back a wreck—it was a wonder that his slight
frame had withstood those dreadful months ; he was invalided
home, and well-nigh died at Bath. Despard, unluckily for
himself, took little harm from the experience. His creditable
service was acknowledged by his promotion to a captaincy
in the 79th Regiment—not the Highland corps of to-day,
but the "Liverpool Blues," a short-lived battalion raised
in 1778 and disbanded in 1784. Despard never joined it,
or did duty as a regimental officer. If, like Nelson, he had
been invalided home in 1788, and transferred to some other
sphere of war, far from the West Indies, he might have died
a loyal soldier.

Next year he was given a very responsible charge. The
majority of the British settlers—log-wood cutters for the
most part—who plied their trade on the coast of Honduras
or on the Mosquito shore, had been forced to retire to the island
of Roatan, which lies some ten miles off the mainland. It
was a convenient port of call for privateers, and a small garrison
was kept there, supplied from Jamaica. Hither Despard
was sent with a temporary commission as Lieutenant-
Colonel.

It is now that we find Despard showing the first signs
of the want of sense of discipline which was to be his ruin.
On arriving at Cape Gracias a Dios, the angle of the coast
from which Honduras slopes away west and Nicaragua south,
he found there his superior officer, a Colonel Hodgson, who
was theoretically in charge of all the surviving British settlements on the Central American coast. Despard's biographer,
Bannatyne, passes over what then happened in the most
matter-of-fact way, as if it presented no special cause of surprise.
"On arriving, he found His Majesty's service likely to be
injured by the appointment of Colonel H—— to chief command. This officer was so obnoxious to the inhabitants
that they refused to serve under him, and at the same time
presented a unanimous address to Colonel D—— offering
to put themselves under his command. To prevent the
colony from being lost to the crown, he accepted their offer,

and assumed the command." Hodgson had to depart to Jamaica. His successor—whose rise to authority reminds one of the simple methods in vogue among the buccaneers who haunted this same coast a century before—though technically only Governor of Roatan, assumed charge of the whole region. He justified his lawless action by success ; for he organized an expedition which captured the Spanish fort upon the Rio Negro, the main hostile establishment in the neighbourhood, and with the aid of the Mosquito Indians he dominated the whole shore as far south as the San Juan river.

So in 1783, when the Treaty of Versailles was signed, and Great Britain was forced to accept the terms imposed on her by France, Spain and the Americans, she had, thanks to Despard, some pledges left to barter with in Central America. Much had to be given up—the Rio Negro Fort, the Isle of Roatan, and all the trading posts south from Cape Gracias a Dios. But she was left " the Bay of Honduras Settlement," as it was then called, what we now style the colony of British Honduras. Despard was given the delicate and difficult task of administering the colony, with the modest title of " Superintendent of His Majesty's Affairs within the district which, by the late Treaty of Peace, has been allotted to the Log-Cutters upon the Bay of Honduras," and the still more modest salary of £500 a year. He was left in an absolutely autocratic position, without any colleagues or council, and he administered the settlement with no official staff save his admiring secretary and biographer, James Bannatyne. The only appeal from him was primarily to the Governor of Jamaica, and, in a last resort, to the Secretary of State in Whitehall.

For seven years Despard ruled British Honduras, in one constant round of disputes and protests. The Spaniards were not his main trouble, though occasionally they made attempts to enforce the exact terms of the treaty of 1783 by violence. The real trouble of the Superintendent came from the British settlers. There were two groups of them always at feud. The one consisted of the 700 original inhabitants of the " Bay Settlement," the small log-cutting and trading community which had always been established there.

The other was formed by the expelled adventurers from the Mosquito Coast, Roatan, and the other points which had been given up to the Spaniards. Many of them had served in the more or less irregular bands which Despard had led as "Provincials," in the San Juan expedition and the capture of the Rio Negro forts. They were a pugnacious and self-assertive crew, and were the Superintendent's old friends, who had aided him to expel Hodgson. Now, when a group of new settlers falls in among an already existing community of a similar class, which has established rights, trouble is sure to follow. The exiles outnumbered the original colonists—there were 2,000 of them, counting their negro slaves and dependents.

There was no doubt ample room in the settlement for everybody; but the old inhabitants had partitioned off the more eligible tracts, near the rivers and round the settlements, into spheres of interest which they had been accustomed to exploit. Wherever the Mosquito Coast men ran up their huts and began to fell timber, they were—so they said—warned off as trespassers on the beat of some claimant who had often not been seen near the spot for years. Hence affrays and litigation. And the Superintendent, acting as court of appeal with some accessors selected by himself, always sided with the new settlers. This drove the "original inhabitants" to angry protest, and Despard did not tolerate criticism.

Looking through the tedious archives of British Honduras in the Record Office, one soon discovers the way things worked. Mr. James Usher, one of the magistrates, resigns, and justifies himself by an "Address to the Inhabitants" which ends—"Should I advance that the Court of Appeal is illegal, oppressive and unjust, that Trial by Jury is thereby done away, and that decisions made when there is not a full board are entirely the Superintendent's decrees, I shall, I suppose, be prosecuted. If the smiles of power are to be obtained by no other method than cringing, creeping and fawning, let those court them who will; for from my own knowledge of the Superintendent's former opinion of his present favourites, I do not hesitate to say that now 'the Post of Honour is a

private station!'" Usher was right in supposing that he
would be prosecuted : he was arrested by Despard and charged
with publishing " a false, seditious and malicious libel, evidence
of a depraved mind and a diabolical disposition." But the
Grand Jury of the Colony was full of "old inhabitants "—
they were the wealthier part of the community—and " ignored
the bill" : I have seen their *Ignoramus* scrawled across it.
Enraged at Usher's escape, Despard on his own authority
declared all the police and judicial institutes of the Colony
cancelled and abolished. After an interval of autocratic
rule he held a poll for a new bench of magistrates, and struck
out on technical grounds some of the persons returned. His
opponents wrote fierce protests to Jamaica and Whitehall
against " the barbarous commanding officer on the Honduras
Coast."

The desks and waste-paper baskets, both of the Governor
of Jamaica and the Secretary of State at Whitehall, grew all
too familiar with petitions and appeals, and lengthy replies
by the King's Superintendent. Apparently these distant
potentates shelved the question again and again : it was
a "tale of little meaning though the words were strong!"
But at last a new Secretary arose in Whitehall, Lord Grenville,
a stiff and untiring man who, unlike his predecessor, was
one of those who read his American dispatches—as had his
unfortunate father, George Grenville, in 1765. He came
to the conclusion that there must be something wrong in
the Bay Settlement, and, without relieving Despard from
office, told him to come home, as investigations into his rule
were about to be made. The King's Superintendent sailed
at once, and reached London in May, 1790. His biographer
tells us that he was well provided with documents proving
the popularity which he enjoyed with the " vast majority "
of the inhabitants of the Colony—*i.e.* the new settlers—and
that he wished for nothing so much as a public inquiry into
his whole conduct since first he took command at Roatan
in 1781. He was not to get it. Instead he found himself
entangled in the meshes of red tape. For two years he was
having interviews with under-secretaries, answering interro-
gatories, drawing up minutes in defence of particular acts.

With constant references to Jamaica and Belize, the matter dragged on interminably. Despard became one of the regular hangers-on in the ante-room of the Secretary of State, always awaiting an ever-deferred decision. It came at last, after two long years, and was most unsatisfactory. He was not to be prosecuted, said Lord Grenville; indeed, it was hard to see that any valid charges could be formulated against him. But when Despard expressed his intention of returning at once to resume his rule in Honduras, he was informed that the post of King's Superintendent was abolished; he had reverted to the position of a half-pay colonel, and might apply for other employment.

But no employment came his way. Despard was a marked man, as he soon found—noted down (and quite rightly) as quarrelsome and tyrannical. There would be no more colonial jobs for him. His first outburst of anger took the form of sending in to Whitehall interminable bills for money spent, or alleged to be spent, on Government service in the Honduras. They were disputed, and never settled. Then came a new mental development in the disappointed ex-autocrat. He suddenly saw that all was rotten in Great Britain, that the Constitution as administered by Mr. Pitt was a solemn sham, that the country was being exploited by a ring of aristocratic jobbers, and that the people must be freed on the new French lines of Liberty, Equality and Fraternity. In short, he joined the steadily dwindling band of enthusiasts whom the historians call the "English Jacobins," the flamboyant band of admirers of the French Revolution who made so much noise in proportion to their numbers between 1793 and 1798.

There is a terrible gap in the domestic history of England still waiting for the writer who shall work out the inner annals of the "Corresponding Society" and the other disloyal associations of the early years of the Revolutionary War. Till it is filled, I fear that the exact place of Despard in the agitation cannot be determined. This, however, is certain, that in 1798 he was one of the small group of traitors in London who were in correspondence both with the Irish rebels and with the French. Their agents, Binns and Allin, were captured, along with the priest O'Quigley and Arthur O'Connor, as they were trying to pass from Kent to the Continent. Despard's name appears in connexion with this plot both in Castlereagh's secret correspondence and—what is more damning—in both the deposition of O'Quigley himself and in the autobiography of Wolfe Tone, wherein he is spoken of as the selected leader of the party who were ready to do something in the way of practical insurrection, in order to help the Irish rising of 1798. Naturally, therefore, he was among the limited number of persons who were arrested by Pitt and clapped into prison : the Habeas Corpus Act was suspended at the time, and had been for several years. I take it that O'Quigley's and Tone's evidence is good enough to upset the easy Whig tale, which is repeated in many partisan histories, that Despard was an innocent man, who had made himself unpopular with the governing bureaucracy by clamouring for an investigation of his doings in Honduras, and by his claims for a settlement of his accounts, and that he was put into prison merely to keep him quiet. What is certain is that he was confined without a trial for more than two years, and only released in the winter of 1800–1, when the French War was obviously verging towards its end, and when the dangers of domestic sedition were thought to be dying down, in view of the approaching general peace. The "Corresponding Society" was long dead ; its members, for the most part, had relapsed into simple Whiggery, or had retired to nurse their theories in idle discontent.

But the newly released prisoner had lost all power of cool judgment, and was simply set on revenge, in season or out of season. And the fact that he could find no fellow-conspirators of any note or personal importance did not suffice to warn him of the futility of his enterprise. There were some bread riots during the winter of 1801, and election riots of a sinister sort in the following year, when a Nottingham mob is said to have displayed the red cap of Liberty as its standard. The inchoate mutiny in the fleet at Bantry Bay in December, 1801, though put down at once with a firm hand, seemed to indicate that the evil days of 1797 were not so far off as had been thought. There was enough trouble on

foot to encourage a rancorous fanatic such as Despard had
now become. "The people are everywhere ripe," he said,
"and anxious for the moment of attack, particularly in
Leeds, in Sheffield, in Birmingham, and in every capital city
of England, and here, in and round London, they are ripe
too. I have travelled about twenty miles in the day, and
the people, wherever I have been, are ready."

His view was that the whole of industrial England was
seething with discontent, and that to produce an explosion
it was only necessary to start with an armed revolt in London.
The blow must be struck at head-quarters, and then the whole
realm would flare up. The initial difficulty was the collection
of the nucleus of determined men who were to start the rising.
It is here that the insane rashness of the scheme emerges.
After a year of propaganda Despard had collected as his
lieutenants and co-organizers only the very dregs of the old
"Corresponding Society," a handful of London tradesmen and
artisans of the Jacobin type. Of all of them only one, Emblin,
a watchmaker in Chelsea, had been a well-known member
of the "Corresponding Society," and had sometimes gone
on its errands to sound in vain the official Whigs. For the rest,
they were busy, and often apparently very magniloquent, talkers.
Many contemporaries—for example, that very Radical Whig,
Major Cartwright—and almost every historian who has
written during the last hundred years, have declared Despard
a lunatic. I am constrained to take a different view. Two
governing facts must be remembered, which were obvious
to every discontented man in 1801, but have been completely
forgotten. The first fact was that every one then alive who
had reached the age of thirty could easily remember a moment
when London was for three days in the hands of a wild and
mischievous mob, which did whatever it pleased in the way
of arson and pillage. And this mob had no organization
or definite political ends, being called into being by the work
of a single crack-brained enthusiast. I refer, of course, to
the Gordon Riots of June 2–9, 1780. It was open to any
malignant plotter to believe that a similar, but far more
formidable, mob could be raised by a man or men who had
created a basis of secret societies to work and officer it.

But we must also remember that, only three years before Despard started his propaganda, there had been a much more serious phenomenon seen than even the Gordon Riots —a widespread mutiny of the armed forces of the Crown. The Navy had then been the body affected, and all that had happened at the Nore and Spithead was well remembered in London. Nothing had come of that mutiny, partly because the leaders were unknown and incapable men, partly because the sailors were rather strikers agitating for better conditions of service than rebels wishing to overthrow the Constitution of their country. But the Mutiny at the Nore had terrified the whole nation, and rightly, since if the French had put to sea while it was in progress, any sort of disaster might have happened. Then there had been a mild echo of naval mutiny as late as the winter of 1801–2 in Bantry Bay. Despard thought that he could organize a similar rising in the Army. The conditions of the soldier's life were little, if at all, better in 1800 than those of the sailor's. There were many ill-managed and discontented battalions. Despard thought that he could organize inter-regimental secret societies, which would gradually prepare the way for a sort of military rising comparable to the Mutiny at the Nore. It was to synchronize with a civil rising comparable to the Gordon Riots. There is no doubt that he had hit upon the Bolshevist idea of the "Soviet of Soldiers and Workmen." Personally he seems to have specialized on the First and Third Battalions of the Grenadier Guards, to one of which (and mostly to the Third Battalion) nearly all the numerous soldiers whose names are found in the record of his trial as defendants or as witnesses, or merely as individuals mentioned in the story, seem to belong. No doubt these battalions appear mainly because they were garrisoned in London, where they were accessible to the members of a conspiracy domiciled in the metropolis. The start was made with men who had good reasons for recklessness. We note in the dock or the witness-box corporals who had twice lost their stripes, men who had been repeatedly flogged, and others who had been deserters and had been recaptured. Granted a nucleus of reckless and discontented men, a kind of systematic proselytism could begin. But

the danger to the conspirators was that in feeling about for
converts they were certain ere long to hit upon the wrong
man—some soldier who had obvious reasons for grumbling,
yet who was not prepared to become a rebel. The striking
thing is, that of some hundreds of men who must have known
with more or less certainty that something sinister was brewing,
not one went to delate the plot to his colonel. To betray
comrades in that way would have been contrary to all the
traditions of the barrack-room.

Some of the companies of the Third Grenadiers must have
been riddled with sedition. The men were attending in small
parties at propagandist meetings held in at least a dozen
different obscure taverns in the East End and Southwark.
For every individual who became a regular conspirator, swore
his oath, and received his ticket, there must have been half
a dozen who refused to commit themselves, who drank the
beer and gin of the society, and went off with a vague promise
that they would think matters over. Probably for most
it was merely a superior and rather exciting form of " grousing."
There was, however, a small number of discontented and
ambitious soldiers who took the matter seriously, and were
active agents in the plot. The two whose names occur most
frequently were John Wood of the First and John Francis of
the Third Battalion of the Grenadiers. The name of one
or other of them appears in the evidence of nearly every one
of the witnesses at the trial of the conspirators. Both were
busy swearing in members of the secret society, and Francis
had been nominated a " colonel " in Despard's organization.

The civil branch of the conspiracy was organized in bodies
of ten men, each recruited by a " captain " who was responsible for their loyalty. Each five captains were responsible
to a " colonel," and the " colonels " were grouped locally
in divisions, of which we only know that there was one in
Southwark, one in Marylebone, one in Spitalfields, and another
" from Blackwall and upward," each composed of several
" subdivisions " under a colonel. Over all was the Commander-in-Chief, Despard himself. The really dangerous
element was the military branch—it is said that there were

over three hundred of the Third Grenadier Guards, and some thirty or forty of the First Battalion, who had sworn the oath.

The majority of the affiliated members never saw Despard, but favoured individuals were privately introduced to him by one of their " colonels " at some obscure rendezvous, if it was thought that they might be useful. More often orders were issued and meetings convened by one of what was called " the Executive," of which we can only say that John Francis, John Macnamara, an Irishman, a man called Pendrill who was never brought to trial, and one or two more, were members. The secret recognition sign of the society was a card, which contained the oath administered to members on their initiation. It was headed—" Constitution : the Independence of Great Britain and Ireland. The Equaliza-tion of all civil, political and ᐟreligious rights. An ample provision for the families of heroes who shall fall in the Contest. A liberal reward for distinguished merit." Then came the actual oath—" In the awful presence of Almighty God, I, A—— B——, do voluntarily declare that I will endeavour to the utmost of my power to gain those rights which the Supreme Being, in His infinite bounty, has given to all men : that neither hopes nor fears, rewards nor punishments, shall ever induce me to give any information, directly or indirectly, concerning the business of this or any similar society, so help me God ! " After reading this formula aloud to the initiator the new member kissed the card.

The meetings of the fractions of the organization were numerous, garrulous, and well watered with various strong drinks. Those admitted to the august presence of Despard himself were given brandy and water ; at the general gather-ings beer, porter and gin are more frequently mentioned. There is a glimpse of one conference which makes one long for a verbatim report : it is given by one Thomas Blades, a perverted soldier. " On a Sunday night John Francis met me and asked me to go down to the Black Raven. We found there Wood, Wratten, Tyndall, Macnamara, and six or seven Irishmen, all in a state of intoxication—about twelve or thirteen persons in all. *The discussion we had then was*

concerning forms of government." Imagination fails to picture
the details of a debate on high political theory between three
mutinous privates of the Guards, three discontented London
tradesmen, and seven Irishmen all very drunk!

By the autumn of 1802 the bolder spirits began to clamour
for practical deeds. The "Executive" seems to have considered that it was time to move. Despard had hitherto,
as it seems, been against immediate action—as well he might
be. The Peace of Amiens was toning down political bitter-
ness, and spreading false hopes of quiet and prosperity. He
had said "there was nothing to be done, he was expecting
news and money from France." This curious phrase, if properly reported by the witness—one of the soldier-conspirators
—was notable : it is the only sign that Despard was in touch
with the Continent. It is quite possible that he may have
been sounding the French Government through some of his
friends, the exiled Irish rebels, as Robert Emmet was certainly
doing at the same time.

Whatever may have been the case with regard to hopes
of foreign aid, there is no doubt that matters quickened up
in the society during August and September. It was determined that there should be a rising in November. At one
meeting a soldier-conspirator confessed that "we all drawed
our bayonets, and swore that we would have a time fixed
for a grand attack on the Tower, before the company broke
up." The day chosen was that of the opening of Parliament,
November 23. It remained that the details should be settled.
On this there was high debate and interminable discussion.
The minor people had each his plan, in which he himself
was to have the leading part. The most effective project
was certainly that for seizing the Tower. The desperate
men would rush the arms-racks of the battalion, arm the
other malcontents, and carry away the rest of the corps by
surprise and terror, for they would be unarmed. This plan
must have involved the shooting of the officers, but there
is not a word said about that detail in any of the depositions.
The Tower was full of munitions of all kinds, and these were
to be distributed to the mob which the society thought that
it could raise in the East End and the Borough. There

was another scheme for a dash at the Bank of England, where were a certain number of muskets—six hundred it is said —stored in the vaults. But it was apparently Despard himself who insisted that an essential part of the insurrection must be the murder of the King. The personality of George III had counted for so much in the suppression of the Gordon Riots twenty-two years before, that it was held that without him the constituted authorities in London would be helpless. Three witnesses at the trial deposed to the exact words that the Colonel used : " I have weighed the matter well, and my heart is callous." The plan was to stop the King's state coach between St. James's Palace and Westminster on the day of the opening of Parliament. He would come out of the back door of the Palace, and the escort of Horse Guards would be waiting for him some way down the Mall. There would be a crowd assembled to watch the show, and the conspirators would mingle with them, and run in upon the coach just as it was starting, and before it had picked up the escort. " Take and shoot two of the horses and the carriage must stop," said Broughton, one of the Colonel's chief confidants. Some one then asked, " But who would execute so dangerous a thing ? " Despard replied, " That he would do it with his own hand." There was then much talk on a less practicable scheme—three or four witnesses depose to it. Wood, of the First Grenadiers, said that his company would be finding the guard over " the Great Gun in the Park "—i.e. the old gun from the *Sovereign of the Seas*, which stood at the back of the Admiralty till it was replaced in 1803 by the Turkish cannon from Egypt, now on the Parade hard by. He could arrange that he himself and a confidant or two should be sentries at the gun ; they would privily load it and fire it into the Royal coach as it defiled at a foot's-pace in front of the muzzle. We have curious reports of the reception of this scheme. The witness Emblin declared that he said, " Good God ! do you consider how many people will be there that day, and how many lives you will take ? " Broughton answered, " Then, damn them, let them get out of the way. It will play hell with the houses at the Treasury and round about there." Some one objected,

"The cannon may be trained too low or high and miss His Majesty." Broughton replied, "Then, damn him, we must run in and manhandle him." All this was in Despard's presence.

The evidence agrees that there were to be at least three separate *coups de main* carried out on November 23. One was to be the murder of the King in the Mall or the Horse Guards Parade, carried out under Despard's superintendence, and followed by a raid on the Houses of Parliament; the second was to be a mutiny of the Third Grenadiers at the Tower; the third was to be the seizing of the Bank of England. "If we have the Tower and the Bank we have everything," were Despard's words, according to one witness. He added that the coaches starting for the country must be stopped, and that the "telegraphs"—*i.e.* the semaphores communicating with Dover, Portsmouth and other garrisons—must be destroyed, in order that matters might be finished in London before the news got round the country.

Would the scheme ever have worked? There were desperate men in it, and something might have been done, but one has a suspicion that at the last a great many conspirators would have found it convenient not to be present at the appointed rendezvous. Possibly the King might have been murdered—conceivably the mutiny at the Tower might have come off; but it is incredible that any measure of success would have followed. The mob was relied upon as the main weapon, and the mob was unorganized, and the destined leaders belonging to the conspiracy were few and obscure. Not far from London were thousands of troops, at Windsor, Chatham, Colchester, Portsmouth, Canterbury, etc., who do not seem to have been affected by the military plot; there is very little trace of any attempt to spread the propaganda among them in the depositions of any of the witnesses. It is specially mentioned that none of the regiments of Household Cavalry, though they were quartered in London, were the least affected. There might have been some bloody work in the streets that day, but it seems unlikely that anything more serious would have happened.

But the striking-power of Despard's gang was never to

be tested. The reckless way in which possible recruits were sounded, and were often admitted to some of the secrets of the Association, had its inevitable results. For the last four or five months the Government had been in possession of a good deal of information concerning the conspiracy. Besides vague reports as to secret meetings of soldiers and others in various taverns about the Tower, they got in July a definite story. It was told by one Thomas Windsor, a private in the Third Grenadiers, an old soldier of eleven years' standing. This man came to the office of Mr. William Bownass, an army agent, and told him that there was mischief afoot in his battalion, that a secret society had been working in it for some months, and that he himself had just been sworn in as a member, though he had no intention of joining in the mutiny. He had only taken the oath in order to see what was up. As a testimony of the existence of the movement, he produced the oath-card on which he had been sworn. Bownass told him to retain his membership, to keep his ears open, and to report to him from time to time what was brewing. For the last four months of the history of the conspiracy, Windsor was sending in reports from time to time, which went to the Home Office. Till September there was nothing on which Despard and his lieutenants could have been arrested, except the charge of forming a secret society and administering illegal oaths. The Ministers resolved to let the matters come to a head before striking. In October the definite assassination plot cropped up, and it was getting time to act. When it came out that the meeting of Parliament was to give the signal for the revolt, measures were taken to be a week early with the conspirators. The plot was to burst out on November 23. Seven days before, a great force of "Bow Street Officers," under Mr. John Stafford, chief clerk of the police office at Union Hall, surrounded a tavern in Lambeth called the Oakley Arms, and there arrested all the members present at one of the meetings of the society. They were about thirty in number, including Despard himself, "the only person there with the appearance of a gentleman."

The arrest seems to have been a tame affair. On the entry of the constables the Colonel and his friends were found seated at a long table in the club-room of the inn. "Some of them were for getting up and looked rather alarmed." They were told to keep their seats, that a warrant was out against them, and that they must submit to be searched. Despard was "rather angry and indignant"; he walked up and down protesting, asked to be shown the warrant, and said that he would not allow a hand to be laid on him. He was searched nevertheless, but no paper of any importance was found; indeed, the only compromising documents discovered that night were five of the printed oath-cards which served as the private tokens of the society.

The Grand Jury of Surrey found a true bill against the Colonel and his associates on January 21, and the trial came off on February 7, 1803, at the Sessions House, Newington, before Lord Ellenborough, the Lord Chief Justice, Sir Alexander Thompson, Sir Simon Leblanc, and Sir Alan Chambre. The prosecution was conducted by Spencer Perceval, then Attorney-General, but destined a few years later to be Prime Minister and to fall by the hand of an assassin. Despard asked that his trial might be conducted apart from that of the rest, and this was granted him. He had as his counsel Serjeant Best, afterwards a judge of the King's Bench, and Mr. Gurney.

Four persons who had been in the plot—three soldiers and the watchmaker Emblin—were allowed to turn King's evidence, thereby saving their necks. On these four men's depositions the case against Despard mainly rested; but five or six more witnesses, mostly soldiers, were produced to prove that they had been sounded by one or other of the chief agents of Despard, and had gathered enough about the object of the plot to make them determined to keep out of it. None of them had "split" upon their comrades till the crash had come. Their stories bore every mark of being given with reluctance. The most damning evidence was concerning a meeting at the Flying Horse Tavern on November 12, when the Colonel had laid down the details of the assassination of the King to a select committee, and it was curiously corroborated by the landlady of the inn, who said that, standing in her bar, she had heard in the next room

Despard break out in a very loud voice with the words—
" I have weighed everything well, and my heart is callous,"
which were attributed to him by several of the other witnesses.

Serjeant Best refused to give any explanation of Despard's presence at the Oakley Arms on November 16, or
of his tavern colloquies during the preceding year.   He simply
pleaded that the Colonel's early career rendered it unnecessary
to go into such things.   He produced Lord Nelson as a witness,
to prove that Despard had been a loyal and zealous officer
in the old American war : but Nelson had not seen him since
1780.   Best's junior, Gurney, who followed, took another
line.   It was easy enough to blacken the characters of the
witnesses for the prosecution.   They were ruffians, informers
acting in collusion, *agents provocateurs* : the plot was a figment,
like the imaginary Popish plot in the reign of Charles II.

Lord Ellenborough invited the Colonel himself to make
any observations that he thought fit, to supplement the
pleading of his counsel.   It was expected that he would
either deny the existence of any plot, on his honour, or else
take the other line—avow himself a Republican and a patriot,
and justify his plans by a tirade upon the unconstitutional
and corrupt form of government under which his country
was suffering.   Despard did neither, but simply observed,
" My lord, my counsel have acquitted themselves so ably,
and so much to my satisfaction, that I have nothing at all
to say."   In short, he refused to deny that a plot had been
formed or that he had a part in it.

The jury was only absent for twenty-five minutes, and
returned to find the prisoner guilty.   They added that they
recommended him to mercy because of his former good character and eminent services.   This, I think, was less a testi-
monial to Despard than a mark of the general enthusiasm
of the day in favour of Nelson, who had spoken up so strongly
for his old comrade.

On the next day but one, twelve of Despard's associates
appeared in the dock.   The jury convicted nine of the twelve ;
the other three were acquitted.   The Crown exercised its
prerogative of mercy in the cases of three more, for whom

[*Reprinted from* THE ENGLISH HISTORICAL REVIEW, *January* 1928.]

The Last Days of Colonel Despard

No one has as yet taken the trouble to write a complete history of the 'English Jacobins', the desperate admirers of the French Revolution who did not swerve from their original enthusiasm, even after the execution of Louis XVI and the Reign of Terror had shocked most of the Whigs into an acquiescence in William Pitt's excommunication of Gallic ideas. How strong was the surviving fraction of the party which had once thought of fraternizing with the early revolutionaries across the water, we do not know. It existed, and individual members of it certainly dallied with treason after the declaration of war with France in 1793. But their numbers and their power to stir up trouble have never been estimated. How many readers of ordinary English history books have ever heard of Colonel Edward Marcus Despard, late governor of British Honduras, whose extraordinary plot to set up a 'Soviet of soldiers and workmen', to seize the Tower, assassinate the king, and proclaim a republic, caused a momentary sensation in London in 1802, but has been completely boycotted in most histories of the official Whig sort ? I took the trouble some fifteen years ago to exhume the record of this rather grim personage, but found very little documentary material to help me to complete the picture of his personality and that of the soldiers and artisans who went to the gallows with him.

Quite unexpectedly there came to my hands of late an un-published piece of evidence as to the character and bearing of Despard from a hitherto unsuggested source. It is a report addressed to Lord Pelham, secretary of state for the Home depart-ment, by the Rev. William Winkworth, of St. Saviour's, South-wark, who was acting in 1802 as chaplain of Horsemonger Lane Gaol, in which Colonel Despard and his accomplices were confined before and after their trial. Attached to it is an extract from Mr. Winkworth's diary concerning the characters and personalities of the colonel's adherents. These papers came to me from Miss Catherine Winkworth Mackintosh, of Heathfield, Sussex, whose family had inherited them from their mother, a granddaughter of the Rev. William Winkworth. Finding them among the docu-ments, she recognized their considerable psychological and historical interest.

It is clear that Colonel Despard was a typical eighteenth-century figure, a believer like Robespierre in a vague 'Supreme Being', and a contemner of all established forms of religion, and obviously of all governments that he chanced to dislike. It may be remembered that, at his trial, it had been expected that he would either dispute all the evidence against him as suborned perjury, or else declare himself openly a revolutionist, who believed in the right to use force against tyrants in power. He did neither, refusing either to deny that there had been a plot, or to justify it on first principles. He simply pleaded his undoubted good service of many years in the army, and refused to explain the mysterious colloquies with discontented soldiers and others at which he had been proved to have been present. He produced Lord Nelson as a witness to his excellent conduct in the expedition to Nicaragua in 1779, but would give no explanation of the reasons for which he had been imprisoned in 1798–9, or of any of his recent political activities. There can, I think, be no doubt that he was a typical British Jacobin, and a most dangerous personage.

C. W. C. OMAN.

I.

(MS. begins without heading—a rough draft without title or preamble—
but obviously addressed to the Home Secretary)

My Lord

Having this day officially attended the execution of Col: Despard and his Associates, and supposing that your Lordship might wish to be acquainted with their behaviour during the time they have been under my ministerial care, I beg leave to submit the following statement for your Lordship's perusal.

My first visit to the Colonel was on the day the Special Commission was opened. Having introduced myself as the Chaplain, I said I supposed he was too much engaged in preparing for his trial to attend anything else. He answered, ' I have always through life made a point of doing my own business myself, though on the present occasion I shall have Counsel '.

I understood him to mean that he would dispense with my assistance, and said ' I did not then come so much with reference to the duties of my office, as to see whether he had all the accommodations his situation would admit of '. He replied he had expressed his obligations to me for my attention to him in this respect, and thinking that I felt hurt at his first address, repeatedly apologized and wished me to believe that he had a respect for my office ; and also mentioned that he had read a great deal of Theology and that he had made up his mind on religious matters. I thought it prudent at that time to avoid all controversy, and was taking my leave by offering my assistance to procure him such comforts as were in my power, when he asked whether the Judge had delivered his charge. I ans⁴ yes, and that the Grand Jury were then sitting on his case.—His behaviour on this and every other occasion was very polite.[1]

The day after his trial, I sent him a note, intimating that, if he was not too fatigued, I would pay him a visit, or would wait upon him the next day. After two attendances, I got an interview. The usual salutations being past, I asked him whether, being an Irishman, he had not been educated in the Roman Catholic Religion, in which case he might have a Priest to attend him, otherwise I was come to tender my services. He replied he had sometimes been at eight different places of worship on the same day,

---

[1] After I retired, he said rather shrewdly, ' So the Clergyman has been to see me before the Bill of Indictment is found ! '

that he believed in a Deity, and that outward forms of worship were useful
for political purposes: otherwise he thought that the opinions of Church-
men, Dissenters, Quakers, Methodists, Catholics, Savages or even Atheists
were equally indifferent.' I urged the propriety of a public acknowledgement of God as the supreme governor, and universal Friend ; and which
sentiment appeared to have been adopted by the whole human race, either
from an original common, though generally corrupted tradition, or from
a universal sentiment, unaccountably though strongly imprinted on the
human mind. He then offered some criticisms on the words Altar and
Ecclesia, which if my memory does not fail were quotations from Thomas
Paine's Age of Reason.—I then presented Dr. Doddridge's evidences of
Christianity, and begged as a favor that he would read it. He then requested
that I would not ' attempt to put shackles on his mind, as his body
(pointing to the iron on his leg) was under so painful a restraint, and said
that he had as much right to ask me to read the book he had in his hand
(a treatise on Logic) as I had to ask him to read mine ', and before I could
make a reply Mrs. Despard and another lady were introduced and our
conversation ended—At our parting said ' he should always be glad to see
me as a *friend* ', laying a strong emphasis on the last word. I left the book
on the table, but have reason to think he never read it.

Several other times I went up to his room, but the moment he saw me,
he apologized that he was very much engaged, by which I understood he
did not wish to see me, and I ceased my visits till the day before his
execution, when, in the presence of the Keeper, I informed him of his fate.
He was a little agitated and complained of the shortness of the warning,
and of his being the only exception of the four recommended to mercy.
I told him his case might be peculiar and proper for exception. I then
asked him if he would permit me to visit him in the evening, when he
begged to be excused. I asked him if he was fully determined to go out
of the world without making any profession of Religion ! but he requested
I would not trouble him ' on this subject '. I said he must be sensible that
what I had done was no more than my duty, which he acknowledged,
but wished to be left to himself.

He went to bed before 8 o'clock, but soon got up again, and, as the attendant informed me, walked in a state of agitation backwards and forwards,
frequently fetching very deep sighs, and broke out in a kind of soliloquy,
' No—Never—not for all the treasure in the Treasury nor for all the jewels
the King has got '. Though necessarily brought to the Chapel door this
morning whilst I was performing Divine Service, he refused to come in.—
He complained to me, in an anti-Room, waiting whilst his companions
were fixed to the fatal tree, ' that he was cruelly used by government ', but
what he said was the substance of his speech to the multitude, which no
doubt your Lordship is before this acquainted with, therefore I will not
trouble your Lordship with a recital. He died without even joining with
us [*Crossed out*: ' with me and the other prisoners '] in the Lord's Prayer,
though repeated in his hearing.

The other prisoners, in a general way, behaved with decency and
propriety, except Francis and Wood, the two soldiers, who were sometimes,
particularly the former, very violent. But all of them complained of false
evidence produced against them ; on my observing to them that this was

perhaps only in some legal points, Graham was convinced, and all acknowledged that they knew for what purpose the Association was formed.—
This morning I asked them severally (except Macnamara who, being a
Catholic, had his own Priest to attend him) previous to the administration
of the Sacrament whether they were not guilty, which all except Francis
confessed. Wood said he had rather die now, for he believed he should
never be so well prepared again. Francis, tho' strongly pressed, was unwilling to say that he was wrong in this affair. I reasoned with him on
the absurdity and wickedness of denying so plain a fact, for whatever might
be said in extenuation of the guilt of some others, *his* crime was apparent
to every unprejudiced mind who knew anything of his transactions. ' That
he particularly, being in His Majesty's pay, was especially bound by general
duty, as well as by his oath of allegiance, not to conspire against the King,
and that he had broken his oath.' He replied ' that he had not broken his
oath, and that he did not intend or wish to hurt any of the Royal Family'.
Though, my Lord, I was not satisfied with him, yet, knowing the violence
of his spirit, I thought it prudent to urge him no further, lest he should
become passionate and thereby cause confusion and retard the execution.

As I understood that Macnamara was supposed to know more of the
conspiracy than the others, except Despard, I this morning spoke to
Mr. Griffiths, the Priest, to request that if he found he knew anything
material, that he would enjoin him to divulge it to a proper person, and
mentioned Sir Richard Forde, which he promised to do, but nothing
transpired. . . .

[*MS. ends.*]

II.

*Memorandum on foolscap paper (seems to be a rough copy with several
errors and corrections)*

It may perhaps be satisfactory to some individuals to have a description
of the persons and other circumstances of Colonel Despard and his fellow-
sufferers. I therefore subjoin the following, which is the best account I
have been able to procure.

Colonel Despard was rather above the middle size, remarkably well
proportioned, fifty-two years of age but looked much older, owing most
probably to his having passed seventeen years of his life between the Tropics
in military service. He has left a widow, but whether any offspring I
cannot tell, as no other relation besides her, as not [*or* as such] visited
him during his confinement. In justice to Col. Despard I here take the
opportunity to say that, though he made no profession of Religion, his
conversation was never profane, nor did he at any time during his confinement speak disrespectfully or contemptuously of anybody, except the
evidences against him. In my letter to the High Sheriff I have stated a
circumstance which upon further information I find is not quite correct, as
to the time and expression, but no variation in substance—When I went
to the prison on the morning of the execution, the man who had sat up
with him a part of the night, told me of a speech that he made the preceding
evening, which has appeared in my printed letter, and not having an opportunity to see the man again till after my letter went to the press, I could
not alter it. But the fact is this.—After the Col. had taken leave of his

friends, he walked about the room, apparently agitated, and frequently sighed. He then layed down on the bed, and after some time exclaimed with vehemence, ' ME—No, never. I'll divulge nothing, no, not for all the treasure and jewels the King is worth.' The attendant went to his bed and asked him if he was asleep ? He replied no. ' Do you know what you have said ? ' He answered ' Yes, and I said it that you might hear '.

As I am assured that no overtures, either direct or indirect, were made to him by Government, it is difficult to determine to what this speech could refer. But it is evident that it was his wish that it should be made public, and my noticing it will answer that purpose. It has been said in the public prints that, just before he was turned off, that the Col. said something to Francis about the weather. That he spoke to Francis I can testify, but it was in so low a tone of voice that I could not distinguish what was said, and I much doubt whether it could be heard by any one else.—At our final parting he wished me health and happiness.

John Francis was a native of Worcestershire, aged 29, bred a shoemaker, and for the last ten years had been a soldier. In his person was tall, well proportioned and handsome. [*Crossed out* : His constitution was considerably broken.] He has left a widow and two small children.

John Wood, aged 25, a labourer and soldier, has left a widow only. His person was tall and thin and of a pleasant countenance.

James Sedgewick Wrattan, born in Kent, aged 33, by trade a shoemaker. Has left a widow and two small children. His person was of the middle size, very thin, pale complection and mean in his appearance.

Thomas Broughton, a carpenter, aged 25, born at Stamford in Lincolnshire, was short, sallow complection, and generally had a smile on his countenance. A widow and two small children survive him.

Arthur Graham, aged 53, by trade a slater, was born in Westminster, and has left a widow and one daughter grown up. He was tall, a sallow complection, and had a sottish appearance, which might be expected from his immoderate use of spirits. He told me that, on the loss of an only son at sea, he took to this unhappy practice, which I believe in some measure was the cause of his untimely death.

John Macnamara, a native of Ireland, 40 years of age, by trade a carpenter. He was of the middle size, stout made, of a florid complection and pleasing appearance. Had been married to his second wife only a month before his apprehension. He left a son by a former wife able to support himself.

[MS. ends.]

the death penalty was commuted for long terms of penal servitude.

On Monday, February 21, the Colonel and his six companions —John Francis and John Wood, both of the Grenadier Guards, Thomas Broughton, carpenter, John Macnamara, an old member of the "United Irishmen," James Wratten, and Arthur Graham, artisans, were executed in public, in front of the Surrey County Jail at Newington. Despard showed no signs of weakness or of repentance. He refused to see a clergyman of any denomination, and displayed a sort of stoic composure. On the scaffold he made a short speech, in which he declared that he was no more guilty of the crime of which he was accused—treason—than any of those who were listening to him. By this he obviously meant that to attempt to overthrow the existing regime was not treason, not that he had made no such attempt. For he added that he had spent his life in the service of the nation, and was suffering for his endeavour. The method of the execution was not according to the barbarous formula for high treason —the seven condemned men were merely hanged ; after half an hour they were cut down, and their dead bodies were beheaded—the executioner holding up the head of each with the words, "This is the head of a traitor !" This was the last occasion but one on which decapitation was used. Thistlewood's case in 1821 was the only subsequent example.

Thus ended a plot undoubtedly real and dangerous, yet as undoubtedly doomed to failure from the first, because its framer had lost all sense of balance and reality. It was the product not of well-reasoned judgment, but of injured vanity and rancorous megalomania. The autocrat of Belize had been ignored by Ministers and flouted by under-secretaries. I cannot but believe that he was out for revenge for his injured self-esteem, not inspired by a Jacobin frenzy for Liberty and Equality to be won by the way of assassination and military mutiny. Of such conspirators one can only say

"ὣς ἀπόλοιτο καὶ ἄλλος, ὅ τις τοσαῦτά γε ῥέζοι."

ARTHUR THISTLEWOOD AND CATO STREET

The man who is outside the common humanity of his own generation, who takes the manners, the morals, or the enthusiasms of one period into another, may be magnificent or sinister, pathetic or grotesque. Sometimes he is all four at once. English history is rich in such eccentric figures, but none is more curious as a character study than Arthur Thistlewood, the " British Jacobin," who reproduced the cheap humanitarianism, the reckless bloodthirstiness, the bombastic phraseology and the autolatrous megalomania of the Parisian demagogues of 1792 before the eyes of the England of Sir Walter Scott and Miss Austen, and who furnished the young Thackeray with the most gruesome anecdote of his boyhood. In the orthodox Whig tradition, on which nineteenth-century history is generally written, he is lightly passed over, and not without reason. For the acts of the Tory Ministers in the distressful years that followed Waterloo have to be decried wholesale, and the words and deeds of the wild fanatics, who frightened Liverpool and Addington into repression, have therefore to be kept dark—or at least relegated to short and vague paragraphs and footnotes.

Arthur Thistlewood, the legitimate spiritual heir of Guy Fawkes, came within a measurable distance of slaying Canning and Wellington before their time. He had made elaborate preparations for parading the head of Castlereagh on a pike along Oxford Street and Holborn, after the slaughter of the whole Cabinet. Nor does it seem at all impossible that he might have carried out his bloody scheme. Insurrections may be foreseen and nipped in the bud ; on the other hand, assassination is a hard thing to guard against, as witness the fates of Alexander of Russia and Frederick Cavendish, of Abraham Lincoln and Sadi Carnot. The more obscure and the fewer that plotters are, the more hard are they to discover. The very fact that Thistlewood's murderous gang was insignificant in numbers, and composed of unknown men, might have enabled him to carry out his appalling plan. For common prescience could not have availed to avert such an unlikely danger, and no victims could have been more helpless than a party of Ministers off duty, and dining quietly in a private house. But for the want of caution that led the arch-conspirator to broach his designs to two ill-chosen recruits, one of whom was a systematic traitor and the other too much of an honest man, he might have made Grosvenor Square the most tragic name in modern English history. As it was, he only succeeded in conferring a half-forgotten notoriety on Cato Street, Edgware Road. But the mere thought of what he might have accomplished makes the brain reel. Imagine Liverpool and Castlereagh, Wellington and Canning, Eldon and Addington—not to speak of minor figures like Vansittart, "Prosperity" Robinson, and Lord Bathurst—all cut off simultaneously by the assassins' swords and bombs. There would have been incendiarism and riot to follow, but it is certain that the affair would not have ended, as Thistlewood hoped, in a general rising of the lower classes of London, culminating in the successful proclamation of a Republic, with himself as "President of the Provisional Government." Most probably the result would have been the instant repression of the turmoil by military force, followed by a sort of "White Terror." After such an atrocity the Tory Party would have been confirmed in power for a whole generation, and it must have ruled with a revengeful vigour compared to which Addington's and Castlereagh's measures of repression in 1816–20 would have been child's play. There would certainly have been no Reform Bill in 1832. Would there have been an ultimate British Revolution of a very venomous sort some years later ? Assassination breeds repression, and repression breeds revolution. Let us be thankful that Mr. Thistlewood's caution was not equal to his energy, and to his compelling power as a leader of men.

He was not young when he first came before the public eye. He was born in 1770, the son of one William Thistlewood, land agent to the Vyners of Gantby, in Lincolnshire, a considerable county family. His father was well-to-do, and he received a good education : he wrote a fair eighteenth-century style of the turgid sort, occasionally lapsing into bombast—as when he spoke of "the purple stream that circulates through a heart enthusiastically vibrating to every impulse of patriotism and honour." [His own, of course.] But it cannot be denied that he possessed a certain eloquence —as witness his dying words :—

"A few hours hence and I shall be no more : but the nightly breeze, which will whistle over the silent grave that shall protect me from its keenness, will bear to your restless pillows the memory of one who lived but for his country, and died when liberty and justice had been driven from her confines by a set of tyrants, whose thirst for blood is only equalled by their activity in plunder. For life, as it respects myself, I care not ; but, while yet I may, I would rescue my memory from the calumny which (I doubt not) will be industriously heaped upon it, when it will be no longer in my power to protect it. My every principle was for the prosperity of my country. The height of my ambition was to bring welfare to my starving fellow-citizens. I keenly felt for their miseries, but when their miseries were laughed at, when because they dared to express those miseries they were cut down by hundreds [an exaggerated allusion to ' Peterloo '], barbarously massacred, and trampled to death, when infants were sabred in their mothers' arms, and the breast from which they drew the tide of life was hacked from the parent's body, then indeed my feelings became too excessive for endurance, and I resolved on vengeance. I resolved that the lives of the instigators of massacre should atone for the souls of murdered innocents."

This sounds genuine enough, when spoken on the edge of the grave. But though Thistlewood ended, we cannot doubt, as an honest fanatic, his life was no more of the idealistic or the Spartan type than that of many of the Jacobins whom he so much admired. He was always restless and thriftless. He was trained as a surveyor, but never took to the profession, and remained a burden on his father long after he had reached manhood. By an odd, unexplained chance he happened to be in Paris for some months during the Terror, and what he saw there of the power of the mob and the mob-leader remained fixed in his mind, to bear fruit in later years. But on his return from France he did not (as we might have expected from his later career) dabble in any of the revolutionary agitations of the 'nineties. Quite the reverse—he accepted an ensign's commission in the 1st York Militia, and later (1798) became a lieutenant in the 3rd Lincoln Militia. He is reputed to have been an active officer and a "good drill," but to have been a loose liver, a persistent and unlucky gambler. In 1804 he courted and married a lady a good many years older than himself—a Miss Jane Worsley. She possessed a good income, and he retired from the militia and settled down in Lincoln to live on her money. Unfortunately for him she died less than eighteen months after the marriage, and as her property was settled on her nearest of kin in default of issue, Thistlewood was thrown upon the world almost penniless. The heirs made him a small allowance. Soon after he had to quit Lincoln, on account of unpaid debts of honour. He had continued his gambling when he had not the wherewithal to settle up. After a period spent in low water, he emerged for a moment into renewed prosperity —an uncle died and left him a farm valued at £10,000. He sold it, not for cash down, but for an annuity; after two years the guarantor of the annuity went bankrupt, and his security disappeared. For a second time he sought salvation in matrimony, taking to wife Susan, daughter of Mr. John Wilkinson of Horncastle, a prosperous butcher. She was philosophic enough to accept and rear a son whom Thistlewood produced—the offspring, not of his first wife, but of an amour. Her dowry served to stock a farm near Horncastle; and here, periodically assisted by loans from his father and elder brother, Thistlewood maintained himself more or less for some years. He was not a competent agriculturist, but prices ran high in the last years of the struggle with Napoleon. Then came the "slump" in corn after the war was over, when the quarter of wheat fell from 80s. to 52s. in a few months. It ruined Thistlewood along with many other fair-weather farmers. Finding that he was losing rather than making money, in consequence of high rent and high taxes, combined with low prices for produce, he got rid of his farm, and came up to London in 1814 with his wife and his son, "not in actual want, but his finances

were at a low ebb." Apparently he had sold his lease for
something ; his wife, " a smart, genteel little woman," had
still some resources, and both he and she probably contrived
to extract occasional doles from their relatives in Lincolnshire. What was Thistlewood's original scheme of life on
arriving in London no man can say. But very shortly after
his establishment there he began to appear as an agitator
of the extreme Radical sort. He has left no account of the
causes of his sudden launch out into politics, beyond vague
declamation about his sympathy for the distressed and unen-
franchised masses. This will hardly pass as an explanation :
his previous life had not been that of a philanthropist. Vain,
ambitious, bankrupt for the third or fourth time, soured by
perpetual ill-luck that mainly came from his own thriftless-
ness, he attributed his present poverty to anything rather
than his own fault. London was seething with political discontent, but it was mostly inarticulate and leaders were
wanting. " Orator " Hunt and " Dr." Watson were certainly
not abler men than Thistlewood : marking their notoriety, he
evidently saw no reason why he should not rise as high. His
tongue was ready and eloquent, his vehemence tremendous, his
personal influence over other men was clearly exceptional ; his
hatred for those who administered England was no doubt real
—to them he ascribed his own indigence. He had the ruined
gambler's grudge against all who had scraped and saved ; the
shopkeepers of London, he once observed, were an aristocracy
as pernicious as the Tory majority in Parliament—he should
rejoice to see their shops looted and their tills cleared out.
But no doubt the governing inspiration in his mind was his
memory of the Paris of the Jacobins : he had seen what mobs
could do when the fabric of the State was rotten, and he thought
—not wrongly—that he himself was singularly gifted for
a mob-leader.

From 1816 onward he was one of the most prominent
figures in that small band of agitators who advocated physical
force as the remedy for all ills, and who broke completely
away from the Whigs and their constitutional methods. He
was heard advocating violence at every open-air meeting,
and that his words were not vain declamation was shown by

the fact that he headed an armed party at the abortive Spa
Fields riot of December 2, 1816, and tried—carrying a tricolour
flag and followed by a constantly dwindling crowd that finally
melted away to nothing—to break into the Tower. He was
tried, along with the younger Watson, for this escapade, but
was fortunate enough to be indicted for high treason, not
for riot : the jury acquitted them of the weightier charge,
because they thought they ought only to have been tried
for the lesser offence. Encouraged by his escape Thistlewood continued to preach violence, till he was at last arrested
for having sent the Home Secretary Addington (Lord Sidmouth)
a challenge to a duel. For this he suffered a year's imprison-
ment in Horsham Gaol [1818-19], but came out from it not
cured of his pugnacity or his megalomania, but almost beside
himself with long-suppressed rage. This was the summer
of the " Manchester Massacre," the untoward affair when
the Lancashire Yeomanry rode down a riotous assembly
that had met to hear " Orator Hunt," where five people were
crushed to death, and many scores more hurt by being trampled
upon or cut about with sabres.

Thistlewood sat in judgment upon the Ministry, and
condemned them all to death, for what was in truth the act
of a scared magistrate and a body of amateur soldiers, who
had lost their heads when the mob closed around them. He
went about London trying in vain to induce the leaders of
the Radical Party to authorize an armed insurrection to avenge
what he styled High Treason against the People of England.
But no one of any weight or importance would listen to the
proposal. Thistlewood said that if they were not cowards
they were traitors : he believed that if he could get at the Home
Secretary's papers in Whitehall he would find that Orator
Hunt received a secret pension, and probably Cobbett also,
" for all his writings, he had no doubt that he was a spy
too."

For months the would-be insurgent tramped the streets
trying to organize a rising, but with small effect and ever-
growing rage. We have a description of him at the time :
" Five feet ten inches, with a sallow complexion, long visage,
dark hair, a little grey ; dark hazel eyes with very arched

eyebrows, a wide mouth and a good set of teeth ; he has a
scar under his right jaw ; he is slenderly built and has the
carriage of a military man. He usually wears a long blue
coat and blue pantaloons." From another and most unfriendly
source we hear that "his countenance, always forbidding,
seemed now to have acquired an additional degree of malig-
nancy. When in custody in 1817 for the Spa Fields affair
he was a stout active man with a fearless and determined
cast of features. Within the last six months he has under-
gone a change—his countenance has grown squalid and emaci-
ated, his dress shabby." He was generally observed walking
—almost running—through the streets with eager impetuosity,
his shoes and hat untidy and much worn, as if he were continually posting about on some absorbing and interminable errand
which brooked no delay. And, in truth, the errand existed
—all that autumn and winter he was trying, with no great
success, to collect the nucleus of the revolutionary army with
which he would sweep the streets and proclaim the Republic
at the Mansion House. As the possibility of "straight-
forward insurrection"—his own phrase—receded farther
and farther into the clouds, be began to vary his plans with
schemes of mere vengeance, the murder of one or more of
the leading Ministers—Sidmouth for choice, both as his own
personal enemy and as the Home Secretary directly responsible
for the "massacre" at Manchester. This was no new idea :
it was afterwards remembered that direct incentives to assassination of individuals occurred in several of his speeches
as far back as 1817. The statement often made, or hinted
at, by Whig writers, to the effect that he only lapsed into
murderous plans under the instigation of the man George
Edwards—of whom more hereafter—has no foundation. He
was ready for any bloody design long before he first met
Edwards in June, 1819.

Thistlewood sounded many scores of Radicals, great and
small, working on, as he tested his man, from general plans
of violence to more definite proposals for the removal of
individual "tyrants." The large majority drew off at the
first hint at murder. "I may be a great fool, but I was not
foolish enough to enter into such a scheme," said one *habitué*

of riotous meetings, when tempted by two of Thistlewood's acolytes. "I did not think they would ever get any persons to be so mad as to join them." Nevertheless, the plotter did, by infinite pains, succeed in collecting a small band of desperadoes, who did not shrink from the idea of assassination. There were two types among them—a minority were Jacobins of Thistlewood's own type, like the shoemaker Brunt, who acted as his second in command. This man was a prosperous workman, who often made 40s. or 50s. a week, and kept an apprentice ; he was the only one among the gang who ever had money in his pocket, and he readily disbursed it on "the cause." He was a great reader, saturated with the works of Tom Paine and other freethinkers, and had the whole vocabulary of French republicanism at his command. Unlike most of the others, he was neither starving nor of evil reputa- tion. He was as perfect a fanatic as his leader—so, it would appear, were one or two of the other conspirators. But the majority were broken men, on the edge—or over the edge —of starvation, whom Thistlewood had attracted by the idea of a general overthrow of existing society. Most of them, as their counsel pleaded at their trial, were probably thinking more of the plunder of the shops of London than of the pre- liminary murders that were to herald the night of pillage. The most violent of them was a bankrupt butcher, one James Ings, whose square brutal face contrasts curiously with the cadaverous countenances of the rest in the little gallery of portraits that illustrates the contemporary publications of 1820. His ferocious language, and his grotesquely boisterous conduct on the scaffold, were long remembered. Down to 1819 he had a fair record for honesty—not so the remaining members of the gang, who were as choice a set of scoundrels as could be fished from the gutter—Davidson, a plausible cant- ing mulatto, who had earned good money as a cabinet-maker, till he was expelled from a Wesleyan congregation to which he belonged for a series of indecent assaults'on Sunday-school girls ; Tidd, a cobbler, whose speciality during the late war had been enlisting into many regiments and absconding with his bounty money ; Robert Adams, an old soldier, whom his own fellow-conspirators described as a professional

swindler; and Dwyer, who is accused of maintaining himself
by blackmailing persons of immoral life. Thistlewood was
not unaware of their characters—but he had to get his instru-
ments where he could find them. Among others he took into
his confidence George Edwards, already mentioned, a very
clever dissolute fellow, by trade a modeller of statuettes, who
had been much about at Radical meetings of late, and distinguished himself by advocating outrages of an ingenious sort.
Thistlewood described him as "poor and penniless, without
a bed to lie upon or a chair to sit in : straw was his only bed
—his only covering a blanket ; and, owing to his bad character
and his swindling propensities, he was ever driven off by his
landlords." Yet the conspirator eagerly welcomed him as
a recruit. He was far more intelligent than most of the
gang and full of wiles. This was Thistlewood's first mistake,
for Edwards, though not a systematic *agent provocateur* of
the Government, as many alleged at the time of the trial of
his comrades, had earned money before by giving secret
information to the police, and was ready to earn it again.

We have the word of Canning himself for the fact that
George Edwards was not a regular Government spy—he was
not in the employment of Bow Street, nor did he receive
an allowance. He volunteered information and got a dole
occasionally, and he had never received any large sum till he
earned blood-money to the tune of £1,000, when the plot was
discovered, by betraying the whereabouts of Thistlewood.
During the winter of 1819-20 he apparently communicated
several times with the police or the Home Office, but could
give them no definite information, because the plot had not
taken shape. Thistlewood was ripe for murder, but had
settled neither his victims nor his exact *modus operandi*. He
continued collecting associates and getting together stores of
arms—the last no easy task, because of the insufficiency of
his exchequer. But hidden about at the lodgings of various
conspirators were some dozens of swords, bayonets, and
muskets, an immense number of pike-heads—some made
of sharpened files, but quite effective—about 1,200 rounds
of ball-cartridge, and a quantity of bombs and grenades.
One of these was of specially large size, and calculated to

produce a tremendous explosion. There was also a provision of fireballs for incendiary purposes.

The plot was taking shape by January, and Thistlewood had fully made up his mind that the preliminary step to a general rising should be the murder of certain Ministers, whether in the street or at their offices, when his plans were put out by the death of the old King George III. This took all official persons to Windsor for some days, and disarranged the routine of business. It was not until February that things had become normal again, and Thistlewood could trace and mark down his intended victims. By this time he had come on an idea which surpassed in completeness and ingenuity all his previous schemes. The members of the Ministry were in the habit, from time to time, of dining together in each other's private houses in rotation at "Cabinet Dinners." The next was to be at the house of the Earl of Harrowby, Lord President of the Council, in Grosvenor Square, on the south side, at the corner of Charles Street, on Wednesday, February 23. Thistlewood would thus find his "tyrants" concentrated in a very accessible spot, with no further guard than Lord Harrowby's butler and footmen.

Having armed themselves at some convenient rendezvous, the conspirators were to go to Grosvenor Square in twos and threes, and were to disperse themselves unostentatiously in the neighbourhood of the Lord President's mansion. Thistlewood, about the time that dinner was half over, was to knock at the door, carrying a red box, such as are used for ministerial correspondence. While he was explaining to the porter that a dispatch of great importance must be handed at once to Lord Castlereagh, other conspirators were to press in to the open door behind him, knock down or kill the servants in the hall, and rush for the dining-room. Bombs were to be thrown upstairs and down, and a select party were to burst into the dining-room and murder the guests. All this is undisputed, and was acknowledged by several of the conspirators. Details were added by the informers at the trial which may or may not be correct. Thistlewood, so it is said, intended to present himself before the startled Ministers with the words : "My Lords, I have got as good men here as

your Manchester Yeomanry—enter citizens and do your
duty !'' When the killing was done, the butcher Ings was
to cut off the heads of Sidmouth and Castlereagh, and to
place them in two bags which he carried for the purpose. When
the city should have risen, as Thistlewood hoped that it would,
the heads were to be placed on pikes and carried in front of
the mob in true Parisian style. It is certain that Ings, on
the fatal night, carried two large bags and a butcher's knife
—but his defenders suggested that the receptacles may have
been for Lord Harrowby's plate rather than for Lord Castlereagh's head. Who shall decide ?

It was hoped that the news of the wholesale slaughter of
the Cabinet would cause a general turmoil in the streets.
This was to be helped by incendiary fires. One of Thistlewood's trusted lieutenants, a man called Palin, was furnished
with a quantity of fireballs, which he was to throw, or cause
to be thrown, into various inflammable places, of which one,
we are told, was the hay store of Albany Street Barracks,
and another an old house near Furnival's Inn. He had three
coadjutors allotted to him, but it is doubtful whether they
would have effected much, when the signal should have been
given on the fateful night. For Palin, according to the evidence of one of his comrades, had primed himself up for the
business with liquor, and was quite incoherent and incapable.
Another party, headed by a man named Cooke, was to endeavour to seize the guns of the Light Horse Volunteers at their
drill-hall in Gray's Inn Lane, and those of the Honourable
Artillery Company. There is no proof that any serious
force was ready at Cooke's disposal—apparently Thistlewood
had arranged for him to be supported by some Irish labourers
living in Gee's Court, St. Giles, with whom he was in communication. But it is evident that his real hope was in the general
assistance of the mob, when the news should have got about.
If all went well, the main body of the gang, who had been
charged with the actual assassination, were to press eastward
along Holborn, gathering up Cooke's party with the cannon
from Gray's Inn Road, and were to seize the Mansion House.
Thistlewood was to install himself there as president of a
'' Provisional Government,'' with Ings as secretary. The

proclamations which they were to post up and publish were duly prepared. Of what, meanwhile, the Guards and other troops garrisoned in London would have been doing, Thistle-wood does not seem to have taken account. There is no mention of them in the evidence of his accusers or of his defenders—a strange piece of reticence!

On Monday, February 21, Thistlewood hired as his armoury and as the base from which his operations were to start, an empty three-horse stable in Cato Street, Edgware Road. This obscure thoroughfare was little more than a lane or mews—it connected John Street and Queen Street, which both run into the lower end of Edgware Road on the right (or eastern) side. No doubt Thistlewood must have been fascinated with the name of Cato Street, with its suggestions of stern ancient Roman republicanism. But the premises were not imposing—three stalls and a coach-house below, a large loft and two small living-rooms above. They were, how-ever, amply sufficient as an arsenal, and thither the muskets, swords, pikes, and grenades were transferred from their several hiding-places.

The first news concerning the final development of Thistle-wood's plan did not come, as might have been expected, from the informer Edwards, though he had given some general warnings, but from Thomas Hyden, a dairyman, who came up in great agitation to Lord Harrowby, as he was riding in Hyde Park on the morning of February 22, and besought him to put off at once his dinner of the next night, or he and his friends would be murdered. This person had been solicited on the previous Sunday to come into the plot by a man called Wilson, one of Thistlewood's minor satellites, and had been told enough to frighten him nearly out of his wits. He tried to catch Lord Castlereagh on the Monday, but failed to get access to him, though he made four calls. Wherefore he waylaid the Lord President next morning, and was more successful. This, according to Lord Harrowby's evidence at the subsequent trial, was the first definite news of Cato Street that came to hand: "We had general information that some plan was in agitation, but knew neither the time nor the particulars." It is quite untrue to say—with some

Whig historians—that the whole matter of the dinner-party was settled with the spy Edwards as a trap for Thistlewood.

But it is quite clear that later on the same day on which Hyden confided the matter to Lord Harrowby, Edwards gave similar information to Lord Sidmouth at the Home Office. For the Ministers by that night had private advice that they were to meet, not at Grosvenor Square, but at Fife House. The preparations for the dinner, however, were allowed to go on, nothing being said to Lord Harrowby's servants as to a countermand. Thistlewood's emissaries watched Grosvenor Square all day, and saw nothing to undeceive them.

Considering that the main outlines of the plot were in the possession of the Home Office by eleven o'clock on Wednesday morning, it does not seem that the arrangements for the arrest of the conspirators were so well concerted as they should have been. The main responsibility was in the hands of Mr. Richard Birnie, the magistrate at Bow Street : he took with him for the business Ruthven, the chief of his patrol, and eleven others of his men only, armed with short cutlasses and pocket-pistols. He was informed that he should have military support, and relied upon it. But from an exaggerated idea of the importance of keeping all preparations secret till the last possible hour, no definite information was given before evening to the Colonel commanding the 2nd Battalion of the Coldstream Guards, in the Portman Street Barracks, from which the detachment was to be drawn. At a quarter to eight the picket on duty was suddenly turned out and ordered to march : it was, by the chance of the roster, under Lieutenant Frederick Fitzclarence—one of the numerous natural sons of William Duke of Clarence—who received at the last moment the instruction that his party—a sergeant, a corporal, and twenty-eight privates—were to aid the police in the seizure of armed conspirators in Cato Street, Edgware Road. The soldiers were not in the least acquainted with the task that they were to perform : they supposed that a fire had broken out, and that they were required to guard property from a casual mob. No guide was sent with them, nor was anyone from the police patrol left to pick them up. It was only when their officer halted them at the corner of

John Street and Edgware Road, and directed them to fix
bayonets, observe the strictest silence, and follow him with
caution, that they became aware that something abnormal was
in hand. They had just resumed their march and reached the
angle of John Street and Cato Street, when they heard, quite
clearly, a single shot, followed by a scattering volley, proceeding from a building sixty yards up the road. Whereupon
they doubled up towards the sound, and came into the midst
of the turmoil which had just started.

It was, apparently, not long after eight o'clock when Mr.
Birnie, the magistrate, gave orders to commence operations
without waiting for the soldiers—either because he thought
that the muster of his little band of police had been detected
by the sentinels of the conspirators, or because the hour
was growing so late that Thistlewood might sally out on his
errand, before the doors of his refuge were blockaded. In
the open street he and his gang would not so easily be arrested
as when they were crowded together in the narrow loft above
the stables. Accordingly Birnie gave the foolhardy order to
his handful of followers to enter the building and seize its
inmates, though they were known to be armed and desperate
men, and to outnumber the attacking party by two to one.

Birnie did not lead the assault himself, but turned over
the charge of the forlorn hope to Ruthven, the chief of the
patrol. The dozen police broke open the door of the stables,
and found themselves confronted by two armed men—Davidson, the mulatto, who had a musket across his shoulder,
and Ings, the butcher, who had a pistol and a sword and was
girt with the belt from which hung the gruesome bags which
have already been mentioned. Whether from fear or from
mere surprise, neither of the sentinels fired, but one of them
shouted up the stairs in a thundering voice, " Look out above ! "
Ruthven called to some of his men to seize the sentinels, and
charged at the steep stairway with the rest. He himself
reached the top, followed by only two officers, Ellis and
Smithers—the rest were stumbling up the narrow ascent,
which would only take one man abreast. The assailants
got a momentary glimpse of the loft crowded by about twenty-
three men, some of whom were loading pistols and muskets,

others girding on swords and cutlasses. What followed was a matter of ten seconds : taking one step into the loft, Ruthven held out his staff of office and shouted, "We are officers—surrender your arms"; according to one witness he added, "here's a pretty nest of you." The conspirators instinctively fell back against the walls, all save Thistlewood, who stood in the doorway of one of the small living-rooms at the end of the loft, with a long German fencing-sword poised in an attitude of defence. Ellis, the second patrol-man, who had reached the top of the stair, levelled a pistol at him and cried, "Drop your sword, or I fire!" The third officer, Smithers, then ran in on Thistlewood, with bare hands, to seize him ; but the conspirator replied with a cool and deadly thrust which ran Smithers through the heart. The point of his weapon went so far that it turned against one of the ribs where it joined the spine. Ellis then fired at Thistlewood and missed him. The first shot set pande-monium loose ; some one cried, "Throw them downstairs," some one else, "Out with the lights." Four or five wild shots were fired upon Ruthven and Ellis, and then all was dark, for the eight candles were overturned, and the gang plunged in a mass at the head of the stairway, to get loose from the trap in which they found themselves. The two surviving patrolmen were knocked head over heels down the steps, and the conspirators poured down after them and fell upon the eight or nine officers who had not yet mounted. There was a clash for a few' seconds—about twenty shots were fired, and then the gang broke out successfully, after wounding five of the police—one was shot through the head, but not mortally. As they charged forth they liberated their two sentinels, Ings and Davidson. The whole started to run in the narrow street—right and left. Those who turned to their right, to the smaller exit into Queen Street, got off, including Thistlewood himself, who, as he ran, made a furious stroke at a harmless passer-by, one William Samson, whom he mistook for an enemy trying to intercept him. The man, fortunately for himself, was wearing an unbuttoned greatcoat—the sword caught in the folds and did him no harm. The less lucky portion of the gang, who had swerved to the left, towards John Street, ran into the arms of the Coldstreamers, who were hurrying up at the sound of the firing. These were mostly caught, some of them fighting hard. Tidd, when seized by the sergeant of the picket, fired on him —the ball went up his sleeve and then grazed his temple. Lieutenant Fitzclarence had a scuffle with another, who cut at him with a sword and then wrestled with him, till he was dragged off by two privates. When all the alarms and excursions were over, the Bow Street officers searched the loft, and found there not only the corpse of Smithers, but two miserable wretches who had buried themselves in a heap of shavings and straw in the corner, being too terrified to flee. One of these, a little snub-nosed Irish tailor named Moniment, was the second of the two conspirators who was allowed to turn king's evidence : the other was a starving wastrel named Gilchrist, who had only been brought into the conspiracy that same evening—literally gleaned from the gutter. So ended the skirmish with the capture of only eight of the twenty-five persons who had been present at the meeting—Ings, Wilson, Tidd, Davidson the mulatto, Bradbourn, Shaw, Gilchrist, and Moniment.

On the next day three more important arrests were made, those of Robert Adams, the old guardsman, Brunt, the shoemaker-politician, and Thistlewood himself. The latter was certainly taken by the treachery of his accomplice Edwards, the spy, for he had never returned to his own abode, but had taken refuge in an obscure lodging-house, 8 White Street, Little Moorfields. No one but Edwards had accompanied him thither, or knew of his hiding-place. He was surprised in bed, with all his clothes on but his coat and boots, sleeping the sleep of exhaustion after his wild night's work. Being, as he thought, safe where he was not known, he had taken no precautions against surprise, and was pounced upon by six Bow Street officers before he could even cast off his blankets. Several other arrests were made that day of persons, some of whom had, and some had not, any real connexion with the plot.

The prisoners were in a very evil case. This was a hanging job—if not a hanging, drawing, and quartering job—as they all knew. There would be no chance of getting off lightly, on the plea that their assembly was a foolish escapade with no deadly purpose behind it. That they had been betrayed by some one deep in the affair was evident, for the Cato Street stable had only been hired two days before the affray. The traitor—whoever he might be—would know all about the projected assassination, the fire-raising, the design for seizing the cannon, and the rest. Wherefore the fanatics, such as Thistlewood, Brunt, and Ings, despaired and raged. But the meaner spirits, who had joined in the plot for plunder, began to think of the chance of turning king's evidence and saving their necks. It might well be that the Home Office had not sufficient detailed information to make out a complete case, and would be glad of more. Within a few hours several of the conspirators were sounding their jailers as to the chance of escape by the way of confession. This is generally the case when a gang of political plotters has been captured, as Irish experience shows. After the Phœnix Park murders not only Councillor Carey, but others of the murderers—some say the majority of them—tried to buy their lives by treachery at their comrades' expense.

Now the Government had at their disposal for direct evidence only Thomas Hyden, who had honestly given information the moment that the general scope of the plot had become clear to him, and who knew no more than outlines, and the odious Edwards—whose part in the affair they would gladly minimize, since the revelation of his long and hypo-. critical spying into the projects of Thistlewood would disgust public opinion. He had let the plan develop, had loudly commended it, and had suggested ingenious, if futile, additions. If he could be kept out of court altogether, the prosecution would be the better for it. Wherefore tacit offers of immunity were made to two of the would-be purveyors of king's evidence—Robert Adams the old soldier and the Irish tailor Moniment. The former had been very early and deep in the conspiracy ; the other knew less, but was a special recruit of Brunt, Thistlewood's chief lieutenant, and could tell all about him. To corroborate the evidence of these two worthies there was an ample amount of outside witnesses, neighbours who had seen mysterious meetings and secret stores of arms, and people who, like Thomas Hyden, had been solicited in more or less open fashion to take a hand in what (following the phraseology of the South Sea Bubble) we may call " an undertaking of great advantage, to be presently divulged." It was accordingly resolved to keep Edwards in the background, and to rely in the prosecution on the evidence of Hyden, Adams, and Moniment, supported by the immense quantity of small detailed facts that could be supplied by persons whom chance had brought into contact with the conspirators. After all, it was impossible for them to explain away the muskets and swords, the 1,200 rounds of ball-cartridge, and the explosive bombs which had been found in their hands. The easy suggestion that the whole matter was a " massacre," an unprovoked attack by the minions of Bow Street, could hardly stand in face of the fact that the patrolmen had lost one killed and five wounded, not to speak of two soldiers slightly hurt, while none of the prisoners could show more than a few bruises. They made the most of them. Ings complained that he had actually been " collared and beaten about the head with a constable's staff, so that it swelled most dreadfully." For an innocent being armed with a cutlass, a pistol, and a large butcher's knife, this was indeed unmerited brutality.

The actual trial of the conspirators took place fifty days after their arrest. The affray in Cato Street had happened at eight on the night of February 23. The inquest on Smithers, with verdict of wilful murder against Arthur Thistlewood, ten more persons named, and " others unknown," had been held on the 25th. On March 2 the prisoners were brought before the Privy Council and examined, with the result that a " Special Commission of Oyer and Terminer " was issued for their trial, both for high treason and for the murder of Smithers and the wounding of certain other persons. On March 27 the Middlesex Grand Jury found true bills for high treason against Thistlewood and ten other prisoners, and for murder against Thistlewood and five more, who had been in the loft where Smithers was killed. Davidson and Ings, the two sentries, who had been below at the time, were not included in this charge, nor were several others of the gang. The names of the two approvers, Adams and Moniment, did not appear in either list—a sign that they were to be utilized for King's evidence.

On April 15 eleven prisoners appeared at the Sessions House, Old Bailey, for trial. These were Thistlewood, Brunt, Davidson, Ings, Tidd, and six minor figures, Wilson, Harrison, Bradbourn, Strange, Cooper, and Gilchrist. Besides the two informers, two persons who had taken a considerable part in the plot were missing from the dock—Palin, who had been in charge of the incendiary department of the business, and Cooke, who was to have led the party which was told off to seize the cannon in the Gray's Inn Road. They had succeeded in disappearing; much activity of Bow Street Runners, and the offer of handsome rewards, had failed to produce them, and they never were seen again : probably they had slipped away from London within a few hours of the affray. Of the twenty-five who had met in Cato Street on February 23, some ten or eleven got off undiscovered; but, so far as the evidence of the two approvers went, they were mostly mere " supers " in the drama. The only one who rouses any interest in the reader of the trial is a person, unknown by name to both Adams and Moniment, " a big man in a long brown overcoat," whom they had never seen before ; he had addressed the gang on the fatal evening. " They were there to serve their country, and if anyone was afraid of his life, he ought to have nothing to do with a concern like this—the one thing to beware of was drunkenness, which would be ruinous to a cause like theirs." He was clearly an earnest recruit for the plot, but a late comer, since two men deep in the matter did not know his name.

The eleven prisoners were arraigned together. Some little delay was caused by Ings refusing to plead in the usual form that he would be tried " by God and his country." He wanted to substitute " by the laws of Reason "—a fine French touch, though he was no doubt borrowing from Tom Paine, and not from any foreign source. All duly answered " Not guilty," whereupon Lord Justice Abbott announced that Thistlewood was to be tried by himself, and the others in succession. As things fell out, the chief, Ings, and Brunt had separate trials : Tidd and Davidson the mulatto agreed to take their fortune together : the remaining six were dealt with in a group. The whole chain of five trials was spread over fourteen days, from Saturday, April 15, the morning of the arraignment, to Friday, April 28, when sentence was delivered to all the accused together.

The main psychological interest of the trials consists in the curious attitude taken by the prisoners as the case against them was slowly worked out. A conspirator has it open to him to plead one of two things—either he is a "martyr," that is, he acknowledges his intent and glories in it, or he is a "victim," an innocent man who is accused by perjured villains of being concerned in a plot of which he knew nothing, or which never even existed. Each of these poses is excellent in its way, but in strict logic they are incompatible with each other. One cannot be both an unjustly-accused innocent man and also the martyr of a great cause. Revolutionaries on their trial have often failed to see this simple fact, and claim both merits for themselves. At one moment they are the prey of lying and corrupt witnesses, and make appeals to the immutable laws of justice ; at another they slide into a vindication of the crime of which they are accused, and boast of their share in it, as a supreme title to respect from their countrymen. This confusion of poses was very evident both in Thistlewood's own defence and in that of several of his followers. Instead of endeavouring to prove that the Cato Street meeting was harmless, or the whole plot an invention of the police and the Government, they spent a vast amount of time and energy in discrediting the character of the witnesses brought against them. Adams and Moniment were traitors, and a traitor should not be credited—even (apparently) if his allegations are borne out by innumerable scraps of corroborating evidence from sources which cannot be impugned. But the most telling part of the defence was an attempt to throw all the responsibility for the plot on to the shoulders of the invisible Edwards. There is good reason to think that this was a policy settled among the accused from the first. Moniment was a miserable little coward,

but there seems every probability that he was telling the
truth when he said that Thistlewood instructed him to this
effect on the day after their arrest, and long before the trial
had begun. "I was handcuffed to him : he advised me
when I came up to say that I had been brought to Cato Street
by Edwards. I asked him how I could say so, when I had
never seen such a man as Edwards in all my life "—it was
Brunt who enlisted him. "Thistlewood said that was of
no consequence. If asked what sort of a man he was, I was
to say that he was a little taller than myself, and dressed
that night in a brown coat." I fancy that from this hint
we can reconstruct the reason why Edwards is always turning
up in the statements of the prisoners, even in improbable
conjunctions, and why either he or Adams is credited by them
with the more startling and atrocious proposals. They even
said that Edwards invented the plot himself—which, considering Thistlewood's previous record, is absurd. "He knew
all the plans for two months before I was acquainted with
them," cried Ings. "I am like a bullock drove into Smith-
field market to be sold. I consider myself murdered if this
man is not brought forward : I am willing to die on the scaffold
if he goes there too. And that man Adams has got out of
the halter himself by accusing others falsely : he would hang
his God. *I* would sooner die five hundred deaths than be
the means of hanging other men." But the falsehoods attributed to Adams, when the accused went into details, turned
out not to be misdescriptions of the character of the plot
but errors as to the names of people present on different
occasions, or as to the number of candles in the loft on February
23, or the attribution of words to one rather than another
of the conspirators.

But, in fact, all attempts to malign the character of witnesses
—which was in several cases bad enough—were useless in
face of the mere facts of the affray. The prosecution had
the easy answer : "If these men were persons of abominable
character, if one is a professional blackmailer, another a
notorious swindler, a third 'a villain of the deepest atrocity
—his very landlord refuses to give him a character,' how came
it that you were, as you acknowledge yourselves, associating

with them for weeks and months in the greatest familiarity ? "
It was a case of *noscitur a sociis.*

The counsel for the prisoners—there were four of them,
Messrs. Adolphus, Curwood, Walford, and Broderick—had
an unenviable task because of the way in which their clients
persisted in " giving themselves away." Adolphus, the leader
for the defence in Thistlewood's case, spent the greater part
of his energy in trying to demonstrate that the conspirators
could not be guilty of high treason, because their means
were insufficient to attack the fabric of the English Monarchy.

" It is unworthy of the Government of this country to prosecute as
traitors some dozen ragged beggars impatient of extreme poverty.
Barracks were to be taken, cannons carried off, Ministers assassinated,
the Mansion House occupied, by some fifteen or twenty men—twenty-
five was the highest number that is spoken to. He believed that the
real object of the party was mere robbery—they might set fire to some
houses to obtain plunder in the confusion that might thereby be created.
These, to be sure, were heinous intentions, but they did not amount to
high treason. The Jury had heard the manner in which some of the
prisoners spoke of the shopkeepers of London—it showed their object
was plunder, and the bags produced were made for the purpose of holding spoil, not the heads of Cabinet Ministers."

All this, though ingenious enough, must have been most
distasteful to Thistlewood, who objected to being degraded
from the position of a patriot chief to that of the head of a
gang of burglars. The pains of the barristers were wasted
for a client whose exposition of his situation was as follows :—

" With respect to the immorality of our project, I will observe that
the assassination of a tyrant has always been deemed a meritorious
action. Brutus and Cassius were lauded to the very skies for slaying
Cæsar. Indeed, when any man, or set of men, place themselves above
the laws of their country, there is no other means of bringing them to
justice but the arm of the private individual. If the laws are not strong
enough to prevent them from murdering the community, it becomes
the duty of every member of that community to rid his country of its
oppressors. High treason was committed against the people at Manchester. If one spark of honour, one spark of patriotism, had still
glimmered in the breasts of Englishmen, they would have risen to a
man—insurrection had become a public duty. The banner of independence should have floated in the gale that brought the tidings of the
wrongs and sufferings of the Manchester people to the metropolis. Such

was not the case : Albion is still in the chains of slavery—I quit it without regret—my body may be immured beneath the soil whereon I first drew breath. My only sorrow is that this soil should be the theatre for despots, for slaves, for cowards ! ''

Translated into Brunt's less flowery style, the same sentiments appear in the following form :—

"Lord Castlereagh and Lord Sidmouth had an antipathy for the people, and if he did conspire to murder them, was that high treason ? He readily acknowledged that he had agreed to assassinate the Ministers, but he was no enemy to his country. He was an enemy to a borough-mongering faction, which equally enslaved King and People. He had joined the conspiracy for the public good. They might quarter his body, they might inflict on him any kind of torture, but they could not shake his resolution or subdue his spirit.''

Ings, an uneducated man, and not a great reader like Brunt, spoke only a few words, but they made the same point.

"His Majesty's Ministers conspire together and impose laws to starve me and my family and my fellow-countrymen. And if I was going to assassinate these Ministers, I do not see that it is so bad as starvation. The Yeomen at Manchester had their swords ground—and I had a sword ground too. I do not see any harm in that. I would rather die like a man than live like a slave.''

Not all the accused spoke up like this. Davidson, the mulatto, mainly harped away on the infamy of Edwards, though he raised a curious constitutional point. In Magna Charta it was provided that if the King violated the terms he had sworn to observe, the barons might rise in arms against him.

"Such an act in old times was not considered treason towards the King, however hostile it might be towards his Ministers. But this does not apply to me—I had no intention of joining any scheme whatever, either to put down my King or to murder his Ministers. I have been entrapped by those who, for private purposes of their own, have had my life sworn away.''

Several others of the less notable conspirators said no more than they had been drawn into the plot by villains, or that all the evidence against them had been perverted.

In every case the successive Juries of the five trials brought in verdicts of guilty. It is hard to see how they could have done otherwise. The sentences of all the conspirators were delivered together by Lord Chief-Justice Abbott. In form the death penalty was passed on all : but the judge, while rehearsing it, held out hopes that some of the condemned men might look for mercy. Within twenty-four hours it was intimated that only five—Thistlewood, Brunt, Ings, Davidson, and Tidd—were to die : Harrison, Wilson, Cooper, Strange, and Bradbourn were sentenced to lifelong transportation to New South Wales. Gilchrist was respited and afterwards given a pardon—inquiry had proved that he had never met Thistlewood before the night of the affray, that he was absolutely starving, and had been brought to the fatal meeting by Cooper on the promise of a meal. It was doubtful whether he had ever understood what was in hand. At the last moment the conspirators had absolutely raked the gutters for recruits.

The kind of execution by which the five men condemned to death perished was a curious compromise between old and modern forms. They were hung till they were dead, and their corpses were then beheaded. The idea that decapitation was the proper punishment for high treason still lingered, but sentiment and public opinion had so far changed since the great executions of 1746 that death by the axe was not enforced, and the horrid ritual of quartering was completely abandoned. Colonel Despard and his gang in 1803 had been hanged and then decapitated, as we have already seen. All the prisoners showed great resolution during the three days that they had still to live. Thistlewood, Brunt, Ings, and Tidd refused to see any minister of religion, declaring themselves Deists, and strenuously rejecting the notion that they needed any man's intercession before the Supreme Being. Davidson first sent for a Wesleyan preacher, and afterwards accepted the ministrations of the Ordinary of Newgate. He showed great contrition, received the sacrament, and spent his last hours in almost unceasing bursts of agonized prayer. On the scaffold he displayed as much courage as any of the other four.

The execution, which took place on a specially prepared platform of unusual size erected in front of the Old Bailey

Sessions House, took place at a quarter to eight on the morning of May 1. The crowd assembled was the largest that London had seen for many years—perhaps the largest that had ever gathered to such a scene, for the metropolis had doubled in size since the Jacobite rebels went to the block in 1746. Executions of highwaymen, murderers, or forgers were common enough, but this was to be something out of the ordinary : " Colonel Despard's job " in 1803, and Bellingham's hanging in 1812, could not compare with it for notoriety. But the precautions taken by the Government rendered the proceedings orderly enough—there was a large display of constables, and a force of soldiery, horse and foot, was on guard to repress possible rioting. To prevent people from being crushed by the swaying of the multitude, successive barriers of posts, bars, and chains had been put across the open space before the Sessions House and the streets that converged on it. Thus the spectators were cut up into a sort of " water-tight compartments," each block separated from the others. The early comers took their posts overnight, and whiled away the time of waiting by watching the carpenters erect the scaffold by torchlight. It was finished by dawn. At five o'clock in the morning the spaces from which there was a view were completely packed, including the roofs of houses for many hundred yards away in all directions. The reporters of the day remark that it was astounding that no accidents of any importance took place in such a vast crowd. Some people were, of course, taken with fits or fainting ; a line of men clinging to a light iron railing by St. Sepulchre's Church brought it down by their weight, and fell on the people below them, but no one got more than bruises.

The fact was that it is strong emotion—anger or fear—that makes crowds dangerous, and this multitude had come together merely to see a show.

" The conduct of the countless thousands assembled," writes an eyewitness, " was peaceable in the extreme. Curiosity seemed powerfully excited, but no political feeling was manifested by any part of the crowd, and they awaited the termination of the dreadful scene in silence. Sometimes a low murmur ran through the multitude as some new incident in the proceedings attracted their attention, but it was a murmur of surprise and interest, which never took the tone of clamorous disapprobation."

At the very last moment of the execution there was a horrid outburst of levity among some of the spectators, which must be described in its due place.

At a quarter before eight the prisoners made their appearance on the scaffold, led by Thistlewood. The bearing of the chief and of Brunt and Tidd was stern and self-contained : Davidson kept muttering prayers all the time of waiting. But Ings created an unseemly disturbance : he kept singing for some time in a discordant voice one of the Reformers' songs, " Oh, give me death or liberty," till Tidd turned to him and said, " Don't, Ings. There is no use in all this noise ; we can die bravely without being noisy." This only made the wretched butcher colloquial instead of musical. He kept up a fire of loud observations, advising the hangman to " Do it well, pull us tight." He nodded to people in the crowd, observing that " he saw a good many friends about." He shouted to them, " Here I go, James Ings, the enemy of tyrants," and, again, " This is soon going to be the last remains of James Ings." At the final moment, after turning to Jack Ketch and shouting, " Now, old gentleman, finish me tidily," he looked toward the crowd and, leaning forward, roared out three distinct cheers in a hoarse and broken voice. Thistlewood ignored him : his only recorded utterance on the scaffold was that he said to Tidd just before the platform fell, " Now we shall soon know the Great Secret."

After the trap had worked, the conspirators were left hanging for half an hour. Their bodies were then lifted into their coffins, with the heads hanging over the upper ends. The decapitation followed. A masked man in a blue coat and grey trousers came on to the scaffold and severed each head with a knife, not an axe.[1] When he had dealt with each

[1] I received a curious piece of information concerning this knife from the venerable Sir George Higginson only last summer (July, 1922). His father, an officer of the Guards, belonging to the company which was held in reserve inside Newgate, was asked to breakfast with the Governor of the prison after the execution. While they were at table

corpse the assistant executioner held up the head by its hair, and proclaimed to the assembled multitude, " This is the head of a traitor," in the ancient style. The crowd at first disliked the horrid sight : as Thistlewood's head was cut off many averted their eyes and others groaned. They looked with more steadiness at the decapitation of Tidd, Ings, and Davidson, some hooting and hissing at the operator. But when the turn of Brunt's corpse came a hateful incident followed. Thackeray related it as the most horrid story that had reached his ears when he was a boy. The masked man, on rising from his stooping position over the coffin, dropped the head, which rolled across the sawdust. Some brute in the crowd cried out, " Yah, butterfingers ! " and a number of others about him burst out into a horse-laugh.

It is said that the impression made by this hideous mirth on the rest of the spectators, and the report of it to the authorities, was the cause of the abolition of the ceremony of decapitation, which has never since been seen in England. Later traitors have always been merely hanged. Probably some general readers remember the Cato Street conspirators mainly because they were the last criminals on whom the ancient ritual of decapitation was carried out.

an excited official came in, and had a whispered conversation with the Governor. He soon departed, taking off the large carving-knife from the sideboard : Jack Ketch had forgotten to bring his full equipment of necessary tools !

III

RUMOUR IN TIME OF WAR [1]

For the first two years of the Great War part of my work was in Whitehall, where every morning I took up my blue pencil, as one of the much-cursed tribe of Censors. Those days now seem a long way off : I am not going to talk of the "secrets of the prison house," which indeed have now lost the greater part of their interest. It might be tedious to say what one thought of war-correspondents and war-orators, publicists, journalists, and propagandists, domestic and foreign, enemy and ally, their psychology and their methods. But I made some notes on a subject of general historical interest, which was always coming up during the Great War, though one had thought that the times and conditions were so changed that it would never emerge again as a practical phenomenon worthy of serious notice. I allude to the genesis and development of Rumours, Reports, and Legends of a false or exaggerated sort, during times of military or political crisis. The topic is enormous : two considerable volumes, I believe, have been written of late by a French publicist on "*Les fausses nouvelles de la Guerre.*" My own object is no more than to illustrate the psychology of Rumour, from incidents that occurred during the eventful years 1914–1918.

Between history previous to the nineteenth century and that of the last three generations, there is, in this province of research, one essential dividing point—the introduction of the Electric Telegraph, which not only made the transmission of true information infinitely more rapid, but also secured the contradiction of false information within a reasonably short space of time. In the days of the Greeks and Romans, or the Middle Ages, an immense lie about events

[1] This essay was delivered in its original shape as an address to the Royal Historical Society on February 14, 1918.

in a remote corner of the world might have free currency
for months : one about events only two or three hundred
miles away might remain uncontradicted for many days.
Even a highly organized system of posts, such as prevailed
in the Roman Empire, and in a less degree in the ancient
Persian Empire and the thirteenth-century Mongol Empire,
worked in a comparatively slow fashion, and in time of trouble
served less usefully than one might have expected, because
the public was naturally and rightly suspicious of official
communiqués. A Persian king or a Roman emperor could
not be expected to give sincere and full information about
palace conspiracies or provincial rebellions, for the benefit
of his discontented subjects in distant corners of his realm :
and the public was well aware of the fact.   On the other hand,
private letters not given to a Government messenger would
naturally travel slowly, and if wars or civil strife were preva-
lent, would not arrive at all, or arrive after unconscionable
delays. Hence Rumour, ΦHMH, the *Fama* that Virgil
describes, with her myriad eyes and her myriad tongues,
had a scope and a surviving power that seemed absurd to us
a few years ago, in the quiet days before the Great War, when
we wrote facile platitudes about the credulity of our predecessors in the Elder World, at which, in view of certain wild
days of the recent war-years, we feel that we must no longer
scoff.

The old-fashioned rumour was generally "tendencious,"
i.e. bore witness to a psychological state of expectation of
certain desired or dreaded events, and declared that they
had actually taken place. A fine example is the story of
Herodotus about the "divine rumour" which ran round the
Greek confederate fleet at Mycale in 479 B.C., that "on this
day the allies have achieved a decisive victory over the Persians in Bœotia."   It happened to be true—but was no doubt
merely the reflection of a reasoned expectation of such a victory.
May we not add as a similar case the story of the sage Apollonius Tyanæus, who exclaimed one day in the market-place
of Ephesus that the tyrant Domitian was being at that very
moment assassinated in Rome ? He *said* he had a vision
of the scene, but was it not the realization of a rational expecta-

tion ? I found a most curious parallel to this story of Apollonius in a modern Serbian book. On the day when Prince Michael Obrenovitch was murdered at Belgrade, a certain peasant supposed to be gifted with second sight cried out in the market-place of Ujitza, some 100 miles away, that " they are slaying the good prince." When the news of the sad event arrived next day, he was arrested as a possible accomplice of the conspirators, but was released on being found to be a respectable person with no possible connexion with them. The whole tale of Matthew of Kremna may be found at length in Chedomil Mijatovitch's *Reminiscences of a Balkan Diplomatist*, with some documentary evidence subjoined.

But ΦΗΜΗ was not infallible either in ancient or in modern days, as witness such incidents as the false tale that the Turks had been completely defeated at Kossovo in 1389, which led to bells being rung in Notre Dame and congratulatory letters drafted in Italy—and as a very modern case the rumour that Sebastopol had fallen early in September, 1854, which had achieved such substantial verisimilitude at Vienna that it was telegraphed on officially to London, and led to the firing of the Park Guns for victory—followed by sad disillusionment in a few days, when no confirmation could be got from the East. Both of these were incidents that might very conceivably have occurred in fact, and can best be explained by a mere false prophecy on the part of public opinion, without there having been any dishonest and deliberate intention on anyone's part.

Of course, such fraudulent intent, in rumours deliberately started, is not unknown, though I think much rarer than the other source of error. Good examples are the story that Napoleon had perished in the Moscow Retreat, put about by General Malet as the preliminary of his hair-brained *coup d'état* in November, 1812, which nearly gave him possession of Paris. This was a political lie. The more sordid form of the " tendencious " rumour, the Stock Exchange lie, seems to have had its first elaborate specimen some eighteen months later. In March, 1814, a group of financial operators in London, who had speculated on the early collapse of Napoleon's defensive fight in Champagne, found themselves about to be ruined

on settling day, and worked out a most detailed imposture.
They sent a bogus Russian officer to land from a smack at
Dover, with news that the Emperor was defeated and slain,
while the semaphores were set working to the same effect,
and a separate party of supposed French officers drove through
London with the same news. The speculators were thus
enabled to sell out without being ruined, but were easily
detected by the utilization of the principle of *cui bono*. Who
had profited by the rumour ?   Obviously those who had sold
out, at once and without hesitation, at its first circulation,
and had not waited for the further rise in all stocks which
would undoubtedly have come had the news of the Emperor's
death been confirmed. The incident is best remembered
because the famous naval hero, Lord Cochrane, was convicted,
whether justly or not, along with his uncle and his uncle's
partner, as having been concerned in the putting about of
the ingenious fiction. The case is notable as being both early
and elaborate ; later " stock-exchange flams " might be quoted
by the dozen, but are by no means so interesting.

The sort of false rumours that I have been quoting hitherto
were all concerned with matters of high political or military
import.   But the Middle Ages were no less rife in popular
fictions which were purely anecdotal, marvellous, or intended
to act as moral warnings.   Tales of ghosts, devils, or impossible natural phenomena, of awful instances of divine judgment on criminals, heretics, or blasphemers, used to pass
freely from mouth to mouth; and sometimes even to get
enshrined in a chronicle by some credulous writer greedy
of anecdotes.   For the sort of thing that would nowadays
appear among the "short paragraphs " of a penny newspaper would in the thirteenth century have appealed to the
less severe type of chronicler.   The parallels of the gigantic
strawberry or the five-ounce hen's-egg of to-day were such
faits divers as an apparition of the devil in Essex, or the swal-
lowing up by the earth of a woman at Newbury who was
adding appeals to God to rank perjury.   If the spot in which
the incident was placed was sufficiently remote from the
chronicler's abode, the story might get down in black and
white.   The length of time for which some of these legends

passed current is extraordinary. They emerge substantially identical in outline, but with locality and name and date changed, at very long intervals, and in very different parts of Europe. They were still strong in the seventeenth century, and I should not like to say that they altogether died out in the eighteenth. They were the parents of many ballads and chap-books.

But to resume the main thread of my thesis. The improvement of internal communications, and the spread all over the civilized parts of Europe of a system of public vehicles, stage-coaches, diligences, etc., was a severe blow to the prolonged life of rumours. So was the introduction of the semaphore system of long-distance signalling, which enabled Paris to communicate with Strasbourg, or London with Dover in an hour or two. But semaphores were slow in working, so that only very short and important messages could be passed ; and they were also liable to be held up, not only for hours but even for days, in times of fog, mist, or rain, when it became impossible to see one station on the line from the next, so that the working of its lights by night, or its arms by day, could not be verified across the many miles of space which always divided one semaphore from another.

The real death-blow to the long currency of rumours was only dealt in the middle years of the nineteenth century by the introduction of the Electric Telegraph, which (unlike the semaphore) was absolutely independent of weather and light ; and was also much more quickly operated. In normal times of peace, and in civilized countries, it enabled news to be circulated or contradicted in a few minutes over many thousands of miles. All Europe was ere long bound up in its network, the great expansion being between 1840 and 1850. The first submarine cable to France was laid in 1851, and soon the cable reached all save remote and unprogressive countries like Turkey. In 1854, when the false rumour of the fall of Sebastopol mentioned above was circulated, the only reason for which it was possible at so late a date was that the wires went no farther than Austria, and had not yet been extended across the Danube or to Constantinople. But it was not till twelve years later that long-distance submarine cables were first laid, so that America was still out of touch for anything from ten days to a fortnight. However, after one signal failure in 1857 the permanent Atlantic cable was laid in 1866. Its first notable success, as a transmitter of news outrunning the swiftest steamer, was the arrest of the notorious railway murderer, Müller, the Crippen of his day, who had thought himself safe when he took ship at Liverpool for New York, but forgot that the newly-laid wire would have warned the American police to be ready for him a fortnight before his liner came in.

There was only one limit to the news-circulating and rumour-destroying power of the Electric Telegraph, and that was the Censor in time of war. It soon became obvious that free transmission of military intelligence by war-correspondents and others across the wire, into neutral countries, might be most pernicious to the army whose movements were being reported. The cardinal instance of this is said to have occurred in the Franco-German War of 1870, where early news that MacMahon's army was marching from Chalons northward, heading for Sedan, is said to have reached the German head-quarters staff long before it could have been obtained by cavalry reconnaissance or other military methods. A war-correspondent had been allowed to pass some suggestive details practically implying a march in that direction to Brussels, from whence German agents telegraphed them to Moltke without delay. Hence came, according to the current story, the disaster of Sedan : for the French would not necessarily have been surrounded and cornered if their adversaries had not received an incredibly early indication of their move.

The artificial closing of the telegraphic communication, normal in time of peace, by the censorship of all parties, gave Rumour a new lease of life in time of war. It was quite impossible before 1914 to guess how long and vigorous that lease of life might be. Who would have believed that for a whole week Europe would be ignorant of whether Kerensky or the Bolsheviks were in possession of Petrograd, while both had their reasons for not sending out full intelligence ? The result was the setting forth of elaborate circumstantial rumours from Stockholm and Copenhagen concerning the details of the triumph of each side, all of which had many days' currency before the real facts came out. Again, early in February, 1918, it was wholly impossible to make out from the censored telegraphic dispatches of both sides whether the Rada or the Bolsheviks were in possession of Kieff. When rival censors are at work, both having tendencious purposes, and neither any regard for the truth, the golden age of the unofficial rumour has come again.

I can just remember the similar phenomenon which prevailed during the Franco-German War of 1870-1, when rumours had a mighty vogue. They were generally of an optimistic nature and from French sources. The putters-about of them always pretended to have good news, which the censor was holding back for some occult military reason. The majority of them had reference to the siege of Paris—the garrison had broken out, or one of the German covering armies had been completely defeated.

It must of course be remembered that so long as telegraphic news was absolutely dependent on the wire, all besieged cities were out of touch with their friends in the distance, and could only communicate with them by the rather precarious method of balloons carrying messengers, or the still more risky enterprises of disguised individuals, who crept through the hostile lines of circumvallation, and were lucky enough not to be caught on the way. How many heroic feats, like Kavanagh's carrying of the message from Lucknow to Havelock's camp, through a thousand dangers, have been rendered unnecessary in our own day by the invention of wireless telegraphy! That once astounding but now familiar device enables a besieged garrison to keep up permanent and regular communication with a relieving force, even though a hostile army and a hundred miles lie between them. This was seen in the Great War both at Przemysl and at General Townshend's defence of Kut, where the fortress was able to give the army outside whatever information it wished—in both cases to no successful effect.

But in 1870-1 Paris was absolutely cut off from the French relieving army, though it was no farther off than Orleans. Hence came the numberless rumours, that used from time to time to gladden the heart of provincial France, about successful sorties and breaches in the German line. They could not be contradicted till the next balloon got over the lines of contravallation, and had a currency of many days. Paris, on the other hand, was still more badly placed for receiving news of what was going on outside, and was even more the prey of false tales which there was no means of testing. For to get news into the city was far more difficult than to get them out. As Parisian siege-diaries show, this was the classical epoch of lying rumours in modern times.

The last crop of deceptions of this kind, depending on the absolute inaccessibility of a besieged garrison, which I can remember, were those relating to the alleged storming of the Pekin Legations, and the massacre of all their inmates, during the Chinese Boxer rebellion of 1901. Twice circumstantial tales of a disaster got about, and once they were so detailed, and were uncontradicted for so long, that arrangements (as is still remembered) were made for a memorial service at St. Paul's for the alleged victims. The truth only got known just in time to prevent this celebration from taking place.

Now that "wireless" enables a besieged garrison to give news of itself down to the last possible moment, such an incident would of course be impossible. The only chance of its repetition would be in small and remote places, unfurnished with the modern appliances, and besieged either by savages, or by an enemy who for his own reasons wished to conceal the news of his success for as long as possible, so as to delude relieving forces.

Since the Electric Telegraph has spanned the world, the rumour in times of peace can never flourish with regard to obvious public events—in a very short time it is discovered whether they have or have not happened. But ΦHMH had still one sphere open—a small and undignified one— she can be busy with personal rumours about individuals more or less prominent. She has taken the shape of mere scandal or slander, where she has as her scope no more than tales about the approaching bankruptcy or moral downfall of Lord A. or Mrs. B. Every one has heard false tales in

his day concerning the domestic or financial infelicities of
some notable member of society. But this is not the kind
of " Rumour " with which I am dealing to-day.

Occasionally stories of a circumstantial kind, which happen
to be entirely false, get an unfair start, through becoming
embodied in an official document which has achieved great
publicity, and has circulated freely through a whole country.
Examples ancient and modern are numerous. A very well-
known specimen is the French naval legend of the *Vengeur*,
which tells how on the " Glorious First of June " that line-
of-battle ship, encompassed by many British vessels, refused
to surrender, and went down with her tricolour flying and
her crew singing the *Marseillaise*. Barrère invented the tale
with all its details, and rehearsed it in the Convention, as a
purple patch of consolation to set at the end of a notorious
defeat. As a matter of fact there is ample British official
documentary evidence to show that the *Vengeur* surrendered,
and that her unwounded officers and crew, and some of the
wounded also, were taken off her by British boats before
she went down. But, as Barrère knew when he framed his lie,
British documentary evidence would not be available to the
French people, and his story was certain to get a start of
months, and even years, before any contradiction would be
forthcoming. So well had he calculated, that the *Vengeur*
has not only got into all the popular French histories,
but may still be seen represented in patriotic prints and
pictures adorning the walls of provincial cafés and hotels,
a century and a quarter after the supposed martyrdom of
the ship. Indeed, it is only in the most specialized and well-
documented modern French naval histories that the lie is abandoned. It may still be found in full in the respectable Duruy's
two-volume history of France, which was to the last generation of French schoolboys what Green's *History of the English
People* was to their English contemporaries.

There was a similar legend afloat in Germany in 1914–16,
which had for two years as great a success as Barrère's *Vengeur*
story. It was the tale that, two days before the outbreak
of the Great War, on August 1, 1914, French aviators dropped
bombs far inside the German frontier in violation of all rules

of international law, with the object of destroying railways.
This was a mere newspaper invention, circulated by Wolff's
Bureau through the length and breadth of Germany; but
it was taken up as a useful weapon by the Berlin authorities.
And the story that bombs were dropped near Wesel in the
Rhineland, and also at or near Nuremberg, figured both
in the Declaration of War served on the French Government, in Chancellor Bethmann Hollweg's speech to the Reich-
stag on August 4 justifying German policy, and in the official
communiqués circulated by the press. With this backing it
became firmly established not only in popular legend, but in
the dozens of "General Histories of the Great War of 1914,"
some of them very sumptuous and illustrated, which began
to be published beyond the Rhine. Nevertheless, there was
no truth in the story whatever : the Nuremberg incident
was formally and officially contradicted by the Bavarian
general commanding the military district in which that
city lies. But as it was only contradicted in 1916, when
the story had got well abroad, and only in one or two local
newspapers, the lie had had such a start that it became accepted
history. As to the Wesel flier, who according to the official
communiqué was actually shot down, and therefore must
have been either killed or captured, nobody has ever heard
of him again since August 4, 1914, though his name, the
character of his machine, and the place of his burial or intern-
ment would obviously have been forthcoming at once, if he
had ever existed,—since his crime would have been a precious
asset in the setting forth of the German justification for war.
The French Government issued a formal denial that any
French aviator crossed the frontier on that day, and an equally
formal declaration that the first casualty in the French flying
corps did not occur till more than two days after, long subsequent to the formal opening of hostilities. The German
public did not see French official documents ; and in any
summaries of the events just before the outbreak of war which
you may find printed in enemy lands during the years 1914–16,
the Wesel and Nuremberg incidents continue regularly to
crop up. So efficacious is a good start for an official lie, that
it may long circulate in full vigour. Scores of years after its

issue, only a small number of professional historians in the
country concerned with its framing will know its real character,
and many of them will not go out of their way to stigmatize
it for what it was.

These were "tendencious" falsehoods, made or used by
responsible official persons for a definite political end. But there
are many more instances where a perfectly truthless rumour
has been spread abroad by unauthorized and irresponsible
persons, till it has achieved a widespread circulation, and
has in some cases had considerable results on the envisage-
ment of the situation of the moment by a whole people. Generally such stories are believed because they are convenient
to those who wish to credit them, as throwing moral blame
on enemies, or ministering encouragement to those who feel
their need of it, or giving a plausible explanation of a puzzling
political problem.

To this class of popular legends belong such tales—to
take an old instance—as that of the Warming-Pan imposture
at the birth of the Old Pretender. We cannot trace it to any
definite Whig inventor, but it was a useful lie for the party,
and was believed because it was convenient. It penetrated
at once not only into mouth-to-mouth circulation, but into
pamphlets, popular songs, and even political medals. Many
years elapsed before it died out as a useful taunt to administer
to Jacobites. It was, we may incidentally remark, the last
example in English history of an old type of anti-dynastic
rumour, which was intended to throw doubt on the legitimacy
of a king or an heir to the throne—earlier and exactly parallel
cases had been the Yorkist accusation that Edward Prince of
Wales (the boy who fell at Tewkesbury) was not the true son
of Henry VI, the much more far-fetched Lancastrian counter-
cry that Edward IV was not the child of Richard Duke of
York, and the better-known story put about by Richard III
officially, that his nephews were illegitimate, because their
father had been secretly betrothed or even married to another
lady before he ever saw Elizabeth Woodville, so that his
union with her was bigamous.

A later example of a groundless lie, which ran far afield
and had considerable political results, was the panic during

the French Revolution called "La Grande Peur," a wild story of a hypothetical reactionary plot for a general massacre of patriots, which led to the general embodiment of the National Guard and many isolated outrages against royalists, though it had no foundation whatever. Attempts have been made to trace the origin and deliberate spreading abroad of the rumour to the *entourage* of Philippe Egalité, Duke of Orleans, but with little success. The rumour seems to have had no traceable parentage, but it undoubtedly served the purposes of the revolutionary party. In this case we may say that a phase of national psychology was the real explaining cause—the attitude of fear, anger, and suspicion was the parent of the necessary legend to justify its existence.

That such rumours are not impossible in our own day, when it might have been thought that the facility of internal methods of communication would have rendered them impossible, was sufficiently shown by the story of the "hundred thousand Russian troops from Archangel" which was so universally current for four or five days in the whole of England during the later part of the month of August in 1914. Probably every reader of these pages was more or less the victim of this rumour. I had attached little credit to it till, on the third day of its circulation, I got by one post three letters, one from a friend in South Gloucestershire saying that there were Russians at Avonmouth, only a few miles from him, a second from another friend in the Isle of Wight, saying that he had been watching steamers with Russians on board emerging from Southampton Water, and the third from Oxford, to the effect that numerous troop-trains, laden (as my informant was assured) with Russians, had been passing through Oxford station on the way to Southampton all the previous night. Then, I must confess, my doubts wavered, for all my three correspondents were writing from a very short distance from the places where the Russians were supposed to have been. It was only when days passed, and no credible person would vouch to having had an actual view of our imaginary allies, that one gradually realized that the true parent of the story was the general appreciation in England that reinforcements were badly needed at the front, and a wish that they should appear from somewhere, with a consequent legend that they had actually arrived. In fairness to the public it must be remembered that every one could see good reasons for reinforcing the Western front at that moment, when we were so hard pressed at the end of the Mons retreat. Moreover, there was no actual physical impossibility in transporting considerable bodies of men from Archangel to the Northern parts of Great Britain. The public could not know then, as we all know now, that Russia had no large surplus of trained battalions to spare at the moment ; her resources were believed to be unlimited, and available. Moreover, there was just the slightest base of fact for the rumour, as there chanced to be at the moment a considerable body of Russian military and naval staff officers collected at Edinburgh, who were making arrangements for the development of the traffic to and from Archangel with the British staff in Scotland. And also at the same time appreciable numbers of Russian reservists were passing into Liverpool from Canada and the United States, having been summoned to join their colours in Europe. I believe that at the most there were 5,000 or 7,000 of them, and they were, of course, all without uniforms and not moving in military units. How far this slender base of fact was responsible for the spread of the rumour I do not pretend to say ; but in the form which the rumour took, there was little relation between the foundation and the superstructure.

Yet we should remember that there was nothing absolutely impossible in the story, except the numbers of the arriving allies : for similar movements were in reality carried out in the course of the two following years. On one occasion Oxford station was really full of foreign friends—three train-loads of Italians, Austrian subjects who had been conscripts, had been captured by the Russians, and had volunteered from the Russian prison-camps for service in the Italian Army. They did perform the extraordinary circuit from Galicia, where they had been taken prisoners, through Russia to Archangel, from thence by the Arctic Ocean and the North Sea to Britain, and so by Southampton to France and the Mont Cenis tunnel. And a similar circuitous voyage was performed later, by a body of Austro-Slav enthusiasts, who volunteered from the Russian prison-camps to join the Serbian Army, and came round from Archangel just as did the Italians. The rumour of 1914 was therefore not quite so absurd as some people have styled it. At the same time, I believe that its origin must be sought rather in the psychological needs of Great Britain at the moment than in the small foundations of fact that I have mentioned above. The majority of the people who spread the rumour would have been quite unable to give reasonable grounds for demonstrating that the tale which they were disseminating was physically possible, so far as transport and movement of troops went.

The memory of the imaginary Russians in the autumn of 1914 suggests another curious psychological phenomenon of that time, or rather of some few months later—for it was most diffused in the spring of 1915,—the wild tale of the " Mons Angels." This had a vast popularity in April and May : in the form which it took in most cases it has been traced back to a letter in a local magazine from Clifton. The version there given was that on an unspecified day during the Mons retreat German cavalry had got round the left wing of the retiring British Army, and bid fair to take it in flank and roll it up with disastrous consequences, when a whole troop of shining figures was seen interposed between this advanced cavalry and the British flank. " The Germans to our amazement stood like dazed men, did not bring up their guns, nor stirred till we had turned off and escaped by some side-roads." One of the supposed narrators in this magazine added his personal experience—his company was retreating to a position where it seemed possible that a stand could be made, but before they could reach it the German cavalry were upon them. They turned therefore and formed up, expecting nothing but instant death, when to their wonder they saw between them and the enemy " a whole troop of angels. The German horses swerved round and regularly stampeded. The men were tugging at their bridles, but the poor beasts tore away in every direction from us."

The writer of the article in the magazine was traced, and confessed that the story had not come directly from the supposed narrators, with whom she had no personal acquain-

tance, not even being certain of their names. It was no more
than hearsay. No indication of this had been given in the
magazine, where parts of the narrative were couched in the
first person, as if taken down from the mouth of an actual
witness. There seemed some reason to believe that the whole
story had its ultimate source in a work of fiction, a tale called
The Archers, published in September, 1914, by Mr. Bernard
Machen, in which St. George and a company of supernatural
archers were represented as standing between the retiring
British and the advancing Germans who were outflanking
them. A correspondence concerning this supposed fictional
source continued between Mr. Machen and Mr. Harold Begbie in
the *Evening News* of August and September, 1915, and resulted
in producing the impression that while Mr. Machen's novel
was largely responsible for some of the details of the angel-
story, there was a substratum of other origin. That is, there
were certain British officers who thought that there was
something odd and inexplicable in the way in which the enemy
refrained from pressing the flank of the Second Army Corps
on the morning after the battle of La Cateau. It is now
known that the Germans were dead beat, and had suffered
so severely in the battle that they had no power to press
hard upon the retreating force, which appreciated the danger
of its own position in the acutest way. The troops were tired
out, and conscious that they were in no condition to fight
another action. Among the numerous letters which cropped
up during the controversy in the *Evening News*, there were
two or three which are worth noting. The authors gave their
names, and were undoubtedly present on the spot on that
day. But their evidence is not about "Angels," but about
hallucinatory French cavalry, covering the flank of the
retiring corps, which vanished in an inexplicable fashion
when the crisis was over. One witness, a colonel, writes
[September 14] :—

"The brigade to which I belonged was rear-guard to the division,
and during the 27th we took up a great many successive positions to
cover the retirement of the rest of the division ; by the night we were
all absolutely worn out with fatigue, both bodily and mental. No
doubt we suffered also to a certain extent from shock, but the retire-

ment was continued in excellent order, and I feel sure that our mental faculties were still in good working condition. On the night of the 27th I was riding along in the column with two other officers; we were talking and doing our best to keep from falling asleep on our horses."

The narrator then says that he suddenly became aware of a very large body of horsemen in the fields on the flank, moving parallel with the British troops, and covering them. He watched these squadrons for some twenty minutes, and spoke about them to the two officers who were in his company.

" So convinced were we that they were real cavalry, that at the next halt one of the officers took out a party to reconnoitre, but could find no one there. The night then grew darker and we saw no more. The same phenomenon was seen by many men in the column —of course we were all dog-tired and overtaxed, but it is extraordinary that the same phenomenon should be witnessed by many different people. I am absolutely convinced that I saw these horsemen, and that they did not exist only in my imagination."

The other narrator says :—

" We had almost reached the end of the retreat, and after marching a whole day and night, with but one half-hour's rest, we found ourselves on the outskirts of Lagny, just at dawn. As the day broke we could see in front of us large bodies of cavalry, all formed up in squadrons— fine big men on massive chargers. I remember turning to my chums and saying, ' Thank God ! We are not far off Paris now. Look at the French cavalry.' They too saw them quite plainly, but to our surprise on getting closer the horsemen vanished, and gave place to banks of white mist, with clumps of trees and bushes showing dimly through them. When I tell you that hardened old soldiers were march-ing quite mechanically along the road, babbling all sorts of nonsense in sheer delirium, you may well believe that we were in a fit state to take a row of beanstalks for all the saints in the calendar."

It will be noted that both witnesses speak of the utter fatigue of the marching column : but the one thinks the hallucinatory cavalry was a misrepresentation of shadows of the night and mist by tired eyes and brains, while the other thinks that there was more than imagination at work, only he will not vouch for what it was.

Whatever the right interpretation, there can be no doubt that many men on the exposed British flank, acutely conscious of the danger of an outflanking pursuit, thought that they saw large masses of cavalry covering them, just where they were wanted, for a considerable space of time, and then found that the supposed cavalry had melted away into nothing. Was it a case of the need producing the supposed remedy ? Or may we conjecture that for some time there were real French cavalry on the flank, which withdrew by some cross-road without being noticed at the moment of their departure ? At any rate, there is scant foundation for a legend of angels, though some definite evidence for what the beholders regarded as a welcome appearance of a non-existent force.

The story of the Mons Retreat Angels has undoubted relations in its extreme and fully developed form, after it had been improved by passing through many magazines and newspapers, with an ancient form of legend,—that of the visible supernatural champion who comes to help the army of his race or of his faith in a moment of supreme need. We can trace this back to Herodotus and the ghostly heroes who were seen fighting in the Greek ranks against the Persians. There is a fine example of it in early Roman history, in the story of Castor and Pollux at the battle of Lake Regillus, familiar to every schoolboy from Macaulay's *Lays of Ancient Rome*. But it is by no means confined to classical days— some of the more respectable chroniclers of the Crusades have a circumstantial account of the apparition of St. George, in shining armour and on a white horse, to lead the exhausted squadron of the Crusaders at the great battle of Antioch in 1098. It is more surprising to find that Santiago, who from a pilgrim-apostle had developed into the military saint of Spanish chivalry, not only manifested himself in several battles with the Moors in the tenth and eleventh centuries, but was seen as late as 1519 rallying the *conquistadores* of Cortez, when they were in danger of being overwhelmed by the masses of the infuriated Mexicans. But there is a more extraordinary story than this to finish up the tale of supernatural warrior-leaders. My Serbian friends assure me that there is no doubt whatever that in the Balkan War of 1912 many of the Serbian rank and file thought that they saw Marco Kralievitch, the hero of mediæval Serbia, riding on his white horse in front of the battalions that stormed the almost impregnable Turkish positions in the fighting that followed the battle of Kumanovo. And it was not mere isolated visionaries who declared that they had followed him, but whole companies and brigades. They saw the white horse ride up impossible slopes, and clambering after him burst through line after line of Turkish trenches. After this, who will think the assertions of the companions of Cortez very remarkable ?

A much more commonplace and comprehensible rumour of the recent war is one that was current almost everywhere about the middle of August, 1914, when the news ran that the German High Seas Fleet had come out, and had fought a general action with our own, somewhere in the North Sea. The versions only differed as to the relative losses, our own were always stated to be heavy—the German even heavier. There was no truth whatever in the rumour, which reached as far as Iceland : a friend told me that he had it in full detail at Reikiavik about August 12—the same day that I was told it myself at Pitlochry. This was, I think, simply the result of a universally current idea that the German Fleet *would* come out, for the strategical purpose of threatening the British coast, in order to prevent our army from being sent overseas to Belgium. Public opinion was wrong, and misjudged the psychology of the German Admiralty, which was not at that time prepared to stake its fleet-in-being on a very doubtful hazard, to secure an insufficient end. For undoubtedly at that time the all-highest command on the other side of the North Sea thought that our "contemptible little army" would make no difference one way or the other, whether it crossed or did not cross to the continental seat of war.

It will be noted that most of these rumours had their chance of life granted to them owing to that artificial hindrance to the free diffusion of information, which does not exist in normal times of peace—the existence of the Censorship. I set aside the Mons Angels and Marco Kralievitch as belonging to the frankly supernatural ; but the stories of Russian troops in Britain, or of "scraps" on a large scale in the North Sea, could only be circulated for more than a few hours on the hypothesis that there were political or strategic reasons for the Censor's keeping back the information. The reason would be obvious enough in the case of the Russian reinforcements, less easy to discern in that of the alleged naval battle. But the public always credited the Censorship with gratuitous stupidity, and reticence of the most senseless kind, so that it was not impossible for the circulator of rumours to gain acceptance for his tale for at least a day or two. He could point out cases, indeed, where reticence had in real truth been protracted for an unconscionable time, as for example the late acknowledgment of the loss of a certain well-known battleship early in the war. Every one could guess at plausible reasons for its being held back for a certain time, but it was the prolongation of the time which gave rise to comment. In this case Rumour was (by way of exception) founded on fact: it is one of the few prominent instances of the kind, however, that I can recall. As a rule, the tales, whether optimistic or pessimistic in tone, rested on no solid foundation, and were simply the expression of expectations, well founded or ill founded according to the amount of data at the disposal of the imaginative original starter of the legend. There was a curious example of the kind afoot early in the year 1918, to explain a phenomenon obvious to every one yet inexplicable to the majority.

As every one knows there were no air-raids on London between December 16, 1917, and January 28, 1918. By the time that the January full moon had been reached, all sorts of absurd rumours were current as to some new scientific invention having been discovered (I will not give the elaborate descriptions of it which were detailed to me) which would make all further raids impossible. On the 28th came another aerial visitation in the usual style, and the story of the wonderful invention fell flat. It was simply an attempt to explain an observed fact, made by imaginative people with no scientific knowledge whatever ; for the details given were impossible, as experts explained to me. This was an absurd optimistic rumour : there have been plenty of mistakes of the opposite kind, rumours of an equally irrational pessimistic cast, which anyone can recall for himself. They were for the most part attempts to account for facts that were worrying persons of a downcast frame of mind, by the invention of the most unpleasant possible explanation that could be devised.

In these pages I have been dealing only with Rumour in the strictest sense of the word. There is a whole section of psychological phenomena of an allied sort which I have left untouched of set purpose. This is the section that I may label with the heading of Prophecies. It may not be generally known that there is a small occultist literature in existence with regard to the war of 1914–18; in the National War Museum there lie some dozen books printed in all parts of the world— England, France, America, Germany—which recall the predictions of Nostradamus, Trithemius, Mother Shipton, or (in a slightly varied form) of the late Dr. Cumming and Madame de Thebès. The latter, I believe, died while the war was actually in progress, not without having uttered some of her usual type of vaticinations.

This kind of literature can hardly be called "Rumour," since it is generally printed, and not passed from mouth to mouth, and since it does not pretend to deal with the present but rather with the near future. The few books or leaflets that circulate to-day are the last survivors of a very ancient and prolific race. Prophets who see visions and write them down for the purpose of influencing wars, politics, or it may be morals, have always existed. They run into the lines of the ancient oracles and apocalypses at the one end, and into those of the modern tendencious pamphlet at the other. But I cannot call them Rumours, though they sometimes reflect the current and popular expectations of the multitude. Of course, the file of prophecies would not be complete without one or two pretending to be exhumed from forgotten mediæval volumes, and others identifying the German Emperor (like so many other hated characters of the past from Nero to Napoleon) with the Beast's little horn in Daniel, and No. 666 in the Book of Revelations. The professional prophets were on the whole very unfortunate in their prognostications concerning the details of the late war. Nor can we wonder at it; the expectations of much wiser men than the sort of people who compile such stuff were not fulfilled. Who, in England, France, Germany, Russia, or America, would have foreseen in 1914

the exact sequence of military affairs down to the Armistice
of November, 1918 ?   The makers of forecasts with no pretence
to supernatural knowledge were mostly by way of promising
us an end of the struggle in three months, or a year, or two years.
And the Germans were equally ill-served by their makers
of military prognostications, as witness the six months' submarine work that was to bring the British Empire to ruin,
according to the views of official and highly placed prophets.

With prophecies we may exclude, from the list of things
to be dealt with, dreams, portents, and visions, except when
they have been much passed round by the public mouth or
the printing press, like the Mons Angels, mentioned on an
earlier page. Usually they were literary productions, not
genuine examples of the credulity of the multitude ; and they
had small success for that reason, because the vitality of a
rumour depends on the condition that the recipients and
circulators of it should believe that they are dealing with a
something genuine, and not with a work of fiction.   Perhaps
one may add that dreamers of dreams and seers of visions
share in the curse of Cassandra : they have not as a rule
the art of making themselves credible—they are too often
obviously set on forwarding some theory or crank of their
own, which emerges too clearly, and enables the reader to see
that he is in reality confronted with nothing more than a
tendencious pamphlet in verse or prose.

My subject is one of a rather incoherent character—it is
rather like Virgil's Cyclops, a veritable *monstrum informe ingens*.
The strict logical arrangement rightly loved by the historical
mind is hard to secure, when we deal with such an elusive
topic.   All that is possible is to collect suggestive deductions
from many and various examples of rumour.   And if I am
asked, in the good mediæval style, to put a moral at the end
of my discourse, in the manner of the delightful authors of
the *Gesta Romanorum*, I am afraid that my moral must be
a very old-fashioned one, to wit, that we are the children of
our fathers, that we should not jest too much at "mediæval
credulity," and that we should recognize in the rumour-
phenomena of our own day the legitimate descendants of
those which used to puzzle and amaze our ancestors, whom

we were too often prone to regard with the complacent superiority of the omniscient nineteenth century. The Great War has taught us—among other things—a little psychology and a good deal of humility.

IV

SOME MEDIÆVAL CONCEPTIONS OF ANCIENT HISTORY [1]

To attempt to deal in twenty pages with the historical perspective of a thousand years would be an over-ambitious task, if one endeavoured to complete it in too minute and conscientious a fashion. But the views of our spiritual forefathers the Chroniclers of the Middle Ages upon the annals of Ancient Greece and Rome were so peculiar, not to say so preposterous, that they are worth collecting. For in order to understand the spirit of an age, one should have some conception of its outlook on the past. There were political philosophers even in mediæval days, and the theories of the political philosopher are based on his conceptions of the history of the elder world, and on the deductions which he draws from it. Most chroniclers, it is true, were not so much political philosophers as anecdotal annalists : but many of them were possessed with the same wild ambition for writing Universal Histories that inspired Walter Raleigh in his prison in the Tower of London. And some carried out this ambition, and piled volume on volume with small mercy for their readers. It is worth while to get some general view as to what the elect historical minds of the thirteenth or the fourteenth or the fifteenth centuries thought about the long series of years which counted backward from the birth of Our Lord to the creation of Adam, so conveniently and accurately fixed for 4275 B.C.

Professional historians were not over common in the Middle Ages, but it is to their views that we shall confine our attention. As to the conceptions of the unlearned we need not

[1] Delivered in its original form as a lecture to the Royal Historical Society on February 10, 1921.

trouble ourselves about them—though they have their psychological interest. To the large majority of men the name of Greece suggested very little—not more than that of Egypt or Persia,—and that of Rome not very much. We find it hard to conceive what sort of a person is meant by a " King of Græcia " when he turns up in some Romance in company with a king of Media or a Soldan of Babylon. As to the name of Rome, it certainly brought up to the man in the street three ideas—firstly, that our father the Pope lived there, in due succession to St. Peter. Secondly, that once upon a time there had been a long series of Roman Emperors, much given to putting the Saints to death in more or less barbarous ways. Thirdly, that the pre-eminence of those ancient heathen rulers of the world had descended to the continental prince now bearing the title of Roman Emperor, in some fashion or other on which the learned alone were entitled to have views. But certainly good Englishmen must deprecate the possible claims of that continental prince to be recognized as suzerain in England, as Duke Humphrey of Gloucester did with such firmness at the landing of the Emperor Sigismund in the year 1416.

There was a vague memory in most parts of Christendom that the Romans had once been spread over all the Western world, and had reared those great buildings, monuments, and public works of which traces were scattered everywhere. In many cases the magnitude of them seems to have so much impressed the simple mediæval mind, that they were believed to have been executed by no mortal hand, but by magic or the powers of evil. Examples of this are the Roman road in Northumberland which came to be called the " Devil's Causeway," and the long rampart which shut off Rhaetia and the Agri Decumates from inner Germany, which Suabians and Bavarians called the " Teufelsmauer." But often the tradition of Roman origin had grown so loose that the great works of the Flavians or the Antonines became ascribed to some native hero, or heroine, or semi-divine character, of the conquering races that followed the old civilization, like the *Chaussée de Brunehaute* in Belgium, or the Watling Street and Ermyn Street of England.

But we are dealing not so much with Roman memories enshrined in folk-lore and popular tradition, as with those to be found in books—giving the impression which ancient history left upon the educated and literary classes of the thirteenth, fourteenth and fifteenth centuries.

The first characteristic which strikes us in the mediæval author's knowledge of ancient history, is that it was nearly all composed of second-hand information. Of course the original sources for Greek history were practically closed, by the fact that the Western world was almost entirely ignorant of the Greek language down to the fifteenth century. Men like John of Salisbury and Bishop Grossetête may have had a smattering of it. But, as it chanced, the historians seem to have been one and all destitute of the linguistic knowledge which would have enabled them to go to Herodotus, Thucydides, or Xenophon, if manuscripts of those authors had been forthcoming. All information about classical Greece comes through Roman epitomes of second-rate value. And with regard to Roman history, where language was no bar, it is not too much to say that the Middle Ages had no criterion of the relative importance of sources. Though they might possess Livy and Cæsar—Tacitus was little known —they relied far more on compilations and epitomes, such as Orosius (first and foremost), Justin's abbreviation of Trogus Pompeius, or the lives in Cornelius Nepos. These were the staple foundation of those who wrote on ancient history, but they were supplemented by a profusion of anecdotes picked from the most various sources, from the legends of the Saints, Josephus, Aulus Gellius, Valerius Maximus, Augustine's *De Civitate Dei* (which supplied many a story), and in England at least (though not abroad) from Geoffrey of Monmouth's astounding inventions, which by the aid of ill-digested Welsh folk-lore falsified three centuries of real Roman history.

Now even from such authorities a historian with a good critical instinct could have written a more or less correct outline of ancient history, more especially of that of Rome, though so many primary sources now available to us were not in his power to discover, and although he had much worthless material at hand which we have learned to reject. But unfortunately good critical power was just what the average mediæval historian lacked. It seems that all written books had equal authority for him, and that he had not the *flair* to differentiate the good from the bad,—secondary from primary information. Indeed right down into Renaissance times this was one of the weak points of the scholar—as is well realized by all who remember how many of the early printed books are editions of authors whom we now regard as of very third-rate importance. Occasionally I have found even obvious works of ancient fiction quoted by a mediæval writer, as if they were historical evidence—in the *Polychronicon* Apuleius' story of the Golden Ass is seriously cited as evidence for the perfection to which in ancient days the art of witchcraft had been carried ! The consequence of this want of discrimination and historical perspective was that tales out of the Æneid were treated as being no less grave history than tales out of Josephus, and that the pseudo-Callisthenes received as much respect as a source for the history of Alexander the Great as did Justin or Orosius. Plutarch and Arrian, not being in Latin but in Greek, were of course not available for the history of the Macedonian conqueror.

Any one who looks through a mediæval history of the world will be struck, first and foremost, by the fact that the historians of those days had no dividing line between legend and authentic history. Cadmus was just as real to them as Philip of Macedon ; Romulus as the Emperor Vespasian. The tales of the early gods and heroes did not immediately betray their mythical character to the mediæval chronicler, as they do to us, by abounding in marvellous tales, in hydras and dragons, Cyclopes and Centaurs and Satyrs, and wolf foster-mothers. Such marvels the man of the fourteenth century was quite ready to digest and reproduce, and put in their due place in classic annals. The reason was that he could produce tales exactly parallel to them from his own legendary period, the Age of the Saints, the first four centuries after Christ. If St. George had slain a dragon, why should not Cadmus have done the same? If Hercules was said to have fallen in with the Satyrs, had not St. Anthony met and conversed with one in the Theban Desert? If St. Patrick and St. Hilda had turned noxious reptiles into stone, might not Perseus have done the same to the sea monster when he rescued Andromeda? Simon Magus had flown through the air by his spells—as we see him pictured in many a *predella*—till dashed down by the exorcisms of St. Peter. Was it then impossible that Medea, by equally wicked arts, had performed the same feat? Why should any one disbelieve in harpies and syrens, chimæras and minotaurs, when (as every one knew) there were one-eyed men in Africa, and gryphons in India, and all kinds of monstrous blends of man and bird and beast in the extreme East of Asia, such as the lively imaginations of the compiler of the Hereford *Mappa Mundi* and the illustrator of the pseudo-Mandeville have left portrayed for us. The merely marvellous and monstrous in those days aroused no suspicion in the historian's mind, and was accepted without criticism.

There was, however, one side of all the old classical legendary tales which compelled the mediæval chronicler to exercise in a more or less acute fashion his critical faculty. This was the habitual appearance in ancient tales of the heathen gods and goddesses as distinct and divine personalities. Of course Christian faith distinctly precluded the acceptance of these divinities as gods—the ten commandments rule them out. What then was to be done? The story of Hercules or of Romulus appeared to rest upon just the same authority as that of Alexander the Great or Julius Cæsar. Probably then there was some foundation for it, though it had got down to posterity in the wrong shape.

Now there were two ways in which the chronicler might discover an explanation that sufficed him as to the real origin of such matters. Firstly it was quite possible that the incidents occurred much as they had been related, but that the supernatural element in them had been attributed to a wrong cause. For though it was not permitted by the Christian faith to think of Jupiter or Apollo or Venus as gods, there was no objection to regarding them as devils. This view is often to be found in lives of the early saints, where we find stories of temples or statues shattered by a dragon or demon flying out of them in rage and despair, when conjured by the apostle or martyr who has been challenged by kings or priests to oppose the power of the Christian's God to that of their own local divinity. Many travellers will remember early Italian pictures in which St. Philip is deconsecrating the temple of Mars in this fashion, with a monstrous snake-like devil taking his unwilling departure. But the best story that I know of the kind comes from the life of Gregory Nazianzen. The saint, belated in travelling, took refuge in a dark portico, which at morning light proved to be that of an oracular temple of Apollo. The oracle that day refused to perform at all—the priests discovered that a Christian priest had slept in the shrine, and sent for the saint, to bid him take off the ban which he had unwittingly placed upon the utterances of their god. Gregory did not—as we might perhaps have expected—refuse the request, but, after warning them of the wickedness of their practices, wrote a short epistle, and bade them lay it on the tripod. The epistle ran, " Gregory to Satan : you may re-enter." When it was placed on the tripod, the inspiration returned at once to the priests, and the machinery worked as usual. From which we can only conclude that Apollo was Satan, as it would seem : or at any rate that Satan had control of Apollo, as a minor demon. The legend of the " Ring given to Venus " distinctly makes Venus a satellite of the principle of evil, who is seen walking behind the car of the great master of all bad spirits. But I take it that the Venus of the Tannhäuser legend is rather an old surviving nature-power of lust and luxury, than a mere instrument of the Christian Satan.

An odd variant in the treatment of the classical supernatural by the mediæval mind is a theory that magicians sometimes personated the heathen gods for their private ends. The most typical instance of such a case is that of Nectanebus, King of Egypt, as he appears not only in the *Romance of Alisannder*, but in the sober pages of the chronicler Higden. This monarch was truly learned in all the wisdom of the Egyptians ! And before he took to imitating the gods he had performed some extensive magical operations to the detriment of the navy of Artaxerxes Ochus,

King of Persia. *Per carmina magica*, we are told, *et per fig-menta fantastica*, he composed waxen images of the whole Persian fleet, which he set afloat in a bowl, and then sank by blowing into the water with a magic pipe of ebony. This proceeding had the effect of raising a storm in the Levant, by which the whole of the Great King's ships were wrecked. What would not modern admiralties give for the secret of this device ! But being finally driven out of Egypt, he unex-pectedly manifested himself at the court of Philip of Macedon, when he suddenly appeared to Queen Olympias amid thunder and lightning, with ram's horns upon his head, assuming the character of Jupiter Ammon, because as an African he had a preference for an African god ! Hence came the universal belief that Ammon had been the parent of Alexander the Great.

But there was another way of dealing with the classical divinities which was decidedly more popular. It was much more respectful to an ancient historian to believe that he had been misled by popular exaggeration and rumour, than that he had been deceived by devils or art-magic. This was the method quite familiar to the ancients themselves, and generally associated with the name of Euhemerus, the sceptic 'of the Cyrenaic school, who in his 'Ιερὰ Ἀναγραφή reduced all the gods into historical characters, whose doings had been distorted by tradition. I do not suppose that many mediæval chroniclers knew the name of Euhemerus —but his method was freely used. This produces some grotesque results : in a tabular chronological arrangement which synchronizes biblical and classical history, we find, in the same year as Abraham's descent into Egypt, the note "at this time there appeared near Lake Tritonis a virgin called Tritonis, who was also named Pallas from a giant whom she had slain—she invented the art of wool-weaving, and was therefore hailed as a goddess by the heathen." And so in the same way we find *Liber qui et Bacchus* flourishing in the time of Ehud, Mercury in that of Gideon, and the death of Hercules—by falling into the fire while in an epileptic fit—in that of Tola the son of Puah. Jupiter appears as a King of Crete, who drove out his father, King Saturnus.

He was a mighty conqueror at large, *et quia bellicosissimus et sceleratissimus fuit, a Græcis deus est vocatus.* In the same way Pluto was a cruel and gloomy king of the Molossians, who used to imprison travellers in an underground dungeon ; and Apollo a celebrated physician and archer. To call a man a son of Jupiter, Mars, or Apollo, merely meant to express in hyperbolical terms the fact that he was a person of great powers, bodily or mental. And thus the whole of the ancient classical legends can be reduced to workaday history !

When, therefore, by a rough calculation of generations the old myths had been fitted into a chronological table, they could be written down as excellent history, parallel to the Old Testament story from Abraham to Eli. After this had been done, it became an easy matter to deduce that it was absurd to make one god pervade the whole period. "How," asks Higden, "can Epaphus have been the son of Jupiter and Io, when the latter was contemporary with Isaac, while Jupiter is primarily connected with Europa, who lived in the time of Joshua, several centuries later ? " Why the connexion of Jupiter with Europa should be more convincing than his connexion with Io, passes my wit to tell : but Higden knew. I may here remark that when dealing with the Trojan legends, Vergil is always followed —with occasional hints from Geoffrey of Monmouth—that great source of errors. The mediæval version is therefore always grossly unfair to the Greeks—Homer and the great tragedians being of course utterly unknown. So we get a very Trojan version of the whole affair—generally ending with the migration of Brutus, that well-known kinsman of Æneas, to the Britain on which he bestowed his name.

When we get out of the time of legends, Greek history becomes a scrappy collection of tales of great men,—the outline from Orosius, the details from third-hand anecdotic people like Cornelius Nepos. Of course Herodotus, Thucydides and Xenophon were all unknown as sources. The importance of the Persian wars is vaguely adumbrated, but the ground-knowledge of the period is so faulty that, for example, the author of the *Eulogium Historiarum* consistently calls Leonidas of Thermopylæ the King of the

Athenians! There is a heterogeneous string of tales about
tyrants and philosophers, notably Socrates, Diogenes the
Cynic, Zaleucus, Plato, and Dionysius of Syracuse, drawn
from Aulus Gellius, Valerius or Isidore. But most of these
anecdotes do not partake of the marvellous or supernatural,
and we think (wrongly !) that we are out of legendary times
and touching firm ground of real history.

This is a vain delusion : Alexander the Great is yet to
come.: and with him we are plunged once more into a period
of wild tales, as astounding as those about the early gods
and heroes. For the strange legends chaotically mixed up
with the realities of his eventful life, one source appears to
be mainly responsible—the book generally known as Pseudo-
Callisthenes. There was, of course, a real Callisthenes [I
do not mean an ingenious modern gentleman whose name
is familiar to us all in connexion with Oxford Street], an
unfortunate philosopher who came to a dreadful end for
crossing Alexander when he was in one of his fits of oriental
megalomania. But the astonishing work usually known by
his name was a collection of folk-tales and anecdotic adventures, compiled apparently at the Byzantine Court, and
permeated with Persian as well as with Greek influence, which
was very popular in the West from the time of the Crusades
onward. Most chroniclers borrowed from it freely as a historical source—though in the shape of the *Romance of Alisannder*
it was also current as more or less acknowledged fiction.
The King's life is touched with Christian, as opposed to
classical, allusions in some parts, *e.g.* when Alexander reached
the Gates of Caucasus [not far from Baku] he found waiting
outside them the ten lost tribes of Israel, who requested
his permission to return to Palestine. But hearing from
the high-priest Jaddua at Jerusalem of the wickedness and
idolatry which had caused their exile, he refused them leave
to pass, and bricked up the Caucasian Gates with a great
wall. The moment he got east from Caucasus, he came into
the land of marvels—he received a visit from Thalestris,
the Queen of the Amazons, who prevailed upon him to refrain
from invading her country. When getting near India, he
came on the talking trees sacred to the Sun and Moon, who

prophesied many things to him—among others that he should die if ever he entered Babylon. Further on, he came to the land of the gryphons, and having caught several of the winged monsters, made an unfortunate experiment in aviation, on a car drawn by four of them, which nearly ended his life. Charming pictures of this incident may be found in many illustrated copies of *Romance of Alisannder*.

It is interesting to find that he took with him throughout his campaigns the philosopher Aristotle, as a sort of combination of intelligence officer, engineer and magician. The name philosopher had acquired in the Middle Ages a sort of secondary meaning which often amuses us. It was a general idea that philosophers as a class had always been addicted to dabbling in the Black Arts. Any acquaintance with natural phenomena or mechanical devices was in the Middle Ages liable to lead to a suspicion of nigromancy. For astronomy was hardly distinguishable from astrology, spells were supposed to be part of medicine, and any successful application of mathematics or mechanics to daily life was thought uncanny. So when the mediæval writer ran across a philosopher in ancient history, he at once suspected him of being a magician. Socrates suffered heavily in reputation because of his little inhibitory δαιμόνιον—the personified conscience which warned him against dishonourable acts or thoughts. In the chroniclers it became a very concrete familiar spirit : " *Socrati comes et instructor fuit daemon quidam,*" as we are told, and it taught him strange knowledge. He was once sent for by Philip of Macedon to ascertain the reason why a certain valley of Macedonia was unhealthy, and discovered by the advice of his spirit, and some operations with reflecting mirrors, that the cause of it was the pestilential breath of two dragons who dwelt therein. They were killed by a wily trick, and the region became habitable. Alas, that Socrates was not forthcoming when the British Army suffered so heavily in 1917 from the poisonous exhalations of that Macedonian lake Tachinos, which gave it so many thousands of malaria-casualties ! But Aristotle was a much better-known figure than Socrates, and has a whole romantic history to himself, involved with that of Alexander. He is said to have been the child of one of those spirits which are called *incubi*, because of the marvellous powers of his body and mind. As an example of his arts, we read that when Alexander was besieging a certain oriental city, many of his soldiers fell dead without any visible wound. He called together his philosophers to investigate this distressing phenomenon. Aristotle replied that " they die because on the walls of this city is a basilisc, whose look infects them, and they die suddenly because of the death-dealing power of his eyes." A simple remedy was at once devised by the philosopher, who ordered a very large mirror to be paraded before the walls. The basilisc's curiosity was roused—he looked out into it, and perished at once, slain by the reflection of his own death-dealing glances. And so the city, deprived of its strange protector, fell without further trouble. I am sorry to say that the moral character of the Stagirite suffers sadly in these romances—there is a weird tale of the indignities to which he was subjected by his mistress—of which you may sometimes see a representation in early Renaissance pictures. When Aristotle died he was interred together with his books of magic in a tomb constructed by himself, and guarded by a spell which prevents any one from being able to approach the place. We are, however, assured that in a future age Antichrist will discover a way into the tomb, and by means of the knowledge of the Black Art contained in the books will make himself for a time master of all the world.

Alexander the Great perished, poisoned by his generals Antipater and Cassander, who prepared for him a draught of such acid and caustic properties that no metal or earthenware cup could hold it, but only a receptacle of horn made from the hoof of a horse. They drugged their master with it at a feast, and his inner parts being burned up, he died immediately. With his end comes a very dry section of ancient history, where the late Roman epitomists direct the narrative, with occasional help from the pages of Josephus and Livy. The only really startling legend that I know of attributed to the period of the decadent Macedonian empire is that of Apollonius, Prince of Tyre, from which was drawn

the plot of the " Pericles " attributed to Shakespeare. It
first appears in the Pantheon, or Universal Chronicle, of
Godfrey of Viterbo, and may be found at length in that
strange collection of pseudo-historical gleanings, the *Gesta
Romanorum*.

We can now turn to the mediæval views of Roman history. For the beginnings of the Roman state the mediæval
chronicler had a splendid and most authentic authority—
the Æneid, taken very naturally as a versified chronicle of
primary importance. But there was much useful information also to be picked up from the first book of Livy. And
it may be noted that the tale of early Rome is often told
in strict parallelism with the tale of early Britain, ruled like
Rome by kings of undoubted Trojan descent, whose eventful
reigns could be excerpted from Geoffrey of Monmouth.

In early Roman annals there is by no means that constant
and persistent interference of divine personages with the
course of events which is to be found in the mythical age
of ancient Greece. The supernatural incidents of the Æneid
—the strife of Juno and Venus and the rest—can be cut out
without any injury to its plot. Still gods and marvels do
occur : but they could be dealt with after the manner of
Euhemerus, *e.g.* the story of the divine parentage of Romulus
and Remus can be simply explained in a light not very favourable to Rhea Silvia. Numa's visits to the nymph Egeria
are simply consultations with a " wise woman," which were
common enough in the Middle Ages—and so forth. Some
odd side-issues, however, get into early Roman history from
an unexpected source—local folk-lore. There had grown
up a whole series of legends concerned with the shattered
monuments of ancient Rome, which pilgrims visited, and
concerning which *cicerones* had devised tales so popular that
they gradually invaded history. The one concerning Trajan
and the unfortunate widow, mentioned by Dante, and sometimes illustrated in Renaissance pictures, seems to have origin-
ated from the same statue which now adorns the Capitol
steps, though in the Middle Ages it stood near the Lateran.
This equestrian figure of Marcus Aurelius—an admirable
portrait—seems to have had before it in its original sur-

roundings a small kneeling figure, since removed when it
was remounted in its present position in the sixteenth century.

Now, oddly enough, the statue got wrongly identified,
not only with the Emperor Trajan, and also with the Emperor
Constantine, but (what is really astounding) with the early
republican hero Marcus Curtius, the man who leaped into
the supernatural abyss which opened in the Forum.

Hence we get two diverging tales. Rome was once besieged
by a tyrant, a king of Messina, who had subdued all Italy,
not so much by his arms, for he was small in stature, almost
a dwarf, but by his skill in Art Magic. For he laid on his
enemies a spell which made them unable to lift a weapon
or strike a blow. No man could hurt him. When the city
was in these straits, a young man named Marcus Curtius
discovered a way out of the difficulty : the spell did not
affect animals. Having discovered that the tyrant was
wont to go every morning to a secret place apart from his
army, to renew his spells, he rode out secretly at dawn, caught
the enemy unawares, and trampled him to death under the
hoofs of his horse. The Romans in honour of Curtius put
up this statue, representing him in the act of riding down
the quailing sorcerer. Here it is easy to see that the legend
is made to explain the statue : but what is not so easy is to
see how it came to be connected with Curtius—save indeed
that there are horses in both the stories. But here comes
in the oddest part of the tale—some one rightly identified
the statue as that of Marcus Aurelius ; but the only result
of this was that in some versions of the story the name of
the philosophic emperor is substituted for that of the republican hero, and he is credited with the heroic leap into the
burning gulf.

The perfectly ludicrous form in which the story has taken
shape in that egregious collection of anecdotes, the *Gesta
Romanorum*, is as follows : " In the midst of Rome a chasm
opened, which no human efforts could fill. The prophets
consulted the oracles, and found that unless some man should
voluntarily commit himself to the abyss it would never close.
Proclamation was made, inviting a man to sacrifice himself
for the general good, but with no effect till a knight named

Marcus Aurelius said : " If you will permit me to live as I
please for the space of one year, I will at the end cheerfully
surrender myself to the yawning chasm." The Romans
assented with joy, and Aurelius indulged for that year in every
wish of his heart. Then remounting his noble steed he rode
furiously into the gulf, which immediately closed over him."
I should much like to know what would have been the real
Marcus Aurelius' conception of a pleasant " year off." Of
one thing I am sure,—it would have much surprised any
mediæval knight or annalist.

But to return to early Roman history. When we read
of the sack of Rome by the Gauls, we are rather surprised
to find that they were not Gauls at all, but Britons. Their
leader, Brennus, was ignorantly supposed a Gaul by the
Italians, merely because he came over the Alps. He was
really a British prince, the brother of King Belinus, who
is best known to the mediæval chronicler from his having
left his name to Billingsgate, in London. Expelled for rebellion by his brother, Brennus and his band wandered through
the West, picking up recruits here and there, and finally
ended by sacking Rome and setting up " Cisalpine Gaul " as a
British colony. It was rather unfriendly of him to attack
the Romans—since he and they descended from two Trojan
cousins—Æneas, and Brutus the conqueror of Britain.

Owing to the impudence of Geoffrey of Monmouth, the
father of all this British pseudo-history, we regularly find
the uncouth names of fictitious kings of the house of Brutus
the Trojan cropping up in the chronology of universal history for some 900 years before Christ, among the kings of
Judah and the consuls of the Roman Republic. The wars
of Ahab with Benhadad of Syria are agreably sandwiched
in among the woes of King Lear ; Xerxes and Aristides were
not far from contemporaries of Molmutius Dunwallo, Britain's
first legislator, and King Lud (who has left his name to Ludgate Circus and Ludgate Hill) might have paid a visit to Sulla,
if his inspirations had taken him on the same path as the
adventurous Brennus.

Later on, the Biblical tradition, and excerpts from
Josephus, impinge in many places on Roman history.

Pompey the Great, we are assured, lost his good fortune on the day when he persisted in entering the Holy of Holies at Jerusalem, despite of the protests of the High Priest. But Cæsar was, of course, a much more eligible subject for mythical adornments. Was there not even a "Romance of Julius Cæsar"? All the portents which attended his career are carefully recorded—including the gigantic phantasm which opposed him as he crossed the Rubicon. But perhaps the oddest is a statement that after his death, though he had been killed by more than twenty dagger-thrusts, his body did not show the mark of one single wound. As Cicero was a contemporary of Cæsar, I may mention that his name Tullius was confused with that of Tullus Hostilius, fourth king of Rome, so it is recorded of him by Higden that he was a Volscian by birth, who was wholly illiterate in his youth, and tended the flocks of the Roman people on lonely hills. Beside his dealing with the conspiracy of Cataline, and certain sarcastic epigrams, which have drifted down from early epitomists, the most interesting thing that I can find about him is that he had a wonderful power of penmanship, and wrote the whole of the *Iliad* in such small compass that the manuscript could go into the shell of a walnut![1]

With the coming of the Roman Empire we get into a very peculiar atmosphere. The all-important problem that presented itself to many mediæval minds—for example to that of Dante—was whether Julius Cæsar was to be considered the first legitimate Emperor of Rome, the starter of the great series of names which theoretically ran down to Frederick of Hohenstaufen and Henry of Luxemburg, and which was surrounded with a halo of time-honoured glory—or whether he was not a military usurper who had destroyed an ancient constitutional republic. Dante evidently opted for the former view, as a consistent Ghibelline: since he placed Brutus and Cassius as traitors in that innermost and hottest corner of his Inferno, the mouth of Satan himself. But

---

[1] Is this tale suggested by the Shorthand system ("Tironian Notes"), of which Cicero was the first to make use?

there was a strong tendency of the other kind in the air—some regarded Brutus and Cassius as tyrannicides and vindicators of liberty, and Cæsar as an ambitious person who met a deserved fate. It had been the view of the Roman senate —and became again the view of mediæval republican Italy, where emperors and tyrants were the foes of civic liberty, and civic patriotism was the ideal.

In the reign of Augustus Our Lord was born, and in consequence we have from his time onward a new series of sources which were at the disposition of the mediæval chronicler—the Apocryphal Gospels and the Lives of the Saints. From these come a series of anecdotic episodes, which, when absorbed into the general flow of the Roman annals, produce some amazing variants on received history. Augustus, as several famous Italian pictures show us, received a visit from the last authentic Sibyl, who showed him the Virgin and Child in a vision. At the same time a magic statue that was to stand till the Lord of all the World was born, fell to pieces, and a miraculous fountain of oil sprang from the earth on the Janiculum. The emperor did not live long enough after to see the development of the divine career of which such early information was thus vouchsafed to him. And we need not modify our views as to his character or reign from the new lights vouchsafed to us.

But when we approach Tiberius, we must cast away all our preconceived ideas drawn, from Tacitus and Suetonius. He was the wisest and justest monarch that Rome ever saw, according to the Gospel of Nicodemus, a primary authority for his reign : but he was afflicted with a sore disease, scrofula or leprosy. Now when Pontius Pilate had permitted Our Lord to be put to death, he was stricken with fear and remorse, and sent an account of the whole matter to the emperor, together with the seamless coat of Christ. Tiberius was much affected by the letter, but no sooner had he handled the Holy Coat than his disease left him. Recognizing the miracle, he at once acknowledged the divinity of Our Lord, and sought to place his statue among those of the gods in the Pantheon. This was strenuously resisted by the senate, whose obstinacy so provoked the emperor, that " *in senatum*

saevissime grassatus est." [1]   He slew many recalcitrant magnates—in revenge for this the later Pagan writers have vilely
maligned him, and represent him as drunken, profligate and
cruel.   His end followed not long after—one night as he
walked by the temple of Isis on the river's bank, he fell in,
or perhaps was pushed in by conspirators.   This, we read
to our astonishment, is the incident from which the river
Tiber got its name.   We are not informed what was its earlier
appellation—nor how Livy and Cicero, both accessible authorities, persisted in calling it Tiberis before Tiberius was born.

Though the chronology may seem strange, and the
parentage surprising, Vespasian, we are assured, was a prince
of Galatia during the reign of Tiberius.   His early experiences with regard to Christianity supply a curious parallel
to those of his sovereign.   One of the early apostolic teachers
preached at his court : he was converted and baptized.   Now
Vespasian had from his infancy been troubled with a dreadful,
even a loathsome, affliction.   " *Quoddam genus vermium
naso insitum ab infantia gerebat, quae vespae sunt dictae. Et
inde a vespis dictus est Vespasianus.*"   Now when Vespasian
had been baptized, suddenly all these *vespae* fell
from his nose and died.   Determined to show his thankful-
ness for the miracle, and fired with horror at the story of
the Passion and Crucifixion, he sought Rome, and obtained
from Tiberius Cæsar permission to destroy the Jews and the
wicked city of Jerusalem.   It was granted : and for many
years he was getting together an army for this purpose—
apparently all through the reigns of Caligula, Claudius, and
Nero—a slow mobilization of over thirty years !   Finally
he approached Jerusalem with a copious host, and wreaked
on the Jews vengeance for their crime.   He had hardly completed his task when messengers arrived from Rome to
salute him as emperor—the wicked Nero being dead.

Lest you should think of Vespasian as merely the enthusiastic
leader of an early Pogrom, I must present him to you in
another aspect.   The *Gesta Romanorum* endows him with the
character and legend of Minos.   He is said to have been exces-
sively unreasonable as to the marriage of his daughter, who

[1] Slight traces of this story occur as early as Orosius !

bore not the very Roman name of Aglæ, and was wont to turn all suitors for her hand into a labyrinth, where after fruit-less wanderings they were devoured, not however by a mino-taur but by a lion. His daughter took pity on a certain attract-ive knight, and gave him an endless clue of silk, which saved him from the intricacies of the labyrinth. But the way in which this first-century representative of Theseus gets the better of the lion is charmingly mediæval. He prepared, we are told, a very large ball of the very stickiest glue, and when the lion rushed on him, popped it into the monster's yawning jaws. The creature gave one munch, and immedi-ately found his mouth hermetically sealed. The knight then easily disposed of him, and made his way out of the labyrinth by means of the clue.

I might go on for some time giving further examples of the way in which the most time-honoured folk-tales of the general stock are fitted on to well-known Roman emperors —Trajan, Hadrian, Aurelius, Constantine—or in which their characters have been transformed, in order to fit in to some episodes from the lives of the Saints. But I will not go on to tell you how " Domitian was a very just and merciful prince," or how Philip (the murderer of Gordian III) was the first Christian emperor—a very early tale, for St. John Chrysostom says that he carried out a penance imposed on him by Babylas, bishop of Antioch,—or how Maximian " was a very gentle and peaceful emperor " : on the other hand Julian the Apostate, for whom mediæval chroniclers con-ceived that nothing was too bad, is in one history made to enact the whole appalling career of Œdipus. Suffice it to say that all through the centuries before the Renaissance, in the days when no criterion of historical values existed, and all sources were regarded as about equally credible, the reading of the Roman annals in any universal history presents to the student the most unrivalled opportunities for getting new, startling, and wholly unreliable side-lights on the men-tality and adventures of his oldest Roman friends. I some-times hope that it may be granted to me, in some improbable moment of leisure, to write a general narrative of the first three centuries of our Era, in which no authentic sources whatever shall be employed, and the *Gesta Romanorum* and Geoffrey of Monmouth shall form my most precious authorities.

Without going into Imperial scandals on the one side, or hagiography on the other, I may conclude this dissertation by one short note on the greatest figure of Roman history —neither an emperor nor a saint, but simply "Magister Vergilius," poet and necromancer. Why the author of the Æneid and the Georgics should have become such a dominant figure alike in history and fiction it is hard to discern— but he not only accompanies Dante in his awful visit to the other world, but pervades many lighter tales in a less majestic capacity. Some think that the profound respect for him as the one great surviving poet from the classical tradition, caused him to be invested with supernatural honours, much as Homer was deified in ancient Greece. Sometimes he is next door to a Christian saint, and by an ingenious perversion of well-known passages in his works foresees the Christian not the Augustan Golden Age, and sings not of the young Marcellus but the Messiah. Serious modern commentators have maintained that he took a glimpse into the Jewish scriptures. More often he becomes supernatural indeed, but not saintly; he is a first-class necromancer—"a dealer in magic and spells, in ever-filled purses, in blessings and curses, in prophecies, witches and knells." The names of his mother and grandfather, Maia and Maius, were corrupted into Maga and Magus, so that he could be said to have been reared by ancestors skilled in the Black Art. The incantation scene described in the eighth Eclogue was supposed to imply an over-great knowledge of incantations in the poet himself. But whatever was the origin of the belief, it led to the most marvellous stories, which introduce Vergil as a mighty mechanician and enchanter, superior, perhaps, even to Aristotle himself. He made an invisible wall of compressed air to surround his garden which kept out trespassers without their being able to understand why they could not get through. He also could rear a bridge of air to carry him wherever he chose to go. Naples, we are told, being troubled with a plague of water-leeches, Vergil fashioned a golden leech, which being thrown into the water proceeded to deliver the city from its pest, by devouring all the natural ones. He fashioned for Augustus a set of images called "Salvatio Romæ." They consisted of representations of all the provinces of the Roman Empire, each bearing a bell in its hand. They were endued with such mystic power that when any region was planning rebellion, the image personifying it commenced to ring its bell, and did not stop doing so till the emperor had taken notice of it. Thus Augustus was enabled to direct timely measures for the repression of any sedition before it had time to come to a head. This suggests a primitive adumbration of the idea of wireless telegraphy. But more surprising still is it to find that Vergil also made for the Emperor Titus—he must have been a centenarian by this time—a still more useful machine—an image that, by the mysterious powers with which it was endowed, communicated to the emperor all offences committed in the city in secret. The illustrative anecdote which follows shows that it revealed even such a trifling breach of the law as working on a public holiday. So great was the consequent unpopularity of the machine among habitual offenders, that Titus had to place a guard of soldiers over it, to prevent it from being broken at night. How convenient it would be if England could be endowed by some modern Vergil with an automatic and infallible secret police information department!

Vergil working in the reign of Titus is surprising—but how much more is it to find in the *Eulogium Historiarum* under the year-date 548, and in the Pontificate of Silverius II, the note "Hoc Anno Virgilius Neapoli sepultus est, cum libro suo." He must have survived, then, for some six centuries, and like Aristotle before him, and Michael Scott after, was buried with his book of spells—which have been sought by many but never found.

Truly there was a time when history could not be called a *dull* science, nor its votaries styled pedants lacking in imagination!

V

A FORGOTTEN HERO : BASIL OF CAPPADOCIA

"Let us now discourse of the illustrious Basil Digenes Akritas, the rose of Cappadocia, the most handsome and valiant of all the warriors of his day, who subdued the castles of rebels and the cities of infidels till his fame extended over all lands as far as Euphrates. Cease, O vain singers, to chant the old lying tales about Hector and Achilles. Remember that Alexander the Macedonian conquered the world by the power of his mighty brain and the manifest help of God, but in personal strength and courage was no greater than other men. Above all sing no more of Philopappus and Cinnamus and the much-praised Joannikius—bold outlaws all, I grant, yet boasters who magnified their own exploits. But the feats of arms of Basil the Warden of the Marches are genuine and well-attested, and let no man refuse his credence to them."

So sang the eleventh-century bard concerning his hero, the champion of a great empire that was about to fall, the protector and patron of a Christian land that was to pass a few years later into the hand of the all-destroying Turk. For three generations after Basil's death the old Byzantine boundary, which had stood firm against the shocks of five hundred years of constant war, gave way at last. The infidel broke in, and there was an end of the Cappadocia that the poet knew, with its towering castles, its palaces of marble and mosaic, its golden churches, and its ancient and turbulent feudal aristocracy. We cannot even identify the towers and passes, the streams and villages round which the tale of Basil's life-work is centred. When next a Christian army toiled over those uplands—it was the way-worn marching column of the First Crusade—Cappadocia was a land of ruins, scantily peopled by the migratory hordes of the Seljouks. A local civilization had vanished, of which the lay of Basil the Brave gives the only remaining detailed picture.

That a Byzantine frontier-baron might be a hero of romance is still a somewhat unfamiliar idea. The very word Byzantine has a flavour of decadence and contempt about it. The tale of the Eastern Empire still bears the slur which the malignant Gibbon laid upon it, and its statesmen and soldiers are still conceived as Walter Scott drew them in his *Count Robert of Paris.* Specialists only read the monumental works of Finlay or of Schlumberger, and realize that the men who beat off Persian and Saracen, Slav and Bulgarian and Russian, for generation after generation, were not wholly effete or wholly vile.

Basil Digenes Akritas was in nowise a Byzantine noble of the type which Gibbon loved to paint. He did not sit at Constantinople employed in palace intrigues and slavish courtiership, and working by hook or by crook to win some grotesque title, such as Grand Drungiary, or Protospathiarius, or Logothete of the Post. He never visited Constantinople indeed at all so far as we know, and was purely provincial and military in his tastes—a hard-working and hard-fighting Warden of the Marches, whose individuality, for one reason or another, so much impressed his contemporaries that the memory of him was preserved not only in the ten-canto epic which bears his name, but in proverbs and folk-songs, of which some fragments remain. Two centuries after Basil's death, the poet Theodore Prodromus could find no better compliment for the knightly emperor Manuel I, than to call him " the second Akritas," and in another passage sighed in vain for a blow from the iron mace of the departed hero to sweep away the luxury and self-indulgence of his own day.

Yet, putting poetry and folk-tales aside, we know uncommonly little of the real Basil Akritas. He can be compared with absolute accuracy to the typical paladin of the Court of Charlemagne. Roland, the hero of romance, has quite driven from men's memory the true " Rhotlandus comes limitis Britannici " who fell at Roncesvalles. And similarly Basil, the queller of Amazons and the slayer of dragons,

has eclipsed the tangible Digenes Akritas, the Warden of
the Cappadocian March, and one of the trusted generals of
the Emperor Nicephorus Phocas.

Before we pass on to the Basil of Romance, we may as
well dismiss the real soldier of the Eastern front, who is a
much less interesting figure than his glorified epic shadow.
From the eighth century to the eleventh the house of Ducas
was without dispute the oldest and noblest in Cappadocia.
It claimed to descend from a Roman "dux," a comrade and
kinsman of Constantine the Great. The genealogy is more
than doubtful for its first three hundred years, but 'from
the eighth century onward there is no doubt that it gave
many good generals to the Byzantine army. And in the
eleventh two emperors, who gloried in the family name,
sat on the throne of Constantinople. The local greatness
of the clan of Ducas, and its ambitions, made it a mark for
the hatred of several of the princes, sprung from other and
less noble houses, who ruled the East-Roman realm, and
especially those of the Macedonian dynasty who reigned in
the tenth and eleventh centuries. Leo VI, mostly unjustly
called Leo the Wise, and his favourite Samonas so harried
Andronicus Ducas, the head of his house in 908, that he
threw up his allegiance to the empire, and retired with his
family and his retainers into the heights of Taurus, there
to dwell as an outlaw. While he, his sons, and his men-at-
arms were absent from their camp, it was surprised by the
Emir Mousour, one of the Wardens of the Caliph's western
borders. Among the prisoners whom the Saracen captured
was Arete Ducas, the only daughter of Andronicus. From
the union of parents who first met in this rough fashion,
the Moslem chief and the captive Christian lady, sprang
Basil the Brave, whom after-generations called "Digenes,"
the man of two races, because Arab and Christian blood
flowed mixed in his veins.

Now Mousour was not all Arab—indeed, his father had been
a Christian and a fanatic. The last chief of those strange
Puritan heretics, the Paulicians, who gave the Byzantine
Empire so much trouble in the ninth century, had been a
certain Chrysocheir, a desperate rebel, who, when his sec-

taries were driven out of Anatolia, had taken refuge with the Saracen enemy. The Emir Omar of Malatia had not only harboured the exile, but given him one of his daughters in marriage. Chrysocheir was killed not long afterwards in a reckless foray, leaving an infant son, whom his mother brought up as a Moslem and named after her brother, Mousour, Emir of Tarsus. He became a famous warrior and served his Arab uncle and grandfather as the captain of three thousand light horse. For some years he had been the plague of the Cappadocian border, and his name was cursed as far away as Iconium and Amorium : but he was known as a generous and high-minded enemy.

The sack of the upland camp of the outlawed house of Ducas was the turning-point in the history of this young adventurer. When the captive Arete was brought before him it was a case of "love at first sight." He offered her no violence, treated her with chivalrous respect, and when her brothers came to seek and ransom her, made them the astounding offer that he would cast away his turban and receive baptism if they would give him their sister's hand in lawful marriage. Apparently the spiritual yoke of Islam sat lightly upon him, and he had not forgotten that he was the son of a Christian and an East-Roman father—though that father had been a heretic and a rebel. The offer was too good to refuse—the Emir was welcomed, he carried out his promise, was baptized by the name of John, and took his wife's family name of Ducas. When, after the death of Leo VI in 912 and the civil strife which followed, the Regent-Emperor Romanus Lecapenus came into power, and the survivors of the exiled Cappadocian nobles were restored to their lands and honour, the Emir was received into grace along with them, and granted a fief on the border, which he now had to defend against his former co-religionists. Whereupon the family bard sagely remarked that Love is a power inexplicable and immeasurable. "It rescued a captive, it stopped a raiding army on its march, it persuaded a hero to deny his faith and break his career : and all the world marvelled that one fair damsel by charm and sweetness had wrecked the most famous of all the war-bands of Syria."

Of the marriage of John-Mousour and the daughter of Andronicus Ducas, Basil " Digenes " was the only offspring, though the pair who had first met under such unpromising conditions enjoyed a prosperous wedded life of more than thirty years and lived to see their son become a man of mark. He was, like all his ancestors on both sides, a desperate fighter, and was made at an early age Warden of one of the " Akritic Themes "—*i.e.* frontier marches in the curious Byzantine phraseology. From holding this office and discharging its duties with unparalelled vigour and success, Basil got his honourable nickname of "the Akritas," the Man of the Marches *par excellence.* His military career was distinguished, though from the scanty mentions of him in the chronicles we should never have guessed that it had that romantic side which struck the imagination of his neighbours and retainers. He was present with his contingent at the long siege of Edessa in 942, and succeeded the celebrated John Kurkuas as commander-in-chief on the Eastern frontier in the same year. He fell into disfavour under the reign of that narrow-minded pedant, Constantine Porphyrogenitus, but was restored to favour under Romanus II, and ruled once more his Cappadocian border-province down to the time of Nicephorus Phocas, who treated him with great confidence and distinction. Somewhere about the year 965 he died, still in vigorous middle age, but having most certainly seen more summers than the scant thirty-three which the author of the Epic allots to him. Though married many years back to a distant relative, a lady of the much-ramified clan of Ducas, he left no issue.

So much for the Basil Digenes Akritas of history. Let us now turn to the Basil of Romance. His tale is told by an anonymous bard of the early eleventh century, who wrote before Cappadocia had fallen into the hands of the invading Turk—*i.e.* before 1071 and the battle of Manzikert. He was probably a dependent of some branch of the house of Ducas, since he displays a competent knowledge of its genealogy, and a great pride in the exploits of its elder generations. He was a man of some education, for he quotes Homer as freely as the Bible, and alludes not only to heroes known

from popular folk-tales, such as Alexander the Great, but
to minor characters of classical antiquity such as Bellerophon
and Olope. Other allusions and comparisons show us that
he was also acquainted with a cycle of tales of Byzantine
adventure which have not come down to us, though they
must have been popular in the eleventh century, the legends
of the outlaws of Taurus, whose exploits he continually
disparages. Had some other local bard been singing of them
of late, and was the admirer of Basil set on snubbing a rival ?
But the author of " Digenes," though obviously a man of
some knowledge and culture, was no historian—he thought
that Chosroes, the great sixth-century King of Persia, had
been a Moslem : " He was the first of the sons of Hagar who
overran Anatolia and came to besiege Constantinople, and
Omar, the great Sultan was the second." He mixed up
the two emperors, Romanus I and Romanus II, though
they lived not more than a century before his own time.
He makes famous relatives of Basil come to bless his early
exploits, who had really perished while the hero must have
been in his cradle. And he thought that Carvas (or Caröes
as he calls him), the great Paulician rebel-chief, had been a
Saracen, and not a heretical Christian. But these are trifles
—the poet was clearly above rather than below average
contemporary culture. He wrote, however, not in pseudo-
classical Greek, like contemporary chroniclers, poets, and
divines at Constantinople, but in the spoken dialect, or " vulgar " Greek, of the eleventh century. Of that tongue his
work is apparently the oldest serious document that has
survived. The metre of the poem is what is called " political " verse, lines of fifteen syllables, with a stress laid on
the odd numbers, the 3rd, 5th, 7th, etc. As a typical screed
of it we may quote the exordium to Canto VII, wherein
the bard sets forth the eternal theme that " in the spring
a young man's fancy lightly turns to thoughts of love "—
very much in the style of *Locksley Hall*.

Τὸν βασιλέα τῶν μηνῶν τίς βουληθείη λέγειν ;
Μάϊος ἐβασίλευσεν εἰς ἅπαντας τοὺς μῆνας,
Κόσμος αὐτὸς φαιδρότατος ἁπάσης γῆς τυγχάνει,
Πάντων φυτῶν ὁ ὀφθαλμὸς καὶ τῶν ἀνθῶν λαμπρότης,

Λειμόνων τε περικαλλῶν τὸ ἄνθος ἐξαστράπτον
Ἔρωτα πνέει θαυμαστόν πρόξενον Ἀφροδίτης.
Τότε γινώσκεται σαφῶς τοὺς ὑπουργοῦντας ἔρως,
Καὶ πᾶς φιλῶν εὐφραίνεται τῆς ἡδονῆς μεγάλως.

We may add that the poem contained ten cantos, and that, of these, fragments, amounting to about two cantos, are missing, including (unfortunately) both the whole of Canto I and the greater part of Canto X, in which the death of Basil was recounted. Thus we lack the historical summary which undoubtedly started the poem, and all but a scrap of Basil's dying speech to his wife, with which it ended.

To give an analysis of the whole poem would be tedious : there are plenty of long screeds in this romance, as in most others, where the poet gets drawn away into descriptions of feasts and ceremonies, of hunting and sportsmanship, of the building of churches, palaces and castles, which might belong to any other tale ; they may perhaps give the atmosphere of the times, but they do not forward the story. Doubtless the poet's audience loved to hear the details of a particularly splendid marriage dinner, of a dowry such as no contemporary father could give his daughter, of an ideal castle, or a robe of surpassing magnificence. But it is the action of a tale which settles its merit, not its merely descriptive passages.

Action there is in plenty in the romance of Basil Digenes, but it is not precisely what we might have expected. The main episodes are not concerned with his great regular campaigns : the siege of Edessa is not even mentioned ; nor is his political importance emphasized, though we have an interesting account of the visit of the Emperor Romanus II to the Cappadocian border, and of the reception which Basil made for him.- The words of advice which he ventured to give his sovereign—very free-spoken advice such as one would not suppose that a Byzantine ruler often heard from his subjects—run as follows : " Sire, may you and your host ever fare well ; but as to the gifts and the honours which you offer me, pass them on to less wealthy warriors, for I know that the expenses of your empire are incalculable. The best boons that a great and worthy king can give to his people are kindness for the exile, food for the hungry, deliverance for those unjustly oppressed, pardon for those who have sinned in thought but not in deed, careful investigation before any man is condemned. These, great Emperor, are the works of righteousness, by means of which you may subdue all your enemies. For mere force does not suffice a king for the holding down and administering of his realm : kingcraft is a special gift from the hand of God Most High. And to win the grace of God, I, your loyal servant, as the most useful offering that I can make, hereby renounce for the term of my natural life all the payments which come from your exchequer for the Wardenship of this March. And from this day you may dismiss all consideration of them, and I pledge myself that your enemies shall be made the slaves of your empire." There was undoubtedly in the mention of "those who have sinned in thought but not in deed " and "those who had been condemned without investigation," an allusion to the misfortunes of the elder generation of Basil's own family, who had been driven into rebellion by false accusations and condemned without a hearing. And Romanus, in the poem, catches the allusion, and promises, in return for the offer made him, to restore all the possessions confiscated long years back, at the time of the attainting and forfeiture of Basil's grandfather, Andronicus Ducas.

There is no one of the ten cantos which narrates Basil's campaigns against the Saracens, though there are frequent allusions to them. "·Before his day the Children of Hagar often came into Romania, wasting on every side in Charsiana, and by Heraclea, and by Amorium and Iconium, even as far as Ancyra and beautiful Smyrna and the plains of Ionia along the sea. But since the rise of Akritas, the son of the noble Emir, the Romans may boast that by the grace of God they have subdued all their foes, routing them completely. For from the moment when the noble and valiant Akritas began his exploits in Syria no enemy dared stand against him, and peace and tranquillity reigned throughout

the borders. Syria cowered before him, and his fear spread
all over the lands of Babylon."

But the exploits of Basil which interested the bard were
his wonderful hunting ; his romantic wooing of his cousin,
the fair Eudocia Ducas ; his adventures among the " Apelatai,"
the warlike outlaws of the Taurus ; his quelling of the Amazon
brigand-queen Maximo—an episode obviously borrowed from
the story of Alexander the Great and Thalestris—and his
building of his famous frontier-castle on the bank of Euphrates,
the model of all Byzantine fortresses, whose glories take up
a whole canto, and are not without interest for those who
seek for Byzantine views on architecture, painting, sculpture,
and mural decoration.

The most striking point about this East-Roman knight
of the tenth century is that, unlike his western antitypes,
he is decidedly a cultured person. A Frankish noble of the
Carlovingian romances might be, like Digenes, a sweet singer
and a skilled harper, but most assuredly he would not be
able to read and write, nor have any acquaintance with the
classics. But Basil's father took the trouble to hire a professor from Constantinople, who for three whole years instructed him in Greek literature as well as the Bible. A
Byzantine feudal household was apparently a school of polite
learning—when the lady Arete argues with her son in Canto
V she not only quotes Thetis's advice to Achilles from the
Iliad—

$$\text{'Εξαύδα, μὴ κεῦθε τῷ νῷ, ἵνα εἴδομεν ἄμφω,}$$

but also two lines from the gnomic poets, concerning cares
concealed. And, in another passage, there is, what seems much
more surprising, an echo from Pindar, besides several more
lines from Homer. Scriptural quotations are far more
numerous, and pervade the whole poem—in one passage
the Emir, Basil's father, recites the Apostles Creed, very
accurately rendered into a metrical version, for the confu-
tation of his Saracenic kinsfolk.

Altogether Basil is drawn for us as a figure very different
from the rough Western heroes of his century, and much
more like a young Italian noble of the Renaissance. The
picture of him, as he rides forth in early youth in the train

of his father, certainly recalls the young knights who figure on Florentine frescoes and cassones.

"This marvellous youth had fair curly hair, large eyes, a complexion like the rose, dark eyebrows and a broad chest. He wore over his light shirt a scarlet tunic with golden clasp and buttons, and its collar was embroidered with a pattern of pearls. His buskins were gilt, his spurs jewelled. He rode upon a white mare, whose trappings were ornamented with little bells of gold, which tinkled pleasantly : she had a saddle-cloth of green and rose silk, and her reins were of gold thread plaited. She was skittish and playful, but Akritas had a firm seat and made her obey his will : as he cantered along he looked like a rose tossing on its stalk. In his hand he held a long Arab lance, of green steel inlaid with golden lettering. In the midst of his father's suite he shone like the sun among the stars."

The first exploits of Basil on which the poet dilates were in sporting expeditions in the Taurus. Though only twelve years old, at his first hunt he faced a bear and brained it with a sledge-hammer blow of his fist on the forehead. He then ran down a roe on foot and slew it with his bare hands. Presently a lioness came across the path. "This is a beast that requires the sword," cried his uncle ; "you must not think that you can rend her as you did the roe." Basil nodded assent, drew his weapon, and when the lioness made her spring at him, he stepped lightly aside and clove her head right down to the neck-bone. Whereupon the huntsmen were struck with awe, and they cried, "Holy Virgin, Mother of God ! We witness feats that make us tremble. This boy is no child of our world, he is a gift sent from God to chastise outlaws and brigands, and he will be their terror all the days of his life."

It was indeed as a queller of the famous "Apelatai" of Taurus that Basil made his first mark. The whole border was overrun with them, and his father's duty as Warden of the passes was unending and incomplete. When he reached the age of eighteen he resolved to take up the task of outlaw-hunting, stimulated, it is said, by seeing the dead carcass of a lion which Joannikius, one of the most famous chiefs, had strangled (like Hercules) with his bare hands. "My eyes," he said, "must look on the champions who can accomplish such exploits."

So he set out, leaving his suite behind, on foot with no arms save a javelin and the iron mace which was his favourite weapon. High in the mountains he came upon the water-carrier of the outlaws, filling his skins at a spring, and asked him where his comrades lay. "What does such a handsome boy want with outlaws?" said the man. But Basil replied that he wanted to become an outlaw himself. So the water-bearer guided him to the head-quarters of brigandage (τὸ λῃσταρχεῖον), a strange and fearsome lair. There lay the old outlaw chief, Philopappus, on a bed piled high with the skins of beasts; his guard were around him. Basil gave him polite greeting, and wished him good day. "Good day to you also," answered the old man, "but I trust, for your own sake, that you are not a spy." "Quite the reverse," said the youth; "I want to become an apprentice-brigand with you in these solitudes." "If that is your ambition," said the old man, "you may start your apprenticeship by taking your mace and going on sentry duty at the pass. You will stop on duty for fifteen days, during which you must take no food or drink, nor allow your eyes to close in sleep. That accomplished, you must go out and kill me several lions, and bring me their skins as testimony; and then you must go on sentry duty again." "All that is much too tedious," said the disappointed youth; "I will not do anything of the sort, but as a proof of my capacity I will thrash you all round." So saying he seized his mace and fell upon the whole gang; some he felled with his fists, others he knocked over with his mace, and when he had got them all down he gathered their weapons under his arm and took them to the old man. He threw the bundle at his feet saying, "Receive, O Philopappus, the spoils of all your brigands, and if you are not satisfied, I will give you a thrashing also." The chief did not show fight, and Basil went down the glen, hunted up his escort, and went home rather disappointed with his experiences. But the outlaws had received a nasty shock, and looked forward to the future with considerable dismay.

The next, or fifth, canto of the poem is by far the most interesting of the whole series, being nothing less than the first existing version of a notable love story which runs through all European romance, and is known in this island in the shape of the "Douglas Tragedy" in the Minstrelsy of the Scottish Border, and the "Childe of Elle" in Bishop Percy's *Reliques*. Like the latter, and unlike the former, it has a happy ending; but its close kinship to both may be judged from the short précis which follows.

In a neighbouring province of Anatolia there was a governor, who came, like Basil, from the great house of Ducas : he had three warlike sons and one fair daughter named Eudocia. The fame of her beauty was spread over the whole of Roman Asia. One day, Akritas had followed the hunt for many miles over hill and dale, and got beyond his own bounds. His train had been left far behind, and he had lost his way. Presently he came on a magnificent castle, and recognized that this must be the abode of General Ducas and the fair Eudocia. Riding under its wall he sang with a loud voice a merry stave: "When a young knight has heard of the charms of a lady, and passes by her home without trying to cast eyes upon her, I reckon that he is a dull fellow who deserves no happiness in this world." The retainers who hung about the gate marvelled at his audacity, but marvelled still more at the melody, of his voice, which surpassed the song of the Sirens. The lady Eudocia was sitting in her chamber high up in the castle, and heard the lay. She went to her window and gazed down on the young man. She could not take her eyes off him, and whispered to her nurse : "Lean down, my nurse, and look at this handsome youth." The nurse obeyed, and answered her mistress: "Certainly, my lady, this is the suitor on whom your father might look with pleasure, for he has no equal in the whole world." And Eudocia continued to stand at her window and to gaze upon him. But he, feigning not to see her, began to question the retainers at the gate. "Is not this the palace of the great General, where dwells the damsel whose beauty has been the death of many noble knights?"

Now, Ducas himself had heard the singing, and had mixed with the group at the gate. Not declaring himself, he spoke out of the throng : " Son, know that many young knights, seduced by the beauty of this lady, have tried to carry her off. But her worthy father, knowing of such designs, guards her well : he has laid snares for such criminals : some he has beheaded, of some he has merely put out the eyes."

Now, Basil guessed that this was the General himself, but feigned to think that he was speaking to some retainer. " Do not suppose, sir, that I am one who comes with dishonourable intentions. But snares, I may say, have no terror for me. Would it please you to convey to the General my compliments, and to ask of him whether he would accept me as a son-in-law. I would serve him as a son should, if he would look upon me as does a father." When Ducas heard these words he answered stiffly, " You have already conveyed your request to the General, and he has not the least intention of granting it."

Hearing this, Basil had no fear, but he spurred his horse, rode close under the damsel's window, and cried with a loud voice, " Lady, let me know if I have pleased you ; if you could think of being my wife send me some token, and make me happy and fortunate. But if your desires are set elsewhere, I have no wish to harm you." And so saying he rode away, before her father's retainers could interfere.

Now, the Lady Eudocia had no doubts, and leaned to the side of acquiescence. She called her nurse and said : " Go down and seek out this young squire, and say to him, ' God knows that I like you well ; but I know not your name or race. But if, as I think, you are Basil Akritas, you are noble and my kinsman. The General, my father, will set his guards everywhere, for he knows you and your reckless courage. Run not into any peril for my sake, for my father is ruthless, and would not spare your life.' "

These words the nurse bore to Basil ; but *how*, the bard forgets to say. Did the good old lady seek for him in the hills—which seems unlikely—or did she send some "little foot page," as in the " Childe of Elle " to hunt for him at his own father's castle ? Anyhow, the message got through, and the young adventurer once more came under the wall, and the damsel to her window. "Lean down," he said, "light of my life, that I may see your beauty, and that your love may descend into my heart. For I am young, as you see, and love has never before touched me. I hardly know what it may be. But if a desire for me has taken your soul, fair maid, then know that though your father and all your kin were swords and arrows they should not keep us apart." And Eudocia replied, "Go in peace, but come again, and do not forget me."

Now here, unfortunately, we come to a short lacuna in the poem. We know that Basil rode home, that he dined with his mother, and that she could see that he had some weighty matter on his mind, which he would not disclose. We know that next evening he called for his big black war-horse and rode out armed, with his sword and mace at his saddle-bow, and his lyre slung across his shoulder, praying that the sun would set quickly and the moon shine bright on the roads, for a noble damsel was waiting for him. But, then, a page is missing from our sole manuscript—and whether Basil entered the castle of Ducas by a ladder of ropes, like Lord William or the Childe of Elle, or whether he burst open the great gate with his mace and slew the guards, we cannot tell. The gap ends—and we find him with the lady on his pillion galloping at dawn over rough mountain roads, with General Ducas, his three warlike sons, and all his men-at-arms in hot pursuit.

What follows is pure "Douglas Tragedy." The pursuers draw so near that it is useless to fly farther. Basil halts at a narrow pass, sets down the lady by a great stone, and murmurs, "Now, light of my eyes, see if you have a husband who can fight for you." To which she only answered, "Spare my brothers in the fray." When the enemy rushed in upon him he charged straight down the road, clove the first man-at-arms in two with one blow, and overthrew one after another those who followed. "He was swift as a hawk pouncing on partridges; he swooped down and they were stricken." But three horsemen drew to the side of the road and pushed past him, making for the damsel standing

by the great stone. Basil swerved and cut in between:
recognizing them as the lady's brothers he threw himself
upon them and felled each with a blow of his mace, so nicely
calculated that it threw them stunned out of their saddles,
but inflicted no deadly wound. The surviving men-at-arms
fled. Then arrived the General, whose age had prevented
him from keeping up with the rest of the party. Weeping
and groaning he saw his three sons on the ground among
their slaughtered followers, and Basil standing unharmed
in front of his daughter. But the knight came forward
with clasped hands, like a suppliant, and spoke him fair:
"Lord and master, bless us, your daughter and myself, and
give us no hard words. Your retainers are rude and rustic
fighters—they have no skill. I have given them a lesson
which they will not forget. Grieve not too much, you have
gained a trusty son-in-law; search round the world and you
will not find a better. He is not base-born, nor is he a
coward, and if you will but set him some task, you may
judge of his fidelity from the way in which he discharges
it."

The General made no further ado. "God has settled the
affair," he said, "and given me a gallant son-in-law." And
he proceeded to announce his intention of presenting his
daughter with a competent dowry—twenty quintals of gold
bezants, a wide estate, three hundred slaves—including
fourteen cooks—and a tiara with other precious jewellery.
Basil would have none of it. "I take your daughter for herself, not for the land or money—give all that to her brothers.
Her beauty may be her dowry; I only ask you to accompany
us to my father's castle and bless our union." The General
refused to come—it shamed him to appear without his train
and bridal gifts. In addition, he had three wounded sons
requiring first-aid—not to speak of some mangled retainers.
It was hardly to be expected that he would leave them—
so Basil rode homeward with Eudocia behind him, driving
in front six good war-horses belonging to the sons and retainers of the General. The lady, we are told, ventured
to observe to her lover that she was coming to her new
home in a somewhat casual and impromptu fashion: brides

are generally accompanied by their parents and relations, attended by their maids and men, and wear their best array. To which Basil replied that she need not fret—no one would blame her or him, if they turned up all alone, dusty and wayworn : the circumstances were exceptional.

On the enthusiastic reception of the pair at the castle of the Emir I have no space to linger. The bard gloats over the music and feasting, the presents showered on Eudocia by her new relatives, and the subsequent arrival of her father with a miscellaneous assortment of gifts. It included twelve palfreys, twelve Abasgian falcons, twelve hunting leopards, twelve ladies' maids, twelve chambermaids, twelve brocaded robes of state, a red and gold travelling pavilion of silk, two icons representing the two Saints Theodore set with rubies and amethysts, and what we are told pleased his daughter most—a tame lion. The lady's taste was odd ! In addition he insisted on leaving behind him a large sum of money and the title deeds of a handsome estate.

The marriage festival lasted three months, during which the Emir entertained General Ducas, his whole family, and his suite. By this time one would have imagined that they had seen enough of each other, and that the provinces which each was supposed to administer must have been in a somewhat neglected condition. This would, indeed, seem to follow from the fact that, the moment that the General turned homeward, Basil had to depart to the frontiers with his men-at-arms in order to repress brigandage. " He made his raids along the passes, he wounded many outlaws, and sent many to Hades. And then the provinces of the orthodox Romans could get peace, since they had him as their patron, guardian, helper, and champion against all enemies, after days of so much bloodshed."

We are bound to confess that Basil, though the most uxorious of spouses, must have been a very trying partner in life to the fair Eudocia, owing to his settled habit of " honeymooning " in inappropriate and dangerous surroundings. Every summer, when Saracens and outlaws had been duly dealt with, he was wont to take his wife up into the mountains for a prolonged tour. He hated having troops of

retainers about him, spying out all his ways; so he arranged
that a tent was pitched for him in a shady place, while those
of his escort and his wife's maids were placed far away, out
of earshot and almost out of eyeshot. When he wanted
servants, he had a system by which he put up outside his
tent as many lanterns by night or coloured signals by day
as he required attendants. Presumably a red lantern meant
a call for the chief groom, a blue one for the first ladies' maid,
and so forth. He grew horribly touchy at any violation
of this rule; and we are told that his chief cook, having
once presented himself unasked, received such a box on the
ears that his eyeballs flew out of their orbits "and the poor
man remained disabled for the rest of his life."

Now, there is considerable risk involved in encamping
some hundreds of yards away from one's suite, when the
surrounding hills are intermittently liable to visits not only
from outlaws but from lions, dragons, and devils of the waste.
The summer outings of the fair Eudocia must have been
trying things, not to be looked forward to with any great
pleasure;—even though the scenery was charming, with
camping-places on flower-strewn turf, surrounded by tufted
shady trees, and with a crystal spring rising before the tent
door, and nightingales singing in all the thickets around.

Here are some incidents recorded by the bard. One hot
afternoon Basil slept in his tent, but Eudocia, feeling restless, slipped out to the beautiful spring at the bottom of
the glade and began to dabble and dip in the clear water.
Unfortunately, the glade was the domain of a forest-devil,
who presented himself in the shape of a beautiful youth,
greeted the lady, and soon began to offer amorous advances.
"Hands off, you brute," cried Eudocia, "I am not to be
touched, and if I scream my lover is asleep close by, and it
were well that you had never been born if he catches you."
But forest-devils are reckless creatures—he cast his arms
around the lady and she screamed for help. Basil awoke
with a start, seized his sword, and was at the spring in a
moment—"it seemed as if his feet had wings." The devil
flung Eudocia aside and turned to fight, displaying no longer
a human form but that of a three-headed dragon, with a

long forked tail, vomiting flame from his nostrils. "When he snorted it was like thunder, and the neighbouring trees shook." Undaunted by this startling transformation, Basil fell upon the monster, and after a short combat decapitated it thrice. When his retainers, startled by the noise, came running up from below, he had only to tell them to drag away the creature and throw it over the next cliff.

This would seem to have been sufficient distraction for one afternoon. But we are told that when Basil, still feeling an "exposition of slumber" upon him, had retired to his couch and dismissed his suite, a lion emerged and began to prowl around the tent. Eudocia had to rouse her husband again. This time he took his mace, sallied out against the beast, and slew it with one stroke on the head, which left its hide intact, though its skull was smashed. Again the attendants had to be called up, given the lion to deal with, and sent away.

Eudocia now observed that two such adventures in one afternoon had upset her nerves, and she wished that her husband would give her a little music as a sedative, "Play me a tune on your lyre, and raise my spirit, for the fear of these monsters has given me a feeling of depression." Basil, now well awake, complied with pleasure, and presently Eudocia began to sing of love to the accompaniment of his harping.

Unfortunately, the recent disturbance—presumably the snorting of the dragon in particular—had attracted to the glade a band of outlaws, "three hundred fine young men, all in armour." They listened to the music, crept gently in toward the tent, and when the concert was over gave it a round of applause, and closed in on the musician and the singer. Their chief had the impudence to command Akritas to give up the lady or be slain on the spot. Their numbers were so great that Eudocia in despair cast her veil around her face, and cried to her husband that this was the end of all things. "But the hero was now thoroughly angry: he snatched up his mace and his shield, and flew undaunted into the midst of the band. They struck at him but to no effect, while whenever his mace descended a brigand breathed his last." So many fell that the rest soon fled, with Akritas in hot pursuit slaying the hindmost, "He caught them up with ease, for he could always outrun a galloping horse—as he himself asserted" (says the bard), "not speaking in vanity, but wishing to show what gifts the Creator gives to certain favoured mortals." When he returned to the tent his wife kissed his hand, bathed him with rose water, and gave him a good drink—which was certainly well earned.

Altogether, an afternoon with Basil Digenes certainly surpassed in interest even "an average day in the life of Peter Pan."

We have several cantos occupied with brigand-hunting, in which Basil dealt with outlaws wholesale and retail—sometimes in single combat with a noted chief, sometimes one to three or four, and sometimes in most incredible mêlées with many scores of ruffians at a time, like that described above. Affrays with Saracens were rather less numerous than those with Christian "Apelatai," but there is one Saracen episode which introduces a canto which deals with a curious and unedifying problem—quite out of harmony with the simple psychology of the rest of the poem. One night Basil was sitting with a few of his most confidential friends : the talk fell on love, desirable and undesirable, and presently he was moved to tell them a deplorable tale to show how the lust of the eyes might lead astray even a God-fearing man who supposed himself to have an ideal of honour, and had no possible excuse for his conduct. It was a story which he had better have left untold.

You will remember, he said, the time when Mousa, that audacious highwayman, was the plague of the frontier, before I got it into order. I was out after him with my escort, when we chanced on him and his band pursuing a young man mounted on a mare and leading another horse by the bridle. Just as I came on the scene, Mousa caught up the fugitive and rolled him out of his saddle by a blow between the shoulders : he would have been dead in another moment if I had not arrived. Well, we killed Mousa and delivered his victim. He was a Roman, the son, as he said, of that unfortunate General Antiochus who had been slain with all his brigade three years back, in a raid against Aplorabdis [Abdurrhadi ?] Emir of Mejafarkin in Mesopotamia. He had been taken captive in the disaster, had been a prisoner in a dungeon ever since, and had lately escaped. There was a large sum of Arabic gold in the saddle-bags of his two horses and some jewels also. I handed him over to my men to take back to Chalcogourna, from which we had set out. But I myself took a cast into the desert by way of reconnaissance. I had ridden many miles and seen nothing, when I began to feel extremely thirsty. In the distance I noted a single palm tree standing amid scrub—this gave promise of water, so I pushed for it. There was a spring sure enough ; as I dismounted I heard the noise of lamentation and saw a young woman sitting on a stone by the water weeping grievously. She was by her dress a Saracen, richly arrayed and of great beauty, but pale and distraught. For a moment I took her for a ghost or spirit ; her first words were odd—she cried to me, " Has love brought you also, for your destruction, into the deserts of Syria ? Come, drink of the water and hear my deplorable tale." I tied up my horse, leant my lance against the tree, took a draught from the spring, and asked the Saracen who she was, and why I found her alone in the midst of a desert.

She replied that she was the daughter of the Emir of Mejafarkin, " you will have heard of him—he is the greatest of all Emirs." To her sorrow she had fallen in love with a Roman captive, long detained in her father's dungeon : he said that he was the son of an illustrious general. By working on her father she got him released from his chains, and made him free of the castle. He swore that he had conceived for her a love as great as her own, and that his only desire was to get her over the border, and marry her honourably within the bounds of the Empire. To make this possible she had gone so far as to get herself baptized in secret by an orthodox priest. That spring the Emir and his army went out for a long campaign : her mother chanced at the same time to be stricken with a fever, and there was no surveillance over her. So having collected her jewels and taken a large sum of money from her father's treasury, she eloped with the young

Antiochus. They had extraordinary luck, escaped all pursuit, travelled unmolested several days, and had got within a long ride of the imperial frontier, when they rested for two nights in this desert oasis. On the third morning the unfortunate girl was wakened by the sound of horses' feet, and sitting up, was horrified to see her lover riding off on his own mare and leading away her palfrey by the bridle. She called after him to stop, and ran some way in pursuit, bidding him to remember his promise and their embraces. But he spurred his mare and disappeared, without once looking back. Returning to their camping-place she discovered that he had carried off all the gold and jewels, though he had left their food and other gear behind. She had been deserted in the most callous fashion, without a horse, in a desert place, to become the prey either of lions or of some roving bandit. "My punishment is even greater than my crime : to go back to my father means certain death ; and I have lost my false lover, for whom I abandoned everything. Give me your sword and let me kill myself, and so inflict a merited justice on a wrongdoer."

Thereupon the poor girl tore her hair and smote her breast. I had, said Akritas, the greatest possible difficulty in preventing her from doing herself some violence. I tried to console her with some shade of hope, and said that at least I thought that I had caught her fugitive lover that morning, and that if she retained any liking for him I would make him marry her, that being possible because she had abandoned "the disgraceful creed of the Ethiopians." This cheered her a little : I took her up upon the croup of my war-horse, and we started to ride toward Chalcogourna.

For what followed I have no excuse to make. She was a most attractive girl—her arms were around me all that afternoon—her breath upon my shoulder, her words in my ear. Satan is present everywhere, and my conscience was slack that day. Desire entered into me by all my senses. We camped that night by the wayside, and that camping defiled my journey. The old enemy, the Prince of Darkness, the adversary of mortal men, caused me to forget God, and the vengeance on sin that will come at the Day of Judgment,

when all secret crimes shall be revealed in the presence of
the angels and of the whole human race.

Next morning brought shame and repentance. Arriving
at Chalcogourna, we found the young son of Antiochus in
the custody of my escort with all his treasure. I had to
do something—what was to become of the girl ? I am no
polygamist and am sincerely attached to my wife. The
only solution I found was to call up the youth, tell him
that his desertion of the Emir's daughter had been abominable, and that he had to marry her. I threatened him with
my vengeance if he should misuse her or neglect her, and I
made over to them the great sum of gold and jewels which
had come from Mejafarkin. I said nothing of what had
happened by the way—nor, naturally, did the lady.

And a few days after I went home, weighed down with
a sinful conscience, feeling a heavy burden of remorse, and
raging at myself for my lawless lapse. When I met my
unsuspecting wife I felt loathsome to myself : I had inflicted
on her the worst of all wrongs.

So ends the Canto. The only attenuating circumstance
that I can see for this particularly mean crime is, that Basil
was a good deal more ashamed of himself than most heroes
of romance who in similar circumstances dallied by the way.
It is a curious piece of Byzantine psychology.

Passing over much more brigand-hunting, it may be worth
while to speak of the castle which Akritas built for himself
overlooking the upper course of the Euphrates. The gate-
house was twenty-four cubits high and adorned with gilded
reliefs, the outer ward was four stories high and decorated
with stones of various colours set in patterns. Within there
was an inner ward, twenty-two cubits high, with bronze
reliefs and inlaid with precious marbles. The upper stories
were gilded and the roof was of mosaic work. The state
chambers of the inner ward had windows surrounded by
friezes of a pattern of vine branches with gilded bunches
of grapes. There was a keep set in it which rose to an incredible height. From its battlements one might survey
all Syria, as far as Babylon. In this keep, approached by
a newel staircase, was the private hall of Basil, with a

vaulted ceiling ornamented with marble and pearls, around a central boss composed of a large transparent white stone, in which there was a light which shone brilliantly at night and was visible for miles around. The chamber was square, like the keep, and its walls were covered with mosaics giving the history of all the famous champions of the world—on the one side scriptural subjects, the exploits of Samson and of David, of Joshua the son of Nun, and of Moses, and the story of Queen Candace. On the other were secular subjects—the Anger of Achilles, Bellerophon slaying the Chimæra, the defeat of King Darius, and all the other exploits of the versatile and courageous Alexander of Macedon, and much more.

In the court of the castle was a fountain which threw its waters to a surprising height, by means of an ingenious mechanism invented by Basil himself. There was also a flower-garden and a vineyard, and a chapel dedicated to St. Theodore, which had an altar of silver and holy vessels of gold.

"Let none of my hearers doubt of all this because of the enormous cost of building such a castle. For princes and satraps sent to Basil great presents from afar, and all the nobles of the empire gave him gifts in testimony of their gratitude for his exploits. The Emperor himself often enriched him with donatives. And no man—Roman or Saracen, Persian or Tarsiot—who frequented the passes, ventured to cross without his passport. Provided with the seal of Akritas any merchant could travel without fear, for the outlaws had the greatest dread of him."

Basil dwelt in prosperity all the days of his life; and his only source of chagrin was that his much-loved wife bore him no heirs, "for childlessness is a great grief to all men." His end was not, like that of many heroes of romance, a sudden disaster of blood and ruin. He was still in the full vigour of his age when he was stricken with a wasting disease, for which the best physicians of the empire could find no remedy. According to the bard he had not exceeded the age of thirty-three—but history would seem to show that he must have been over fifty. For he was born while the

Ducas family were in insurrection, and some time before Romanus Lecapenus restored the exiled Cappadocian nobles, *i.e.* between the outlawry of Andronicus Ducas in 908 and the pacification of 919. He died during the reign of Nicephorus Phocas, who did not come to the throne till 963, and not in its earliest years. If Basil was old enough in 944 to be put in command of the army of the East, he is more likely to have been born in 912 than in 919.

Whatever his age, he died in his bed, and his wife Eudocia did not survive him, for they were buried together. The tenth canto, which tells of their end, is mutilated—only some sixty lines of its commencement survive. But its title-heading runs : " This tenth book of Akritas tells of his death, and how his beloved wife died also, and of the lamentation of the whole world for them, and of the honourable and worthy funeral which was made for him and his spouse." The scrap of the tenth canto which survives only gives us the verdict of the physicians, and the commencement of the last adieu which Basil addresses to Eudocia, reminding her of the romantic commencement of their union and speaking of their untiring devotion to each other. It breaks off in the middle. We may presume that the lady died of a broken heart upon his breathless body, like so many heroines of romance. For we need not take into consideration a horrid folk-song of a later age, which says, while speaking of the bodily power of Akritas, that he was so strong that when, in his dying agony, he gave his wife a last embrace he crushed her to death. This, along with many other exaggerations and absurdities found in the folktales concerning Akritas, is quite out of keeping with the poem of the eleventh century, which reflects Byzantine culture rather than wild folk-lore. It may be noted that it is singularly exempt from that sort of supernatural and preternatural incidents in which early romances generally abound. The only exception is the story of the wood-devil, who appeared first as a beautiful youth and then as a dragon, in Canto VII. The rest of the story is but a glorified transcript of the life of a warden of the Cappadocian frontier march in the middle of the tenth century. It may show some faults of taste in the bard, and certain "*longueurs*" of description and repetition, but it certainly gives us a far higher view of the spirit of the East-Roman feudal noblesse than can be got from any other surviving document.

VI

THE CRUSADES

Ever since recorded history begins, and probably for untold centuries before, a never-ending strife between the East and the West has been in progress, and the tide of conquest and invasion has been mounting eastward or westward, only to reach its high-water mark, stand still for a moment, and then commence slowly or quickly to retire. The writers of the old classical world of antiquity saw this clearly enough. Herodotus, the father of all European historians, began his famous book with a tale of legendary raids and counter-raids between Europe and Asia, and traced down from them the great war of Greek and Persian which had formed the all-engrossing interest of his own youth.

Different nations have led the attack in different ages : the Greek, the Roman, the Frankish Crusader, last of all the British, on the one side : the Persian, the Saracen, the Tartar, and the Ottoman Turk on the other. Three or four times Europe has seemed to submerge Western Asia, and to plant herself down there so, firmly that the lands of the debatable zone seemed incorporated for ever with the Western world. Alexander the Great, and after him the Romans, made so thorough a conquest of Asia Minor, Syria, and Egypt, and planted there so deeply the laws and language of the West, that it seemed for long centuries incredible that these regions should ever slip back again into Orientalism. On the other hand the Persians, in the old days before the Christian era, the Saracens of Mohammed in the Dark Ages, the Tartars of the house of Genghiz Khan in the central Middle Ages, the Ottoman Turk in modern times, cut great cantles out of Europe and added them to the East. For six hundred years Southern Spain was an Oriental land,

116

looking to Mecca and Bagdad for its culture and its creed,
not to Rome and the nearer West. For more than four
and a half centuries Constantinople and the lands behind
it were in similar case : it seems that they may be so left
for a few years more—thanks to the internal jealousies of
Christendom, which now, as during the last whole century,
have been retarding the inevitable, and still at this moment
leave the Sultan—though his baggage has twice been packed—
sitting by the Golden Horn.

We are prone to look upon the Crusades as a unique
phenomenon, because of the predominantly religious character
of the impulse which in the eleventh and twelfth centuries
hurled the legions of the Christian West upon Palestine and
Syria and Egypt. A few generations ago historians who
regarded themselves as citizens of the world, and presumed
to look down on the affairs of men from some point of view
of philosophic cosmopolitanism, taught that the Crusades
were irrational outbreaks of blind fanaticism, leading to
endless loss of life and waste of wealth for no adequate end.
They did not see that the great movement was but one of
the most stirring and picturesque episodes of the unending
struggle between East and West. The antagonism between
Europe and Asia was but taking a new shape, and that this
shape was for the moment religious was not the fault of the
West—the first move of that kind had been made on the
side of Asia. The Arabs whom Mohammed's preaching had
roused from their deserts, and flung upon the Asiatic and
African provinces of the Roman Empire, or the Gothic Kingdom of Spain, had gone forth conquering and to conquer
with a purely religious war-cry, " God is God, and Mohammed
is his prophet : the nations of the world must accept the
Koran, the tribute, or the sword." After more than four
centuries of subjection to the Mohammedan danger, the nations
of the West now roused themselves for the due retaliation,
and an impulse, fanatical in shape as that which had moved
the Saracens in the seventh century, now launched the
mailed chivalry of Western Europe against the East, and
produced the great counter-stroke which made Jerusalem,
Antioch, and Edessa for a time the capital of Christian states.

It was one more back sweep of the pendulum, which had
been swinging to and fro ever since the days of Darius and
Alexander the Great. The rate at which the pendulum should
swing forward to East or West, the causes of the coming
of each wave of new conquerors, the race which might lead
the van in each invasion, could never be foreseen by the
wisest of prophets. But the process was always going on;
in 1090 it was high time that one of the backward sweeps
toward the East should begin—as it was high time in 1918
that the most recent of them all, and that in which Britain
was for the first time the leader of the movement, should
take its course. When will the next westward sweep come?
And who will lead it? Can we imagine a formidable combination between Russian Bolshevism and the Pan-
Islamic movement? Or are we to dream of the "Yellow
Peril," the marshalling of the countless millions of China
under some military organization such as that of which
modern Japan has given the example? I cannot say.
But I have little doubt that the pendulum will continue to
oscillate.

Any history book, however slight and short, will give
you the formal causes of the first Crusade—it will tell you
how the Seljouk Turks were thundering at the gates of Constantinople, and causing the Eastern Emperor, Alexius Com-
nenus, to utter constant cries for help to the Christian nations
of inner Europe. You will read how the Turkish governors
of Jerusalem had been maltreating the pilgrims who (through
so many dangers and difficulties) were always making their
way from the Rhine and the Seine to worship at the Holy
Sepulchre and the manger of Bethlehem. You will be told
how Peter the Hermit wandered north and south denouncing
the cruelties of the Infidel, how Pope Urban II summoned
the bishops and princes of the West to the Council of Cler-
mont in 1095, and how when he called upon them to punish
the Turk and the Saracen, and to recover the Holy Places,
the whole crowd started up crying with one voice, "Dieu
le veult"—it is the will of God. You know how duke and
count, baron and knight, man-at-arms and peasant stepped
forward in unending file to receive from the Pope's own hands

the cross which the armed pilgrims were to display as their special badge, and which gave to their bands the name of " Crusaders," and to their enterprise the style of " Crusade."

But this is only the outward and picturesque aspect of the movement. It had many · other aspects—less spiritual and less inspiring, but not less important. It was not the fact that in 1095 Christendom was in worse straits than at any earlier crisis, and that an expedition to drive away the Turk from Palestine was the only way of salvation. Twice before, at least, the aspect of affairs for Christian Europe had looked much worse. Constantinople had been actually beleaguered by the Moslems in 673 and 717, yet no help had then come from the West. Pilgrims had often been maltreated before, yet Christendom had not marched en masse to revenge their sufferings. The new factor in the world in 1095 was not the special cruelty or threatening power of the Seljouk Turks—whose Sultanate indeed was at this precise moment breaking up into fractions, and ceasing to be a danger —but the fitness of the West for opening an active campaign against Orientalism. Europe was in 1095 in better trim for launching a great expedition against the Infidel than she had been at any moment since the break-up of the old Roman Empire. For the first time for many ages she was in a condition to turn her main attention to the struggle with the East.

For the preceding three centuries Christendom had been engaged in beating off three deadly enemies, whose attacks had come all at once. The Vikings from the Scandinavian north had ravaged England, Ireland, France, and Northern Germany, breaking up survivals of old civilization, upsetting dynasties, and sweeping away landmarks. From the East at the same time, or a little later, had come the wild Hungarian horse-bowmen, the plague which swept along the Danube to ravage South Germany and Northern Italy. And thirdly there had been the Mohammedan enemy, still formidable and active, though the caliphate had broken up, and though the attack was delivered not by one great power but by many separate adventurers, Saracen, Moor, and Turk, who worked by land in Asia Minor and Spain, by sea in Sicily and Crete, even in South Italy and for one short period in Provence. There had once been a day in the tenth century when Saracen raiders from Fraxinet on the Riviera met and fought with Hungarian raiders from the Danube, in the very heart of Switzerland, at Orbe in Canton Vaud. It looked as if the defence of Christendom had been pierced through on both sides. Beset by all three invaders at once, Europe had only just held her own for several generations. But the work of Leo the Isaurian, of Alfred of Wessex, and Henry of Saxony, of Otto the Great, and Nicephorus Phocas had not really been in vain. By 1095 Christendom had saved herself ; the two internal enemies, the Viking and the Hungarian, had not been conquered or exterminated, but they had been first beaten off, and then absorbed into the fellowship of Europe, by conversion and the acceptance of Christian culture. And the worst attacks of the third enemy, the Mohammedan, whose religion made him incapable of being absorbed as the Dane or Magyar had been, had been definitely checked on all the long front of his attack, from end to end of the Mediterranean, save at the extreme eastern point. He had long lost all hope of mastering Christian Spain : he had recently been evicted from all the islands from which he threatened Central Europe—Sardinia, Sicily, Crete, Cyprus, were all Christian once again. Only in Byzantine Asia Minor had a recent breach been made, by that disastrous battle of Manzikert in 1071, which gave to the Seljouk Turks Angora and Iconium permanently, and even Nicæa and an outlook on to the Bosphorus for a few years. But this last thrust of the newest Mohammedan enemy of Christendom was to be answered by such a counter-stroke as Europe had never delivered since Pompey the Great went out to conquer the kings of Asia in the first century before Christ, some eleven hundred years before.

There are two ways from Western Europe to the Levant, one by sea and one by land. For the last three hundred years one of them had been dangerous and the other absolutely blocked. The natural road from France or Germany to Constantinople and Asia Minor lies down the Danube and

across Hungary. But since the end of the sixth century
the plain of the central Danube had been in the hands of
wild pagan tribes, the enemies of Christendom and civilization.
First came the Avars, then the still more formidable Magyars,
the scourge of Central Europe. The passage from Germany
to Constantinople was absolutely stopped for more than
three centuries. We must pause for a moment, to realize
the difference that was made in the geographical situation
by the conversion of the Magyars to Christianity under St.
Stephen, in the early years of the eleventh century. The
land-road was opened again ; for the first time for ages
it had become possible to cross the continent of Europe,
and reach the East without leaving friendly Christian
territory.

As long as the land-road had been impracticable, the
only other way of getting from Western Europe to the Levant
had been, of course, by sea. From the ports of Italy the
voyage ought not to have been difficult. But for the last
two hundred years it had been very perilous, as long as the
Mohammedans had naval supremacy in the central Mediterranean. While they held Sicily and Sardinia, and even for a
time Crete and lodgments in Southern Italy, their countless
swarms of piratical vessels made commerce and pilgrimage
alike impossible. The Byzantine emperors were, till the
eleventh century, the only Christian princes who possessed
a war-fleet, and in despite of it they were driven out of their
last hold on Sicily, which, when it was (after fifty years of
interval) won back for Christendom, was recovered, not by
the East-Romans, but by a new power. In the early eleventh
century the Byzantine fleet was keeping the Ægean and sometimes the Adriatic practicable for commerce, but it had failed
to hold the central Mediterranean.

So things remained on the side of the sea till the second
quarter of the eleventh century, when naval enterprise began
to be seen for the first time in the West. The Italians were
at last beginning to take to the water and build war-fleets.
First Venice in North-Eastern Italy, then Pisa and Genoa
in North-Western, developed into maritime powers, and
began to oppose and finally to drive away the Mohammedan

pirates of Sardinia, Sicily, and the Moorish coast. As late as 1011 the last great Mohammedan naval expedition sacked Pisa—but only a very few years after Pisa and Genoa took the offensive and recovered Sardinia from the Infidel. A generation later arose the last, and for a time the most formidable, of the Italian naval powers, that established by the Norman adventurers (close kinsmen to the conquerors of Hastings) in Naples and Southern Italy. In a long series of campaigns between 1060 and 1091 they finally drove out the Moors from Sicily. Then all the Italian naval powers combined to hunt down the Barbary pirates, and by 1095 and the start of the first Crusade, the central Mediterranean was, what it had not been for many ages, once more a Christian lake. The enemy was pursued into Africa, and beaten off the seas. Safe transit from West to East was at last possible.

Clearly then, by the year 1095, there had been established a wholly new posture of affairs in Europe. It was possible to go from France or Germany or Italy to the Levant with safety, both by land and by water. It was this conjuncture which made the first Crusade a possibility, almost a necessity. For already Europe had taken the offensive against the Mohammedan enemy in the western and central waters of the Mediterranean, and was only wanting a start and an impulse to induce her to invade the eastern waters also. The new naval powers, both the three republics and the Norman Princes of Naples and Sicily, were militant and ambitious.

The thrust of the Seljouk Turks at Constantinople and their maltreatment of the western Pilgrims in Palestine were sufficient provocative causes. These acts of hostility, which early generations would have had to pass over, because they would have been unable to deal with them, could be resented with effect by the Europe of 1095. That they were punished, not merely by isolated expeditions of the Italian maritime powers in search of new fields of commercial activity, but by a sudden outburst of energy which affected most of the further nations of Christendom, was largely due to the statesmanship of the Papacy. It was from the first true that " the Crusades were the foreign policy of the Popes." It was Urban II, who, instead of stirring up merely Genoa and Venice and the Normans of Sicily, crossed the Alps and preached the Crusade to all Europe. The Papacy, no doubt, had its own ends to serve in its great contest with the Emperors of the West ; it obtained an immense moral advantage by placing itself at the head of a movement whose inspiration could not but be approved by all Christendom. The Crusades showed the Papacy as a great international power, acting everywhere on the subjects of every king, whether the temporal ruler approved or not. And the ideal set forth was one which made the personal ambitions of emperors and kings, for themselves or their dynasties, appear local, selfish, and mischievous. It is a noteworthy fact that to the first of these great expeditions there went forth no sovereign prince —neither the Emperor, nor the King of France, nor the King of England (imagine William Rufus on a crusade !), nor the King of Hungary, but that the subjects of each of these monarchs, from great dukes and counts like Robert of Normandy, or Robert of Flanders, or Godfrey of Bouillon, or Raymond of Toulouse, down to simple burghers and peasants, started by thousands for the East, at the papal fiat, and with the papal blessing.

Looking at the fundamental causes which flung the armed pilgrims of the West by tens of thousands against the East, both by the sea route and by the land route, with the intention of taking the Holy Places from the Moslem, we can distinguish three impulses—the one religious, the second political, the third arising from naval enterprise. The three ideals were hopelessly intermixed—many crusaders were inspired only by one of them—more perhaps by two—some (such are the complexities of human psychology) by all three at once.

No doubt some of the princes and great multitudes of the minor pilgrims who went forth to Palestine did so on a genuine religious impulse—the same that had been taking a few eager souls eastward to the Holy Places at intervals during the whole of the Dark Ages, when the enterprise had been so far more difficult. It was certainly neither political ambition nor commercial enterprise that led individuals, many of whom were advanced in age, and powerful and wealthy in their own lands, to desert their homes for years, and risk death or captivity in the unknown East. In some Crusaders, no doubt, simple piety was mixed with the spirit of adventure : feudal Europe loved fighting for fighting's sake, as its tournaments showed : and the desire to chastise the pilgrim-persecuting infidel, or to worship at the primitive shrines of the Christian faith, might be none the less genuine because of the alluring fact that hard knocks would certainly have to be given and taken in the process.

But along with the genuine pilgrims there went others whose aims were less idealistic. From the point of view of the Italian republics and the Normans of Sicily, the Crusade was undoubtedly a great venture for naval domination and commercial exploitation in the Levant. Venice and Genoa threw themselves vigorously into the enterprise ; they spoke, like their allies, of the delivery of the Holy Places, but their action shows that they were mainly set on getting control of the great sea-routes to the East. When Syria was conquered, the Italians greedily grabbed every port, to the detriment of the newly crowned King of Jerusalem, and spent enormous pains in diverting to Jaffa and Acre, to Beyrout and Laodicea, the Persian and Indian commerce that had been wont to go overland to Constantinople. They would not allow the feudal princes of Palestine and Syria to get any real control of their own harbours, or to tax the imports and exports that passed through them. It was this self-seeking of the Italians that ultimately proved no small factor in the ruin of the short-lived Kingdom of Jerusalem.

But there were not only religious enthusiasts and commercial monopolists among the Crusaders. The third element was the military adventurers, who were in search of fiefs and castles in the wealthy East,—the cadets and landless younger sons of all the noble houses of the feudal West, with those restless or impoverished landowners who were discontented with their home conditions. It was these land-seeking soldiers of fortune who built up the Frankish community in Syria, such as it was. The religious pilgrims went home, such of them as had not perished : the merchants settled down in some seaport, and ultimately went home also if their venture had succeeded. The free-lances stayed out in the East for good, seized some fief, small or great, and fought against the Moslem to retain it or to enlarge it, for all the days of their life. Adventurers never ceased drifting eastward to the "Holy War" till, in the thirteenth century, it became evident that the game was up, and that it was more promising as a career to become a captain of mercenaries, or a professional rebel at home, than to go out to be slain by Turk or Saracen on the Holy Soil.

All the three aims of the Crusaders were attained, but at the cost of enormous waste of life and energy, due to two main causes—indiscipline and ignorance. The first Crusade, as all know, was nearly wrecked because the great invading horde was led by no single leader of an eminence sufficiently great to command the obedience of his fellows. The crowd of dukes and counts, vassals of different suzerains, were too proud to obey one of their equals. The host was really directed by an unruly council of war, in which every magnate urged his own plan, and finally some strategical compromise was adopted which pleased nobody. Orders were not obeyed —he who chose went off on a side-expedition, or melted away from the banner. It is wonderful that the first Crusaders ever reached Palestine, or took Jerusalem. More than once they were on the verge of ruin, owing to their stupid indiscipline : only their indomitable courage finally pulled them through.

But geographical ignorance was almost as fatal a drawback as want of discipline. The moment that they left Constantinople they were wandering about "in worlds not realized "—any sort of misdirection was possible in days when all East of the Bosphorus was in the land of marvels and legends, whose darkness was only lit up by casual oral information gathered from stray merchants, pilgrims, or prisoners. Even in the Balkan Peninsula the Crusaders made strange errors—one army of South French origin actually marched from Trieste to Constantinople, through the stony mountains of Dalmatia, Montenegro, and Albania, because they thought it would be a "short out," as compared with the obvious route through Hungary: half of them died before they reached the Bosphorus. There was a more disastrous incident still in 1101, when a whole expedition, disregarding the advice of the Byzantine Emperor, who tried to put them right, strove to march on Bagdad *via* Armenia, by a non-existent route. Most of them left their bones in Kurdistan. To be fair, however, to the general intelligence of the Crusaders, we must acknowledge that it was always the landsmen,—the French and Germans in the first two Crusades, the Germans alone in the third, who took the difficult and circuitous route across the Balkan Peninsula and Asia Minor. Even on the first Crusade many of the Italians arrived by water, and when the naval control in the Levant had once fallen into Christian hands, it became normal to use the sea-route, as did Richard Cœur de Lion and Philip Augustus in the third Crusade, and many before them, not to speak of St. Louis in the last great venture of the thirteenth century.

Two juxtaposed facts had much to do with the success of the first Crusade, and the comparative failure of all that followed. The one fact we have already noted—that after the final expulsion of the Moors from Sicily in 1091 the Mediterranean now offered safe sailing for all Christian fleets. The second and simultaneous fact was the break-up of the great Moslem State which had been a few years before dominating all the nearer East. The power of the Seljouk Turks, which had in 1080 been still a single sultanate, which extended all over Asia Minor, Syria, Mesopotamia, and Persia had just fallen apart by civil war into a dozen jarring fragments. The last heirs of the great Seljouk monarch in Persia were no longer obeyed by the minor sultan in Asia Minor, or by the petty emirs who had just made themselves independent at Antioch, Aleppo, Damascus, Mardin, and else-where. And a power hostile to all the Turkish race, the Fatimite sultan of Egypt, had just conquered Palestine. Jerusalem in 1097 was held no longer by those Seljouks who had recently been maltreating the Christian pilgrims, but by an Egyptian governor and garrison. Fighting against

jealous and divided enemies, the Crusaders only just succeeded in conquering Antioch and Edessa, Jerusalem and
Tripoli.   Opposed by a single monarch wielding the resources
of the whole of Syria, Mesopotamia and Persia, they would
certainly have failed, and would never have seen the Holy
Sepulchre, or established the short-lived Latin Principalities
of the Levant.

The best proof of this is that the gradual reunion of the
group of Mohammedan petty states into a single great
monarchy was the ruin of the Crusading venture.   There
was a bare half-century during which those great fighters
the Baldwins and Amaurys increased their borders and held
their own.   But at last a Mesopotamian prince named Zenghi
united the states on each side of the Euphrates, and in 1144
attacked and destroyed the most outlying Christian prin-
cipality, the county of Edessa.   The last chance for the
survival of the invaders came five years later, when the King
of Jerusalem, aided by the depleted armies of the Second
Crusade, laid siege to Damascus in 1149—this was the high-
water mark of the Crusading wave.   If the Franks had taken
Damascus, and cut through completely to the Syrian desert,
the Mohammedan North and the Mohammedan South—
Mesopotamia and Egypt—would have been completely
severed.   But the siege of Damascus did not succeed, through
dissension between the Syrian barons and the Western pilgrims,
and the stroke failed.   Five years later the Emir Nur-ed-din,
son of Zenghi, conquered his neighbour of Damascus, and
became master of Southern as well as Northern Syria.   His
state was getting too powerful to be resisted by the little
Kingdom of Jerusalem.   In 1171 the end became inevitable
when Nur-ed-din annexed Egypt—his generals having made
an end of the last Fatimite Caliph.   The enormous new
sultanate which embraced Mesopotamia, Syria, and Egypt
was too strong to be resisted, especially when its strength
was wielded by Nur-ed-din's great successor, the famous
usurper Saladin (1172-1192).   He crushed the Franks by
numbers combined with good generalship, at the fatal battle
of Tiberias in 1187, and took Jerusalem a few months
after.

The overpowering strength of the great Mohammedan
state thus created was the dominating cause of the failure
of the Crusades. Minor causes there were in plenty—(1)
the feudal organization which made the intrusive Christian
states of Syria, not a single military monarchy, but an ill-
compacted group of quarrelsome feudatories. (2) The want
of a loyal and homogeneous lower class to serve as a safe
basis for society—the tillers of the soil were either discontented Mohammedan fellaheen, or Syrian Christians, who
hated the Western Church only less than they hated Islam.
The army of the King of Jerusalem counted many barons
and knights, but never enough foot soldiery—the material
for it was wanting. Only in time of very dire need would
the Italian burghers of the seaport towns turn out in arms.
(3) The King was always poor, because the greedy Italian
maritime powers had only joined in setting him up on condition that they should have a monopoly of all commerce.
The lively trade which sprang up profited the Venetian Genoese
or Pisan factories, not the King's exchequer. The titular
sovereign had only his small feudal revenue on which to
depend—not a customs revenue or the power to tallage his
burghers, on which other princes could count. (4) Geography
too was against the survival of the Crusading states. If
the Franks in their first rush had occupied all Syria from
the sea to the Arabian desert, the Kingdom of Jerusalem
would have had a defensible boundary. But Aleppo and
Damascus were never won, and the Crusading states remained
a narrow coast slip, all frontier, and all equally exposed to the
enemy. Islam was never cut in two—the route from the
Euphrates to Egypt *via* Damascus, Ma'an, and Akabah was
always open to the enemy, and the doom of the Crusaders
came precisely from the fact that Syria and Egypt were
finally joined under a single great monarch, who was altogether
too strong to be resisted.

That the fall of Jerusalem in 1187 was not immediately
followed by the expulsion of the Franks from the Levant
was due to that much misrepresented enterprise, the Third
Crusade. It is generally spoken of as a complete failure,
because it failed to recover the Holy Places. But this is

to do Richard Cœur de Lion scant justice. He met Saladin
at the height of his power, when he had subdued all Palestine
save a few harbour towns, faced him, and recovered Acre,
then the greatest port of Syria, in spite of all the efforts of
a great relieving army. He finally beat the Sultan in pitched
battle at Arsouf, a famous spot again in 1918, for it is the
precise point at which General Allenby broke through the
Turkish lines, and started that wonderful turning movement which won all Palestine in a week, and ended in the
surrender of 100,000 Ottoman troops. It is true that Cœur
de Lion failed to recover Jerusalem, owing to the mean fashion
in which he was betrayed by his jealous allies. But it was
no small feat to force Saladin to a treaty which left all the
coast, with its harbours and its castles, to Christendom, if
Jerusalem and the highlands of the inland had to be abandoned
as irrecoverable. The best proof of Richard's success is that
what he had won back was held by the Franks for nearly a century more. At the same time it must be confessed that the
surviving remnant of the Kingdom of Jerusalem—it was now
more truly the Kingdom of Acre and Tyre—continued to
exist for so long mainly as a result of lucky chance. The
great Saladin died not long after the treaty of peace of 1192,
and his empire, which had extended from the Tigris to the
Cataracts of the Nile, broke up for a time, being parted between
his brother and his sons. This delayed the final ruin of
the states of Christian Syria for a space, for it is possible to make a long fight against enemies who have jealousies
and divided interests. But the Kingdom of Jerusalem was,
during its last ninety years of life, entirely destitute of any
power to recover itself. Nothing but the ports being left,
the maintenance of the state practically depended on the
Italian commercial powers, who were deeply interested in
keeping their profitable factories safe, but had no reason
to take thought for the recovery of the inland. That would
have been of no use to themselves, though it might profit
the Syrian baronage and the titular king. Hence a passive
defence of the harbours, and truce, and trade if possible,
with the Mohammedan powers, were their natural
policy.

There was still in the earlier thirteenth century some chance that succour might come from outside, to reinforce the decadent Christian power in Syria. The Crusading spirit was not yet entirely dead, and the Papacy still continued its consistent policy of encouraging Eastern expeditions with the old aims. But the leaders of the so-called Fourth Crusade disappointed all Christendom. Instead of reinforcing Palestine, they allowed themselves to be led astray by the selfish and intriguing Venetians, went off to the Bosphorus instead of to Syria, and, like pirates, seized, plundered and occupied Christian Constantinople in 1204. This was one of the greatest crimes of history—perhaps the greatest ever committed under the name of religion—and no excuse can be made for the greedy Venetians, who lured off the princes of the West on a side-issue, profitable to Venice alone, but ruinous to the general defences of Christendom. For one of its side-effects was to let the Seljouk Turks once more into Western Asia Minor, from which they had been driven away by the First Crusade a century back.

There were yet several crusades to come before the Papacy and the Christian West finally gave up the idea of the recovery of the Holy Places. The Fifth Crusade of 1218 is interesting as a strategical variant on all the earlier expeditions. It was launched not against Palestine, but against Egypt, on a hypothesis which was strategically sound, that a blow struck there, at the narrow middle-point of the Mohammedan world, would be decisive of the fate of the whole East. For Syria and Africa are linked only by the narrow isthmus of Suez, and he who could occupy the Nile Delta would cut the power of Islam in two. But the blow was tactically misdirected, since campaigning amid the canals and marshes of Lower Egypt was unsuited for an army composed of feudal men-at-arms, who needed broad plains and pitched battles to display their efficiency. The only way to tackle Egypt by an invasion from the sea, is to land either west of the Delta-Marshes at Alexandria, as Napoleon did in 1798, or east of them, as did Lord Wolseley in 1882, and to avoid the marsh dangers, by refusing to be entangled in them. The enterprise of 1218, though it secured a base at Damietta, flickered out among topographical difficulties. Yet precisely the same mistake was repeated a generation later, when the enthusiastic St. Louis led the great French host of 1249-50 to perish miserably in a blow at Cairo aimed through the inextricable network of the dykes and canals of the Delta. His army, thrown ashore at Acre, might certainly have accomplished much in Syria ; if he had landed at Alexandria, clear of the water-courses, he might have got forward a long way, if he could have solved the problem of transport. But, striking at Damietta, like his predecessors of the Fifth Crusade, he involved himself in the swamps and water-ways, failed in his thrust, was himself finally besieged in his advanced camp, and forced to surrender with the wreck of his host. It was only after his ransom, and release from Egyptian captivity, that St. Louis went to Palestine, and spent more than two years in endeavouring to restore concord among the Christians, and in strengthening and repairing their long line of harbour-fortresses. But he came without the great army that he had wasted in Egypt, and, therefore, his efforts were of little avail.

Yet so long as the Mohammedan powers remained divided, the Christian coast-power in Syria survived. Once for a few years the Emperor Frederic II, by taking part in a civil war between the Eyubite princes, recovered Jerusalem by treaty (1229), but only the city and the pilgrims' way thereto from Jaffa. It was a peace-arrangement which ceased when the next war came, and a Turkish army in the pay of the Egyptian sultan stormed Jerusalem in 1244—the last time, I believe, that it was taken by fighting till 1917. But this rather illusory occupation of Jerusalem for twelve years had no military or political meaning : it was a diplomatic rather than a strategical achievement ; safe access to the ceded city had not been secured, and at the first renewal of war it was bound to fall back to the Sultan, whose territory surrounded it on every side.

If it be asked how it came to pass that the Frankish holding in Syria survived for forty years after King Louis' fiasco in Egypt in 1250, the answer must, I suppose, be that if aid practically ceased to come in from the West (though

one must not forget petty succours like that which the English
prince, Edward Longshanks, brought in 1270), yet for some
years after 1250 the Mohammedan central power was in
trouble. The last Eyubite sultan of Egypt and Syria did
not survive the year in which St. Louis was defeated and
taken prisoner. He perished in a mutiny of his mercenary
troops, the famous Mamelukes, just after his victory. The
rebels made an end of his family in Egypt, but not for the
moment in Syria, where many towns held out for the old
dynasty, but fell to internal strife as to the succession : and
it was some little time before all the old lands of Saladin's
empire were united again under Sultan Eibek, the first of the
so-called Mameluke dynasty. The reign of this short-lived
prince was disturbed by the threat of a great invasion, not of
Christians from the West but of Mongols—a new name for
us—from the East. This vast horde which Genghiz Khan
had set rolling westward from the borders of China was
impending as a common danger over the Mohammedan
East and the Christian East. It was the first serious threat
from Asia that Europe had seen for 200 years. But it was
also a threat to Moslem civilization : after sweeping over and
devastating Persia, the Mongol Khan Hulagu captured Bagdad in 1258, slew (or rather starved) the last Caliph, and
reduced the ancient capital of the Mohammedan world to
a ruin. The Mongols then flooded forward into Syria and
took Aleppo : unless beaten they would next make for
Damascus and Egypt. The Mamelukes stood fiercely to
defend the sultanate they had recently mastered, and after
two years of hard fighting finally achieved a decisive victory
over the Mongol Khan in 1260. It was only when they
had saved themselves from this danger that they turned
at last to the systematic extermination of the Franks of
the Syrian coast-land. The process took about a quarter
of a century, for the Christian harbour cities were strong,
the Italian commercial states had every reason for keeping
them safe, and the military orders of the Temple and the
Hospital provided a solid nucleus of fighting power, though the
old Frankish baronage of Palestine had dwindled away to
nothing. The process therefore was slow, if sure. Bibars,

the fourth and perhaps the greatest of the Mameluke sultans, captured Antioch, the largest city still in Christian hands, in 1268, and Jaffa, the southernmost Christian port, in the same year. From thenceforward the dwindling coast-slip was doomed, and in 1289 Tripoli and in 1291 Acre, the vital point of all commerce, was taken by the successor of Bibars. Abandoning the last few sea-castles, the Franks gave up the game, and retired by sea to the West. The episode of the attempt by Europe to master the Levant had come to a disastrous end. No European army set foot in the disputed lands of Western Asia again till 1798, when Bonaparte's extraordinary and reckless attack on Egypt brought him for a moment into Syria, there to be checked before Acre by the indefatigable Sydney Smith, rather than by the local Mohammedan power. But Bonaparte's raid from the first was an insane *tour de force*. How could he create an Eastern Empire with 30,000 men, when he was not sure of his sea-communication with France, his only base ? Nelson's victory of the Nile had stultified his enterprise ere ever he set foot on Syrian soil.

It was not the Mameluke conquerors of the last Frankish strongholds of Syria who were to be the real gainers by the extinction of the Crusading states, nor were they ever destined to follow up their success by important offensive action against Christendom. During the 230 years for which their power was destined to survive, they accomplished no more than the conquest of the small Armenian kingdom in Cilicia, and some unsuccessful raids on the island-realm of Cyprus. The destruction of the Christian states of the Latin East was rather a necessary preliminary to the last great Moslem attack on Europe by quite another power—the Ottoman Turks. I count this the last great swing of the pendulum westward, not reckoning the awful but transient inroad of the Mongols, which indeed had taken place fifty years before the end of the Kingdom of Jerusalem. The year of terror for Western Europe had been 1241-42 when the immense horde of Batu Khan, after sweeping all over Southern Russia and sacking Kief, had entered Poland, beaten its dukes and their East-German neighbours at Liegnitz, and then thrown itself upon Hungary. The Hungarian kingdom seemed absolutely annihilated at the battle of the Sajo, "ubi fere extinguitur militia totius regni Hungariae," and the Mongols actually pressed down into Dalmatia, and saw the waters of the Adriatic. But they vanished as quickly as they came, and after one winter of acute panic, which spread as far as Italy and England, Christendom breathed again. Hungary and Poland emerged from the deluge battered but safe, and it was only in unlucky Russia, for which Latin Europe had little concern, that the effects of the Mongol inroad lasted for generations—perhaps spiritually even down to to-day. For Russian barbarism is a survival in some sense from the destructive action of the eastern savages of the thirteenth century.

But the Ottoman Turks, not the Mongols, were the peril to Europe in the centuries that followed the fall of the Kingdom of Jerusalem. As long as Christendom had held a great outwork in the Levant, and the heart of the Mohammedan world was always liable to be assailed by a new Crusade, the solid advance of the East against the West was not possible. But the Crusaders of 1204 had knocked to pieces the old Byzantine Empire, the former guardian of the gate against eastern adventurers, and had set up nothing to replace it. After 1291 there was no Christian military power left on guard towards the frontiers of Islam. The Frankish principalities of the nearer East—Cyprus, Athens, Achaia—were miserably weak. The restored Byzantine Empire of the wretched Paleologi was no stronger. The Knights Hospitallers of Rhodes were but a handful of adventurers isolated in a precarious outpost. There was nothing left to resist the Ottoman Turks of Asia Minor, who after small beginnings which date back to the thirteenth century, began to assail Christendom in the fourteenth, and crossed over into Europe—where their remnant still remains encamped—in 1354. By one of the unlucky coincidences of history the one power which seemed likely to replace Byzantium as the guardian of the Balkans —the Serbian empire of the great Czar Stephen Durhan, broke up on the death of that prince precisely at the moment of the Ottoman landing in the Gallipoli peninsula.

Then came the nemesis of the commercial republics of Italy, for whose sole profit the Crusades seemed to have been fought out to an unsuccessful end. For, though the lands of the Levant had been lost, control over the sea and its trade was still retained by them after 1291. The fall of Acre had not ruined Venice or Genoa, who (accepting the situation) made financial compromises with the Mameluke conqueror, and by commercial treaties, kept open the trade routes of the East (mainly now through Alexandria), for another two centuries and more, so long as the Mameluke dynasties endured. But when the Ottoman Turks, whose growing power and persistent hostility to Christendom the Italians deliberately ignored in their blind commercialism, finally built a navy, and captured the long-defended Constantinople in 1453, the face of the world was changed. Venice and Genoa had very deliberately refused to send any adequate help to save Constantinople—the Venetian fleet had actually run up to the Bosphorus, just before the siege, taken on board the greater part of the Venetian colony there, and gone off for good.

The nemesis came in a few years. Mahomet II set himself to create a great naval power, and to cut off all the threads of Western commerce. Before he was dead he had effectually blocked the way to the Black Sea, and had practically mastered the Ægean. Christian vessels could get no further than Crete, Rhodes, and Cyprus. Venice fought hard now, when it was too late ; but her Golden Age was gone for good. Forty years later Selim the Terrible conquered Syria and Egypt, and blocked the sole surviving avenue of Western and Eastern trade, by destroying the Mameluke Sultanate, and capturing Alexandria in 1517. The Turk, in his day of triumph, was altogether fanatical, and anti-commercial ; he wished to have no dealings with the West save with the sword. That which followed—the great sixteenth-century assault of the Ottoman Empire on Central and Southern Europe, culminating at the siege of Vienna in 1529—is another story, too long to be told in these few pages. I take the tale of East and West no further than the time when Venice and Genoa, stripped of their ancient sea-supremacy, no longer " holding the gorgeous East in fee," nor living the wealthy exuberant life that they had enjoyed for the last three centuries, at last paid the

penalty of commercial ruin for their failure to back up the
Christian powers of the East, and were left to moulder,
"stranded shells of former greatness," by the Mediterranean
shore.

Who could have foreseen in 1291 or in 1453 or in 1517
that the next conquest of Egypt and Syria from the West
would be carried out by an invader as remote and improbable
as—let us say—the Mongols were in 1098, when Frank and
Turk and Saracen first contended for the guardianship of
the Holy Places ? I do not, of course, allude to Bonaparte's
fiasco of 1798–99, made with inadequate means and without a
safe line of communication with his base. He merely pointed
out the way, and demonstrated the weakness of the decaying
Ottoman Empire. The reconquest of Palestine and Syria
was to be accomplished by a British army. There was one
well-known Englishman in the first Crusade—the worthy but
unlucky Edgar Atheling. It would be interesting to know
what he would have thought of the prophecy—if it had been
made to him—that the armies of a descendant of his sister,
Queen Margaret of Scotland, would one day, without any
appreciable help from any other Christian power, sweep
the Turk out of Syria in one majestic campaign. The enemy
was still to be the Turk—if Ottoman and not Seljouk, yet
still the same tough fighter in war, and hopeless maladminis-
trator and waster of culture in time of peace. Palestine has
not changed much since 1099—the dry limestone uplands, the
waterless ravines, the thin-spread population, the blazing
sun of summer, the pestilent torrents of the short rainy season,
were the same in 1918 as the Crusading chronicler describes
them as being in his day. But how changed the character
of the combatants—the Crusaders' complaint was always
that he lacked light cavalry—we swamped Palestine with
Australian mounted infantry and Indian lancers, and cut off
and surrounded the last Turkish army by the most beautiful
cavalry manœuvre in recorded military history, which began
with the "second battle of Arsouf" and ended in the capture
of Damascus and Aleppo in an incredibly short term of days.
In 1099 the Turk was essentially a fighter on horseback—a
mounted archer : in 1918 he had become an obstinate sticker

to trenches, with no adequate cavalry arm at all! But I must not dwell on the last Eastward swing of the pendulum. The story of Allenby's Syrian campaign deserves something more than casual comment.

VII

LORD CARTERET

A few years ago one of our popular historians gave fair expression to the feeling of the English reading public, when he labelled the political history of the period which lies between the death of Queen Anne and the Seven Years' War as " remarkable for its distressing commonness and flatness both in men and in affairs." Amid the obscurity of its first half nothing is visible but the burly figure of Walpole ; when the great minister has been displaced, it is only to usher in the tedious struggle of the Whig factions for office—the great battle of the kites and crows, whose details are inexpressibly wearisome to every one save that strangely constituted being the professed parliamentary historian. Happily we have learnt of late that the history of England is something more than the history of parliaments and ministries and congresses, or we should be tempted to surrender the greater part of the reigns of the first two Georges to the annalist and the antiquary.

John Lord Carteret was a statesman of brilliant parts, whose misfortune it was to live in that dullest of times. He was a young man just entering public life when Queen Anne died, and a gout-ridden invalid of sixty-six when Boscawen's cannon in the Gulf of St. Lawrence announced the rupture of the treaty of Aix-la-Chapelle. This fact goes far towards explaining the oblivion into which a man of such mark has fallen, but other causes are not far to seek.

Carteret's whole life was a brilliant failure : the best years of it were spent in futile opposition to Walpole ; and when at last he had succeeded in seizing the reins of power, he was ignominiously thwarted, and ere long overthrown, by his own disloyal colleagues. The policy which he strove to carry out was in its essence the same which afterwards brought

fame and popularity to the elder Pitt. But Carteret failed
in his endeavour to apply it, and has been forgotten : Pitt,
who obtained the free hand which the elder statesman could
never gain, succeeded, and has won the credit of being the
sole inventor and exponent of such views. Beside his practical
achievements Carteret's ingenious but fruitless schemes are
thrown completely into the shade. If the two men are ever
mentioned together, it is only when historians detail the
truculent abuse which Pitt in his free-lance days heaped
upon the " desperate rhodomontading minister " who in 1744
advocated the same foreign policy which was to be the glory
of 1758.

In an age of political pamphlets, memoirs, and diaries,
Carteret steadfastly kept the printer idle. The numerous
unpublished dispatches from his hand show that he possessed
a clear and forcible style : the few private letters which have
survived are sufficient—in spite of Lord Shelburne's verdict
that Carteret " could never write a common letter well "
—to prove that his reputation for incisive humour was not
undeserved. Every contemporary writer agrees that he was
a ripe scholar and a marvellous linguist, that he held his own
with Swift in the contest of wits, and spent long evenings in
thrashing out the metres of Terence with Bentley. He was
reckoned by his friends the best, and by his enemies the
second best, speaker in the House of Lords, and the few
happy phrases of his oratory that have come down to us fully
bear out their verdict. But all our admiration for him must
be at second hand : it is from the impression that he left
on others, not from that which we ourselves receive, that
our notion of his character must be drawn. He has left
no literary memorial of any kind whatsoever behind him.
That his parliamentary speeches should have perished is
nothing strange : they have but shared the fate of those of
every other statesman of the days when reporting was a crime.
But that a man of such pronounced literary tastes should
never have written a line outside his necessary public and
private correspondence is nothing less than astonishing. If
he did not join Pulteney in penning political pamphlets, we
might have expected to find him dabbling like Chesterfield

in miscellaneous essay writing, or wooing the Muses in happier numbers than Pitt, or solacing the weariness of long years spent in Opposition by writing memoirs. Not a single work, however, issued from his hand. The curious inquirer who consults the headings " Carteret " or " Granville " in one of our great public libraries will find nothing under them but one wretched political squib dedicated to Carteret in 1722 by an anonymous Whig pamphleteer. His own contemporaries expected more of him : in 1737 it was noised abroad that he was writing a " History of his own time," and society speculated on the judgments he would pass on its more prominent members. There seems, however, to have been no truth in the report : if projected, the work was never begun.

But in spite of his literary inactivity, and of the singular carelessness which he always displayed as to his own posthumous reputation, we should not have expected that his countrymen would " succeed in altogether forgetting their considerable Carteret," as Carlyle phrased it. He had always been a friend and patron of literary men, not merely of poets and scholars but of historians, such as Harte, the author of the *Life of Gustavus Adolphus*. Probably we may say of him, as of many another statesman, that he lived too long for his own reputation. Had' he died in 1746, men would have said that the most striking personality in English politics had been removed : by 1763 his rise and fall, his talents and ambition, were already on the way to be forgotten.

The verdicts of modern historians on him have been shallow and unjust. One writer speaks of him as " presenting a fearful example of a highly cultivated intellect and a great capacity for business totally ruined and obscured by the pernicious habit of drinking to which he was a slave," another as " a man of genius but of irregular life, capricious and sudden in all his actions." With the story of his career before us, we can see at a glance how futile are the cheap Tacitean paradoxes of the majority of our nineteenth-century writers, who seem to have taken the most fantastic statements of Hervey and Horace Walpole as sober and accurate narration of fact where Carteret was concerned. Even Mr. Lecky's

judicious estimate of the man must be to a certain extent
modified, much more so Macaulay's characteristic epigrams.

As to the attractive side of Carteret's character we need
only say that he had every faculty that could attract admiration and win the love of friends. There is no reason to requote
the opinions which Macaulay collected, from Chatham and
Chesterfield, Horace Walpole, Swift, and Johnson—all men
with whom Carteret had come into hostile collision—as to
his abilities as a statesman. Perhaps we may mention as a
less hackneyed piece of evidence the remark of Speaker Onslow,
another old enemy of Carteret's, that " it was not his aim
to aggrandise himself : he was all for glory, even to the enthusiasm of it, and that made him more scrupulous in the means
he used for his greatness."

That he was perfectly incorrupt in money matters, and
was a heavy loser while he held office under the Crown, is
acknowledged by all. But personal integrity of that kind
can be ascribed to Bolingbroke, to Newcastle, even to Walpole himself. The virtue in which Carteret stands unrivalled
is his utter detestation for the abuses of patronage. No
unworthy relative or dependent ever owed a place to his recom-
mendation : he drove off his nearest friends and most necessary
political allies, when once they began to talk to him of posts
and pensions. The well-known story told by Lord Chief
Justice Willes is a sufficient illustration :—

" Sir R. Walpole promised me to make my friend Clive one of the
King's Counsel : but too late ! When Lord Granville [Carteret's later
title] came to the height of his power, I one day said to him, ' My lord,
you are going to the king ; do ask him to make poor Clive one of his
Counsel.' He turned and replied, ' What is it to me who is a judge or a
bishop ? It is *my* business to make kings and emperors, and to maintain
the balance of Europe.' I replied, ' Then those who want to be bishops
or judges will apply to those who *will* submit to make it their business.' "

To turn to the other side, there is but one serious charge
made against him—that he was addicted to port wine. We
do not wish to give any exaggerated importance to the charge ;
the modern historians who have pitched upon inebriety as
the most prominent feature in Carteret's private character
have gone ludicrously wrong. But it is impossible to ignore

the consensus of opinion in contemporary writers. It is
not enemies alone who say that Carteret loved his bottle
too well; his friends admit it—even his own son-in-law
euphemistically calls him a *bon-vivant*. That the public
voice named his tenure of office " the Drunken Administration " may go for little ; but we cannot fail to see that many
of the best of his sayings breathe a post-prandial atmosphere.
Lord Shelburne himself prefaces one of them by the obser-
vation that before a Cabinet Council his illustrious relative
" had generally dined." It is equally impossible to mistake
the tastes of the man who said that he liked to have Steele
and Addison together for an evening, the one for the start,
the other for the finish ; " for, by the time that Steele had
drunk himself down, Addison had drunk himself up." We
cannot misconceive the meaning of the fits of gout to which
Carteret was a martyr in his later years ; there can be no
doubt that, like many another statesman, he was suffering
from the effects of the Methuen Treaty. There is no proof
that drink ever obscured Carteret's intellect, or that he ever
sank to making a public exhibition of its effects, as not only
the younger Pitt but at least one more recent premier is accused
of doing. But in a hard-drinking age he earned a special reputation for loving his port overmuch, and we cannot ignore the
consequences to his character, and to the estimation in which
he was held. The charge, even when admitted, is not a very
heavy one ; it leaves us perfectly free to hold that he was
not merely magnanimous in his own large eighteenth-century
way, but worthy of liking and esteem to a degree which none
of his contemporaries, save Pitt alone, could attain. A
statesman of that day against whom nothing can be brought
but a too copious thirst and a few rather unworthy political
intrigues, entered into in the heat of a ministerial crisis, may
pass as a man of approved virtue.

In a prolonged panegyric on Carteret we need not indulge :
the strength and the weakness of that remarkable man are
best realized by glancing at the strange vicissitudes of his
career—a career whose early promise and performance were
extraordinary ; whose middle part was blighted by long
exclusion from office under the jealous rule of Walpole ; whose

final act began with such brilliant success only to end tamely in defeat at the hands of the meanest and most contemptible of enemies.

The Carterets are an ancient and honourable family in Jersey, but till Stuart times their reputation was bounded by the limits of that pleasant but not too spacious island. The one notable story in their earlier annals is a legend of the defeat of Du Guesclin by Reginald de Carteret and his eight sons, and of their consequent knighting by King Edward III ; but on this tale sceptics have cast their doubts. The real importance of the house dates only from Sir George Carteret, a zealous Royalist who held Jersey for Charles II down to the month of December, 1651, long after the " Crowning Mercy " had driven the last royal garrisons in Great Britain to despair and surrender. On his restoration Charles for once contrived to remember the services of a faithful adherent. Sir George received places and pensions, and when his heir was slain in early manhood at the battle of Solebay, the king endeavoured to recompense the loyalty of the family by granting a peerage to the old man's grandson and namesake. This George, first Baron Carteret, was cut off like his father before he had time to make a name in the world. He died at the age of twenty-six, leaving two infant sons by his wife Lady Grace Granville, who was to survive him for a full half-century. She was a granddaughter of Sir Bevil Grenville, the hero of Stratton and Lansdowne fights.

John, the famous statesman, was the elder of the sons of the first peer : he was five, and his brother Philip only three, when their father died in 1695. Both the boys were sent to Westminster School. Philip stayed there till the unusually late age of eighteen, was accidentally drowned in the Thames, and was mourned in excellent sapphics by his head master, Dr. Friend. John left the school at fifteen, but had already made a reputation as an unusually clever boy. He seems to have always retained a great affection for Westminster. The young peer was made a " Busby Trustee " before he came of age, and frequented the Plays and other festivities of St. Peter's School long after he had become a pillar of the State.

Of Carteret's Oxford life some suggestive facts are to be found in Hearne's Diaries. He matriculated at Christ Church on January 15, 1706, being then somewhat under sixteen years of age, and had the privilege of paying £2, where his companions contributed 2s. 6d., to the University Chest. He resided four years, but never chose to take his degree,[1] although it might have been obtained easily enough by the favour of the Chancellor, without the completion of the necessary exercises, as were those of most other noble graduates of that day. But Carteret never ceased to be an undergraduate till an honorary D.C.L. was conferred on him at the Encænia of 1756. He studied Civil Law to such effect that, fifty years after he had left the university, he was able to use his knowledge in that branch of learning to confute Lord Chancellor Hardwicke on his own ground. However, he did not design to make himself a mere Civilian : his studies ranged over the whole field of classical and modern literature. He was a constant reader in the Bodleian, and to that fact we owe our first description of him. Hearne, the famous Jacobite sub-librarian, notes him in 1709 as "juvenis ingenii acutissimi, morum suavissimorum, et in primæ classis scriptoribus, cum Græcis tum Latinis, supra annos versatus. In Æde Christi, studiis deditus, vitam agit." On one occasion he took Hearne to his rooms in Christ Church, and showed him with pride some early printed editions of Livy which he had collected. A little later we find him subscribing to Dr. Barnes's "Homer," a very characteristic touch, for the *Iliad* was always his favourite book, and he actually died with Sarpedon's speech to Glaucus upon his lips. The world in after years accused him of having learnt his drinking habits at the university, and it is curious to find that on one occasion Hearne had been holding a sitting with "that great proficient in Greek and all polite learning, my Lord Carteret of Ch. Ch.," whereat they drank Dr. and Mrs. Barnes's healths two or three times over each, not without other libations, we may presume.

---

[1] By a ridiculous blunder biographical dictionaries invariably state that Carteret was made an honorary D.C.L. on April 26, 1706, three months after his matriculation. He has been confounded with his uncle John Lord Granville.

All this sounds like the beginnings of the life of a mere student and bibliophile, but in 1710 Carteret broke with Oxford and her placid delights. He came up to London, and within a few months had married Frances Worsley, daughter of Sir Robert Worsley. The united age of bride and bridegroom did not quite reach thirty-seven, and the courtship was short and sudden : but all accounts agree that the marriage was a most happy one. In that dissolute age Carteret was conspicuous for his conjugal fidelity, and not even the most scandalous of his enemies ever reflected on his morals.

A few months after his marriage Carteret came of age and took his seat in the House of Lords. He does not seem at first to have definitely attached himself to either of the great parties. The Tories were at that moment in the ascendant, and as his father had been a Tory and his uncle was at this very time Secretary at War in Harley's government, it might have been expected that he himself would incline to that side. Indeed, the fact that he had at Oxford been intimate with Hearne, a man to whom all Whigs were as poison, would lead us to think that his Whig proclivities must have been very slight. Of the first four years of his parliamentary career, we can only discover that as late as the winter of 1713-14 Peter Wentworth (perhaps the most intrepid speller of our Augustan age) calls " Lord Carterwright " a " straggling peer " who returned sometimes to vote with the Court party.[1] We cannot say that Carteret definitely declared for the Whigs by voting against the ministerial resolution that " the Protestant Succession was in no danger " ; several undoubted Tories, such as the Earls of Abingdon, Jersey, and Anglesey, joined him in so doing. A better test of his conversion to Whig principles is the fact that in the May of the same year he voted against the Schism Act, which was supported by Anglesey and the other " Hanoverian Tory " peers. From that moment his politics were never doubtful.

Three months after the Schism Act had passed Queen

---

[1] *Wentworth Papers*, p. 367. Wentworth's spelling is wild beyond conception. He calls Walpole " Wallpoole," and Kensington " Kinsenton," habitually.

Anne died, and the Whig Party entered on that long tenure
of office which was to endure for all but a complete half-
century. Carteret had, as it turned out, chosen his side
wisely. Before the new king was crowned he was appointed
a Lord of the Bedchamber, and a few months later he was
made Lord-Lieutenant of Devonshire, though his property
and influence did not lie in that county. Probably Whig
magnates were rare in the Jacobite West, and a man of ability
was required to manage a shire where a French landing was
always possible. While the rebellion of 1715 was in progress Carteret was vigilantly moving about, "improving the
thoughts of the neighbouring gentry, and discountenancing
the seeds of faction that have been sown in these parts,"
as he phrased it himself. But his powers were not destined
to be tried by any outbreak. Devonshire made no movement, and the months of danger passed safely by.

We have now reached the point at which Carteret became
a notable figure in politics. When once he has taken office
and his public correspondence becomes available, the meagre
and fragmentary record of his career grows fuller and clearer.
Up to this moment there was no tangible proof of Carteret's
abilities. Evidently his contemporaries believed in him, but
their belief had not as yet been justified by any notable achievement. There was no doubt that he was a good Whig, that
he possessed a pretty wit, and that, though somewhat of
a scholar and a student, he had a considerable political ambition. But many a young man starts in life with all these
attributes and never makes his mark. Carteret was now about
to be tested by the logic of facts, and to show that his friends'
confidence was not misplaced.

On the hopelessly dull and uninteresting details of the quarrel
between the Whigs who followed Walpole, and the Whigs
who followed Sunderland or Stanhope in the earlier years
of George I, there is no reason to enlarge. Suffice it to say
that Carteret cast in his lot with Sunderland, and by so doing
determined the whole of his own career, for he thereby earned
Walpole's undying enmity, and that enmity was to keep him
out of office for the best years of his life. A happy turn
for the easy acquisition of languages, a good address, and

a talent for picking up miscellaneous information, marked
Carteret out as a possible diplomatist. Sunderland determined to make trial of him in a position of considerable importance, and sent him out as Ambassador Extraordinary to
Sweden.

His Swedish dispatches are most interesting, and a perusal
of them is enough by itself to give a fair idea of Carteret's
character. We are struck at once with the happy combination of foresight and of capacity for sudden action, of readi-
ness and of persistence, which they display, above all with
their sustained hopefulness and buoyancy of spirit in the midst
of countless checks and hindrances.

Six months before Carteret landed at Gothenborg a traitorous
pistol-shot from the rear had laid Charles XII dead in the
trenches of Fredrikshald on November 30, 1718. His sister
Ulrika Eleonora succeeded to a disputed crown, an empty
exchequer, a factious Diet, and four foreign wars. Seldom
has a country reached a more forlorn condition than Sweden
at that moment : the empire which Gustavus Adolphus had
built up was crumbling to pieces from sheer want of men and
money to maintain a war with all its neighbours at once. The
Danes were invading the western provinces from their base
in Norway, the Russian fleet was harrying the shores of Upland
and Sudermania, the King of Prussia had just conquered
Pomerania and Rügen ; lastly, George of England, intent
on revenge for Charles XII's support of the Pretender, and
seeing a fair chance of adding to his beloved electoral territories,
had stretched out his hand for the duchies of Bremen and
Verden. The interests which Carteret—starting at the
age of twenty-eight on his first diplomatic campaign—had
to reconcile seemed hopelessly at variance. England did
not wish to see Sweden too much weakened, yet the King
of England was bent on gaining land from her for his own
private domain. Russia, Prussia, and Denmark were resolved
to get all that they could extort from their exhausted enemy,
while the unruly Swedish Diet refused to hear reason till
the conqueror was at their very gates. "They do not as
yet feel all their wounds," wrote Carteret ; "they are still
warm. The late king put a spirit and a courage and left

a motion in this nation which is not yet expired, though it abates daily and must soon cease."

The reconciliation of all parties concerned and the happy conclusion of four several peaces were probably the cleverest achievement of the whole of Carteret's career. He persuaded the Swedish Government to begin by buying off the enmity of his own master with the required territorial cessions, on condition that England should grant her friendly mediation with the other powers. Then, bringing up the British fleet into the Baltic, he overawed the Russian and the Dane into withdrawal. This was the boldest of strokes, for he had neither permission nor intention to use the fleet for actual warlike operations, and could only reckon on the moral effect of its presence. But he had gauged the situation, and believed that a mere demonstration would be enough. Nor was he disappointed. The appearance of Admiral Norris and his seventy-fours was the signal for the disappearance of Tsar Peter and his marauding squadron. The Danes consented to an armistice, the King of Prussia proved open to negotiations, and signs of peace began to appear on the horizon.

"I don't care for bold strokes," wrote Carteret, "but I have lived by nothing else since I came here. . . . No public minister was ever for a month together upon so bad or so dangerous a situation as I have been. The common people looked upon me as the author of their misery while no succour came. . . . However, I still went on in the same strain, and have worked through with success, so that at present no ambassador was ever upon a better footing in a country than I am."

Ere long Frederick William came to terms, obtaining the cession of Stettin and its district on the payment of two million florins. A curious instance of the king's economy came out in the course of the negotiation. He stipulated that the wagons and horses which brought the Prussian money should be precisely paid for. "So minute a particular," wrote Carteret, "has hardly ever been inserted before in a treaty to be made between two crowns."

When Denmark also had been satisfied by a comparatively small cession of territory and a sum of 600,000 dollars, Carteret's popularity rose to its zenith. The Queen of Sweden loaded him with praises, the ministers were constant in their attendance on him, the Diet expressed its thanks. When he visited Copenhagen he was much surprised to find that in Denmark also he was regarded with high approval, as the terminator of the war. Frederick IV on receiving him commenced with the happy speech : " Milord, comme par votre entremise j'ai fait la paix, et qu'à cette heure mes armes me sont inutiles, permettez-moi que je vous fasse présent de mon épée," handing him at the same time a sword valued at 20,000 crowns, specially made for the occasion.

After Carteret had quitted the north, but entirely in con- sequence of the success of his previous negotiations, the Tsar was induced to make the peace of Nystadt, which restored Finland to Sweden, though it stripped her of her possessions to the south and south-east of the gulf of the same name. Thus the work of pacification was completed.

The bold and skilful diplomacy which had given peace to Europe was less appreciated in England than in any other country. The Government, indeed, was satisfied, but it is doubtful whether the general public had any conception of the matter, beyond the notion that Carteret had used the power of England in order to enable King George to add a strip of Swedish territory to his hated electorate. On the man himself the effect was most marked : it gave him a jovial self-reliance and a cheerful confidence in his own " bold strokes " which were for the future the most prominent features in his character. He had picked up a knowledge not only of Swedish but of German during his eighteen months of sojourn at Stockholm, and had thoroughly mastered the politics of all the northern powers. Consequently it was not unnatural that he should believe that the foreign rela- tions of his country were by far the most important things with which the ministry was charged, and that he should be profoundly convinced that skilful diplomacy could accomplish all things—even the impossible. It can easily be guessed how these ideas clashed with the theories of Walpole, with whom he was soon to be brought into the closest contact. The two men and their notions of England's true policy were abso- lutely and entirely incompatible.

During the last months of Carteret's stay in Sweden the great South Sea crash had occurred. He arrived in England just in time to find his patron Sunderland tottering to his fall, and Walpole preparing to resume his place in the ministry. When the new government was formed, the last trace of the outgoing premier's influence was the appointment of Carteret as "Secretary of State for the Southern Department." This gave him the control of our foreign relations with France, Spain, Italy, and Turkey. The "Secretary for the North," who had charge of Scandinavia, Russia, and Germany, was his future bane, the Duke of Newcastle. Carteret held this post for exactly three years, with very considerable credit to his own powers as an administrator and diplomatist, but with gradually decreasing influence in the ministry. The truth was that Walpole had made up his mind to get rid of him by fair means or foul. He disliked him as an unwelcome legacy from Sunderland, but he absolutely dreaded him as a possible rival in the favour of the king; we may add that on grounds of general principle he objected to having any man of more than average ability serving under him in the Cabinet. George I, as every one knows, was fond of interfering in every branch of European politics. Walpole, to whom all foreign languages were as sealed books, was almost incredibly ignorant of the commonplaces of diplomacy. He lived, therefore, in a constant state of nightmare, picturing to himself Carteret obtaining the king's full confidence by conversing with him in the mysterious German tongue on the affairs of the Continent. Nor was he entirely in the wrong : George certainly displayed some partiality for the young Secretary of State, and even took him over to enjoy the delights of Hanover. This brought matters to a crisis ; for six months there was open war, and then the king was induced to dismiss Carteret from his post. During the period of stress the falling minister was endeavouring to save himself by his personal credit with the king and his entourage. He won the favour of the Duchess of Kendal by undertaking to settle certain private matters about which she was treating with Cardinal Dubois, and afterwards with Orleans' favourite Nocé. By this backstairs influence he

was for a moment maintained ; but when Walpole had set his
mind on a thing, the power of the king or the king's mistress
was a broken reed on which to rely. In March, 1724, Carteret
lost his secretaryship, and his fall was hardly softened by
the fact that he was in the next month presented with the
extremely undesirable post of Lord-Lieutenant of Ireland,
more to keep him out of London than to solace him for his
removal from the Cabinet. Indeed there were many who
thought that Walpole sent him over the Channel merely
that he might wreck his career in that unhappy island, the
grave of great reputations.

With Carteret's removal to Ireland his public correspondence almost entirely fails us, and becomes incomplete and
fragmentary. The controversy about Wood's halfpence was
assuming dangerous proportions at the moment of his appointment, and it was probably Walpole's plan to make him the
scapegoat in the matter, if any such were required. Swift
and the new Lord-Lieutenant had been slightly acquainted
before, and had no unkindly recollection of each other. But
any less adroit and genial personage than Carteret must have
found himself committed to war with the fiery Dean before
a month was over. The sound and fury of the *Drapier's
Letters* are now forgotten, but the ruler who dealt with them
without losing his head must have been a man of imperturbable
temper. Though not personally attacked, he could not but
resent the barefaced sedition which, in his own words, "struck
at the dependency of Ireland on the throne of Great Britain."
Nevertheless, he succeeded in keeping off any actual collision.
One good story is told of the curious relations between Swift
and Carteret, at the time when a proclamation was out against
the more than suspected author of the *Drapier's Letters*, and
yet the two men were continually meeting on friendly terms
in private life. The Dean, making a call at the Castle, was
kept some time waiting in the anteroom, for the Lord-Lieutenant was engaged. Growing impatient he sent in a card
with two lines scribbled on it :—

> "My very good Lord, 'tis a very hard task
> For a man to wait here who has nothing to ask."

Carteret sent out an answer at once in the happy lines :—

> "My very good Dean, there are few who come here
> But have something to ask, *or something to fear.*"

When Wood's execrated patent was finally withdrawn, the discredit of the defeat did not fall on the Lord-Lieutenant. He had so carefully confined himself to a cautious and wary carrying out of orders expressly given in England, that no one could say that he was personally compromised in the smallest degree.

Of the last five years of Carteret's stay in Ireland there is not very much to tell. Swift wrote that "I confess that he had a genteeler manner of binding the chains of this kingdom than most of his predecessors." Nobody who has read Mr. Lecky's chapters on Ireland in his *Eighteenth Century* can fail to catch the allusion. Though personally mild and genial, Carteret was charged with the carrying out of a most detestable policy. During his tenure of office the exclusion of all Irishmen from promotion became more marked than ever. The times were bad, trade continually decreased, yet Walpole was always loading the Irish pension-list with all the jobs that were too flagrant to be carried out in England. The Lord-Lieutenancy must have been no pleasant post for a man who, whatever his faults, had a good heart and an unfeigned dislike to the evils of misused patronage.

In 1730 Carteret returned from his exile, and, resuming the place in the House of Lords from which he had so long been absent, plunged at once into vehement opposition to Walpole's government. For twelve weary years that opposition continued, and it was not till nine of those twelve had elapsed that ultimate success appeared in the least probable. We may fairly say that Carteret wasted on fruitless parliamentary wrangling, and still more fruitless attempts to win the favour of the king and queen, those years of his life when brain and nerves were at their best and strongest. His administrative talents found no better scope than the endeavour to organize a party which always turned out to be in the minority. His skilful diplomacy had to be exercised in futile attempts to gain personal interviews with the queen, or even with those

who were about the queen's person. He leagued himself
with Pulteney and Chesterfield, and Argyll, but neither the
racy political writing of the first, nor the sonorous eloquence
of the second, nor the parliamentary influence of the third
availed him aught against Walpole's skilfully managed money-
bags. He turned to the Tories : he stimulated the vehemence
of Pitt and Lyttelton and the other " Boy-patriots," but his
heterogeneous forces were only mustered in order to suffer
defeat. The man who at twenty-eight had settled the affairs
of Europe was apparently a stranded wreck at fifty.

Constant failure is said to leave men either soured or indifferent. Carteret had too buoyant a spirit to sink into gloom
and despair ; nor did his twelve years' apprenticeship to
adversity cause him to quit political life. After leading a
furious assault on Walpole and suffering the usual defeat he
would retire in complete good humour to his books and his
bottle and wait for the chance of another fight. But there
can be little doubt that his long exclusion from office injured
his character by sapping his sense of responsibility. There
were not unfrequent occasions when his conduct sank into
mere factiousness, and this was remembered against him
when he himself came at last into power. It is easy to understand the irritation of the knot of men of genius whose careers
were spoilt merely because Walpole could not tolerate ability
in his subordinates. But the penalty which they had to
pay for their unceasing onslaughts on the great minister was
to acquire a reputation for levity, and for loving opposition
for opposition's sake.

On the question of the Spanish war, however, we are not
disposed to join the common cry of those who denounce
Carteret and Pulteney for having driven Walpole into an
unjust and unnecessary conflict with an unoffending neighbour.
All such accusations are out of place since the long-hidden
terms of the first " Family Compact " of 1733 can be studied
by the historian. Whether Robert Jenkins, whose name
has been so ridiculously imposed on the war, ever lost his
ear or not makes no difference to us. We know that the
house of Bourbon had bound itself in close alliance to impose
its will on Europe. We know that England was expressly

named as a possible enemy, and that Spain undertook, long
before any offence had been given, and while the most pacific
of English ministers was in office, to endeavour to ruin England's
trade. The molestation which our merchants suffered on
the Spanish Main and in the South Seas was part of a deliberate plan to transfer our commercial advantages to France.
Not merely, then, in the interest of the balance of power
in Europe, threatened by the preponderance of the Bourbons,
but in the defence of our own rights, we were perfectly justified
in taking up the sword. Carteret, more versed in foreign
politics than any other Englishman of his day, thoroughly
understood the state of affairs, and very rightly decided in
favour of war.

Driven to fight against his will, and fighting with an equal
want of skill and of luck, Walpole at last lost his hold on
the House of Commons. Defeated on January 28, 1742, on
the paltry question of the Chippenham election petition,
the great minister resigned. At last the conjuncture for
which twenty able men had been scheming and working for
the last dozen years had come to pass. The victory was
won ; it only remained to be seen who would carry off
the spoils.

Pulteney was the first to whom the opportunity was offered ;
but, with a sudden and incomprehensible fear of the situation
which he had so long been scheming to bring about, that
statesman refused to accept office. Carteret was the next
whose name was suggested to the King, and he proved more
amenable than might have been expected to the royal behest.
There were two courses open to him. He might stipulate
for the entire exclusion of Walpole's party from the new
Cabinet, and build it up by employing all the sections of
the motley majority which had won the victory of January
28, combining the Hanoverian Tories with the various sections
of discontented Whigs. Or he might, with his own immediate
following, join the more moderate members of the late ministry,
and get the benefit of their enormous parliamentary influence.
The former course was the more honest and the more difficult :
to endeavour to combine Chesterfield and Argyll, Pitt and
Cotton, would be undoubtedly hard. The second was the

easier, but the less honourable : the men who had been denouncing Walpole's policy had no right to ally themselves with Walpole's lieutenants. In an evil hour, however, Carteret chose the worse alternative : he joined the new ministry in which Newcastle, Henry Pelham, Hardwicke, Wilmington, and Harrington, all of whom had served under Walpole, were allowed to find places. Wilmington was even given the nominal position of prime minister, though every one understood that he was and would be a mere cipher. On the other hand, Chesterfield, the "Patriots," and the Tories were excluded.

This was the worst day's work that Carteret ever did for himself : he made the treacherous Pelhams his colleagues, and sent Pitt and Chesterfield into opposition. Within two years the Pelhams had intrigued him out of office, and the opposition had made him the best-hated man in England by their incendiary harangues. But it would be wrong to see in the causes of his fall nothing but the intrigues of Newcastle and the harangues of Pitt. There can be no doubt, that the foibles of Carteret had quite as much to do with his disgrace as the machinations of his enemies. He was by nature and training better fitted for a diplomatist than a responsible minister. He hated the drudgery of parliamentary management, and despised the corrupt means which it then required. His mind was so set on carrying out his broad schemes of foreign policy that he could find no time to explain and justify them before Parliament and public opinion. Moreover, as Onslow observed, "he was all for glory." Carteret, indeed, had no vulgar ambition ; we should be wrong if we classed him with the Newcastles or Henry Foxes of the day, as a man who engaged in politics from selfish love of power or desire for mere advancement. His ideal was, to use his own words—flippant in expression but sincere in thought —"to knock the heads of all the kings of Europe together, and jumble something out of it that may be of service to England." But in addition there can be no doubt that he took a keen personal pleasure in his diplomatic schemes. He loved to score a political success, but if success was impossible it gave him almost as much pleasure to fail after a well-fought struggle. The stir and bustle of the statesman's life, the skilful fencing of diplomatic interviews, the handling of the threads of national policy which ramified to every court in Europe, were very dear to him. He had one of those buoyant spirits on which responsibility sits lightly; his cheerful and easy self-confidence saw its way through every difficulty, and his ready wit had an answer for every objection. Newcastle, finding a happy phrase for once in his life, said that "Carteret was one of the men who never doubted." The saying was true enough : his judgment was so quick, and his knowledge in every branch of practical affairs so wide, that he never had to stop to ponder long over a line of action. One course always presented itself to his mind as obvious, the rest were dismissed without a further thought.

In practical politics this faculty of rapid decision was by no means an unmixed advantage to Carteret. So clear was his mental vision that he was impatient with those whose perception was slow, and hardly condescended to explain his ideas to their duller intelligence. To mediocrities who could just see far enough to realize the difficulties of a question, the imperious decisiveness of his answers seemed to spring from mere unreflecting rashness. The favourite name for him in Opposition pamphlets was "Jack Headlong." His dislike to plunge into wearisome explanations and discussion was most of all displayed when continental affairs were in question. Here he claimed a free hand ; when he had accompanied the King to Germany, he proceeded to enter into treaties and agreements to right and left, without giving any notice to his colleagues at home until the matters were settled. We can now see that his schemes were feasible, and his general plan of operations favourable to England. But while he was in fact walking at his ease through the labyrinthine mazes of German politics, those who had not the clue saw in him a blind leader of the blind, staggering at haphazard among snares and pitfalls, and dragging the nation to destruction after him. Unable to penetrate his designs, owing to the gross ignorance of continental affairs which reigned in England, they professed to come to one of three conclusions : either he was " mad," or he was " drunk," or he was betraying the interests of his country to the Hanoverian partialities of the king.

Seldom have more unjust charges been brought against a statesman. His " madness " was precisely what was afterwards regarded as Pitt's inspiration—the idea that the power of the House of Bourbon might be bled to death in Germany. While his colleagues and rivals were thinking of petty expeditions against Dunkirk or Cartagena, Carteret had realized that such pin-pricks could have no effect on the general course of the war. He wished to wear down the enemy by confederate armies on the Scheldt, the Rhine, and the Alps, and trusted that England would open her purse to subsidize them. But men who had not a tithe of his knowledge of the Continent thought otherwise ; they found his scheme visionary and presumptuous, because the proof of its feasibility rested on data which were unknown to them. So his colleagues deserted him, while his enemies laid every folly and baseness to his charge. Pitt, unconscious of his own future, denounced " the execrable minister who seemed to have drunk of the potion which poets have described as causing men to forget their country." Chesterfield described him as one whose only object in life was to pour English guineas into the hands of foreigners, in order that the king might win some petty Hanoverian object.

English public opinion seems to have realized very little of Carteret's scheme for a simultaneous attack on France by all the Powers of Central Europe. When it was reported that at a public banquet he had drunk to the " Restoration of Alsace and Lorraine to the Empire," the news went round that the English subsidies were to be spent in helping Austria to carry on a war of mere ambition and aggression. No one would see that every army that France had to put in motion for the East meant the diversion of a considerable portion of her resources from the defence of her naval power and colonies. The true and happy phrase that " Canada must be conquered on the plains of Germany " had not yet been invented ; the man who was one day to formulate it was at that moment thundering on Carteret's devoted head for daring to sub-

sidize the few thousand Hanoverian troops who had joined
the British army on the Main.

This fatal Hanoverian question, the one point in foreign
politics which every Englishman thought that he understood,
was to be Carteret's rúin. It does not seem to have been in
the least true that he played into the king's hands. If we
had to hire auxiliaries, the battalions of the Electorate could
be trusted far more than those of any other power. The
stories of their cowardice and indiscipline which Pitt and
Chesterfield spread abroad were malevolent inventions,
destitute of any real foundation. Whenever Hanoverian
troops served alongside of British, from Fontenoy to Wellington's Peninsular battles, they always did well. But it was
safe to abuse Hanover : and by dint of repeated assertions that
Carteret had sold his country, the opposition persuaded public
opinion that there was something in the charge.

Then came the chance of the Pelhams. They wanted to
get rid of their headstrong colleague, who sent them from
the heart of Germany imperious dispatches whose meaning
they were unable to fathom, and left them the duty of wring-
ing money for his subsidies out of a recalcitrant Parliament.
Newcastle did not understand foreign politics, but he did
understand the way to manage the baser part of the two
Houses. By November, 1744, he and his brother had their
plans ready. On the first day of the month the Duke handed
to King George a memorial signed not only by the majority
of the ministry, but by the whole of the Whig opposition,
which denounced Carteret, his conduct, and his policy. The
King was unwilling to lose a minister whose knowledge of
German affairs had been so useful, and whose views tallied
to a large extent with his own ; but he was not the fanatical
admirer of his Secretary of State which men had supposed
him to be. By the 24th he had discovered that any ministry
of which Carteret formed a part would be in a hopeless minority
in both Houses of Parliament, and on that day he yielded
to the Pelhams.

Nearly twenty years of life were before the fallen minister,
who had now reached the age of fifty-four. But they were
never to see him again at the head of affairs. For one moment

in the winter of 1745–6, while the Jacobite rebellion was
in full vigour, it seemed that he might be called back to power.
But Pulteney, on whose aid he had been relying, deserted
him in the moment of trial. That "Weathercock"—as
Shelburne remarked—"always spoilt everything." The Pelham influence proved too strong, even at the moment when
Newcastle and his brother had mismanaged affairs, both at
home and abroad, to an extent which made Walpole's failures
of 1739–42 look like brilliant successes. After being Secretary
of State for precisely four days, Carteret—now become Earl
Granville by the death of his aged mother—had to give place
to his old enemies. He relapsed into opposition with his
customary good humour, and employed himself in the study
of his favourite Greek authors and the nursing of the gout
which was fast growing upon him.

By 1752 the last incident of his chequered career took
place. The wheel of fortune brought round his turn when
it was too late : he was now not much better than an invalid,
though his mind and brain were clear enough. In that year
the men who had turned him out of office so meanly came
to him to invite him once more to join them. To every
one's surprise he consented : *non eadem est ætas, non mens,*
was the observer's comment, but this did not cover the whole
truth. Carteret had been from the first wholly destitute of
resentment, even to the verge of faultiness. It was not so
much the active faculty of pardoning his enemies which he
possessed, as the negative quality of being unable to hate
them when they wronged him, the defect that Aristotle once
called ἀοργησία. When they looked to see him angry and
depressed, they found him regarding events with the eyes of
a disinterested spectator of a humorous cast of mind.

"Once, when terribly abused by Lord Aylesford in the House of
Peers, he waited till the oration was over, and then, turning to those
who were sitting by him, said with a cheerful unconcern, not at all
affected or put on, but quite natural, ' Poor Aylesford is really angry ! ' "

Now the English public likes a good hater. It has its
doubts about the sincerity of a statesman who contents
himself with showing that his opponents are illogical or ill-
informed, and prefers to hear him charge them with wilful

misdoing. Nothing is easier than to accuse Carteret of levity and want of principle for taking office in 1752. But it is rather to his conviction that he could be of service to England that his conduct must be referred.

Seldom had one statesman played off on another meaner tricks than Newcastle and Pelham had used against Carteret. But in the day of their humiliation he consented to serve with them, in order that his knowledge of foreign affairs might be useful to the country. At the first Cabinet Council which he attended, he came cheerfully among his old detractors with the remark, "Well, my lords, here is the common enemy returned." For twelve years—till his death in 1763—he was uninterruptedly Lord President of the Council. It is satisfactory to know that he was ere long reconciled to Pitt, who, recanting all his previous abuse, became his friend, and carried out the policy which its original inventor was now too old and broken to execute. "In the upper departments of government Carteret had no equal," said Pitt; "to his instruction I owe whatever I am." It must have solaced the old minister in the long years when, "bent almost double, worn to a skeleton, and with the use of his legs quite gone," he still followed the course of affairs with an eager eye, to watch the working out of his own schemes in the Seven Years' War. He lived to see the Peace of Paris signed, and declared it just and reasonable. The last scene of his life is described in Wood's *Essay on the Genius of Homer*.

"I found him," says Wood, "so languid that I proposed postponing my business (the reading over to him of the preliminary articles of the Peace of Paris) for another time. But he insisted that I should stay, saying it could not prolong his life to neglect his duty, and repeating the following passage out of Sarpedon's speech, he dwelled with particular emphasis on the third line, which recalled to his mind the distinguished part he had taken in public affairs :—

᾿Ω πέπον, εἰ μὲν γὰρ πόλεμον περὶ τόνδε φυγόντες
αἰεὶ δὴ μέλλοιμεν ἀγήρω τ᾿ ἀθανάτω τε
ἔσσεσθ᾿, οὔτε κεν αὐτὸς ἐνὶ πρώτοισι μαχοίμην
οὔτε κε σὲ στέλλοιμι μάχην ἐς κυδιάνειραν:
νῦν δ᾿ (ἔμπης γὰρ κῆρες ἐφεστᾶσιν θανάτοιο
μυρίαι, ἃς οὐκ ἔστι φυγεῖν βροτὸν οὐδ᾿ ὑπαλύξαι)
ἴομεν.

His lordship repeated the last word several times with a calm and determined resignation ; and after a serious pause of some minutes, he desired to hear the treaty read, to which he listened with great attention, and recovered spirits enough to declare the approbation of a dying statesman (I use his own words) ' on the most glorious war and the most honourable peace this nation ever saw.' "

Two days later the old man was dead.

VIII

ON THE DRAWING OF BOUNDARIES
A.D. 1919–21

Since modern history began there has never been a year
in which the boundaries of Europe were altered in such a
drastic fashion as in the twelvemonth of 1919–20, when the
series of treaties which were negotiated at Versailles broke
up the work of three centuries of diplomacy. The changes
made at the Congress of Vienna in 1814–15 used to be considered as broad and sweeping ; very important modifications
were made at Aix-la-Chapelle, and at Utrecht, and at the
Westphalian Conferences which ended the Thirty Years'
War. But these may all be reckoned trifling compared
with the astounding work of 1919–20, when the whole of
Central and Eastern Europe seemed to be thrown on the
table, like a child's puzzle-map, to be reconstructed with
new and unfamiliar combinations of shapes and colours by
unpractised hands. And this was accompanied not only
by countless changes of proprietorship in the whole non-
European part of the Western Hemisphere, but by alterations
in the balance of world power, whose consequences we are
but beginning to understand. Nor is this all—there were
changes in the moral outlook of mankind, changes in social
economy, changes in conception of law and international
obligation. The brain reels when it tries to visualize as a
whole the consequences of the Great War of 1914–18. Whole
volumes have already been written on single aspects of the
new situation. But it is with only one problem that I am
endeavouring to deal. What are the lines on which the
boundaries of states should be drawn ?—for all will acknowledge that there are right and wrong ways of drawing them.
It was my duty in 1918–19 to be very busy with the old
historical frontiers and political maps of the eighteenth and

nineteenth centuries, on which reports and comments had to be drawn up. Hence came the impulse, perhaps a rather presumptuous one, to set forth some general deductions on topics which were puzzling the keenest brains of Europe and America. Let us at any rate see what were the methods of the past, and endeavour to learn from them something that may be of use in dealing with the problems of the future.

What were the guiding principles of the statesmen of the Elder Europe, when they stood at the end of a victorious war, with the map laid out before them ? I think that we may discern four separate lines of thought, on each of which there is much to say.

The first is mere " annexationism," land-hunger gratifying itself by the simple impulse of taking all that can be safely taken, as the victor's right. The second is the principle of " compensations," so dear to the diplomatists of the eighteenth century, which amounted to the general rule that if one state had received an increase of territory, or other advantages, its neighbours—or at least its allies—were entitled to similar augmentation. The third theory was that of "natural frontiers," which started on the plausible assertion that state boundaries ought to follow marked lines of geographical demarcation. The fourth—which often in practice got mixed with the third—was the doctrine of "necessary strategic frontiers," under which the victor pleads that, for his future safety against the possible revenge of the vanquished, he must take over fortresses, ports or strips of territory, to which he has no other claim, moral, geographical, or ethnological. This often becomes in practical application as shameless as the first impulse of mere " annexationism."

Let us consider these four points of view in succession, remembering that there were traces of every one of them in the various claims which one state or another set forth in its plea for consideration, at the time of the making of the new map of Europe in 1919-20.

Mere "land hunger," the victor's claim to take all that he chooses, on no mere pretence of "balance of power," or "strategic necessity," or "natural geographical frontiers," or "racial affinities," or the "protection of oppressed nationalities," is the most ancient and most blatant principle of all. One had supposed that this " good old rule and simple plan," which inspired Nebuchadnezzar or Alexander the Great, was dead since the days of Napoleon's shameless annexations of Rome and Tuscany, Holland and Hamburg, Dalmatia and Catalonia, and all the other unconsidered scraps on which he laid hands without any real claim save that of the sword. The later annexations of the nineteenth century were generally cloaked under one or the other of the less truculent pleas. And the Congress of Vienna when it handed over unwilling populations to alien masters, had the decency to talk of old dynastic claims when it put the Austrian in Milan or restored the Bourbons to Naples, or of the " balance of power " when it perpetuated that already committed crime the partition of Poland. Napoleon III harped on geography and racial affinities when he took over Nice and Savoy from King Victor Emmanuel. So did Bismarck when he stripped France of Alsace—though for the even more iniquitous annexation of Lorraine, or rather of its Metz corner, Germany—or its military statesmen— had to plead the "strategic necessity" justification. When we reflect that these unscrupulous personages thought themselves forced by the spirit of the times to formulate pleas less offensive than the mere right of the sword, it was a distinct moral set-back to find in 1919–20 claims cropping up that had not the decency to cloak themselves under strategical, geographical, or ethnological disguises, and which spoke openly of dividing up the goods of the vanquished. I read plenty of pamphlets and newspaper articles at the time of the Versailles Conference, nearly all non-British I am glad to say—which might have been written by Machiavelli or Napoleon. Fortunately, the greater part of these ambitions have been frustrated, but there are one or two corners in more than one of the recently-signed treaties which have the old twang about them. The greatest sufferers have been the shrunken Austrian and Hungarian Republics of to-day.

Nor has very much been said during the recent years about the second old-fashioned plea, with which the eighteenth-century diplomatist used to work when treaties were on hand—that which put forth the so-called " Balance of Power " as its ideal, and talked of the " compensations " which one member of an alliance owed to the others. This useful and iniquitous word "compensations " presupposes that there are always available lands or sources of wealth that can be cut or pared like cheeses, without any moral hindrance. In practice it always meant the mangling or even the extinction of small (or misgoverned and powerless) neighbours for the benefit of the strong. It may sometimes be the case that small states have continued to exist for no very obvious reason—they may not represent a national unit, or even a convenient geographical unit. They may have been called into existence by a lawyer-like partition of a heritage, or have been created to serve as an appanage or an endowment for some forgotten person or dynasty. Such is Luxemburg to-day ; such were Parma or Lucca the day before yesterday. Nevertheless the principle that states destitute of any obvious *raison d'être* may be swallowed by their greater neighbours, without any reference to their own desires or local patriotism, is not only immoral, but fraught with ruin for the devourer in the end. The example of the Hapsburg empire of Austria is the best warning—built up laboriously by many generations of marriages, exchanges and conquests, out of heterogeneous and unwilling elements, it finally flew to pieces in a moment in November, 1918, because the union had not been with the consent of the united nationalities, but imposed upon them, contrary to their will.

I have nothing to say against voluntary unions, aggregations by mutual consent, whether of units of the same racial group—like the states that went to make the United Italy of 1860—or of units heterogeneous in blood and language, but with closely united geographical or political connexion, like the Cantons of Switzerland, or the Walloon and Flemish halves of Belgium. Such unions no man will condemn. It is the free consent and the will to hold together that matters, not race, or language, or religion—as witness Switzerland. But where the wish to cohere and to coalesce does not exist, the treaty-maker draws his boundaries in vain, however much he may talk of race and language, of manifest geographical destiny, or of commercial ties and unity of culture. Why could Norway never be united to Sweden ? All these compelling causes were in operation to bind them together ; nevertheless after nearly a century of involuntary union they flew apart—simply because the wish to unite never existed ; reason might dictate union, but national sympathy and antipathy is not guided by reason.

The only cases in which annexations on the " compensation " principle have not been obviously deleterious to the annexer, sooner or later, may be found in cases where the people of the land transferred had no particular preference for their former status, or loyalty to it, and no particular objection to the power which was taking them over. When there are two or more states in the same large national group which are competing with each other, it may be a matter of comparative indifference to the inhabitants of a city or a county whether they are inside the boundary of one or the other. This was a common feature in the middle ages, before national states had grown up. In fourteenth or fifteenth century Italy a citizen of Brescia or Verona would undoubtedly have preferred independence in a minute city-republic. But if this was impossible, as sad experience showed, it did not so much matter to him whether he became a subject of the Duke of Milan or of the Doge of Venice. Or similarly a few centuries later, an inhabitant of Arras or Douai or Lille felt no enduring resentment when he was taken out of the dead non-national aggregation that was called the Spanish Netherlands, and put inside the limits of the Kingdom of France. He owed no reasoned loyalty to Philip IV or Charles II of Spain, and took no interest in those distant and unseen personages. He was certainly not worse governed after the change of masters ; he fell in among old neighbours of the same language, religion, and culture. The generation born after the annexation became good Frenchmen, and had no desire to be anything else. A more surprising instance was the contemporary union of Alsace to France, when an annexation (or series of annexations) carried out by the high hand and with no plea of justice, turned out a success, because the Alsatians had in the seventeenth century no loyalty to a non-existent Germany. The idea of United Germany did not then exist : the land was divided into hostile camps which hated each other more than they hated the foreigner. The Alsatians actually gained by ceasing to be outlying subjects of the distant Hapsburgs, or denizens of small and powerless principalities and municipalities, and so far recognized the gain that within far less than a century they had become French in sympathy, and fought more loyally than many old French departments for the Republic of 1792, and the Empire that followed.

All this, we may note, was in days before the modern conception of nationality had developed in many parts of Europe. The difference that was made by the development of that conception was shown by the fact that the Alsatians of 1871 could never be made into Germans again by the re-annexation to Germany carried out by Bismarck, though their ancestors had been made into Frenchmen easily enough two hundred years before. And this was despite of the fact that geography, language, and ancient history were all in favour of the union with Germany, and against the union with France. Yet after fifty years of forcible re-absorption into the modern Bismarckian Empire, the spirit of Alsace remained thoroughly French ; only the German immigrants forcibly planted in on top of the indigenous population were favourable to the restoration of the political situation that had existed throughout the Middle Ages. The explanation simply was that national feeling did not exist in 1670, but had become perfectly well developed by 1870.

But cases like those of French Flanders, or Alsace, where the lands annexed by the Bourbons in the seventeenth century became thoroughly incorporated with the annexing state, because they had no loyalty to the state from which they were taken, were exceptional. Where national feeling, and active dislike to the conqueror, actually *did* exist, at the moment of the annexation, it was not one century or two that could reconcile the conquered to the change. The classical case, of course, is Poland, where the principle of " compensations," the cutting up of an old racial unit by its neighbours for their common profit, was carried out to its most shameless extreme. All those three neighbours, Russia, Prussia and Austria, are very properly expiating their crime a hundred and twenty years after. They sinned against the cardinal law of nationality in their greed ; they bought unwilling and resentful subjects, who could never be reconciled, and who tore themselves loose at the first opportunity. Who would have dared in 1900 to say that such an opportunity would ever come ? Poland looked so helpless— her spoilers were so all-powerful ! But now we have a Poland in resurrection, with free access to the Baltic, and boundaries corresponding to those of the real Polish nationality (not, of course, to the artificial Polish empire of the seventeenth or eighteenth centuries), a state which if only it can learn its lesson and keep free of the old Polish curse of faction, should serve as a barrier against the German *Drang nach Osten* on the one side, and keep anarchic Russia from advancing into Central Europe on the other. It is strange, and inspiring as an example of retributive justice,to see the fate of eighteenth-century Poland revenged on all the three neighbours who plundered her in 1792 and 1795 on the plea of " compensations." They are *now* what she was *then*, writhing in faction and civil tumult, breaking up into fractions, a miserable spectacle. All the morals and sermons that used to be read to the old Polish oligarchy of the eighteenth century, may be rehearsed now with complete justice by Polish preachers to the three robber-states who accomplished the crimes of 1772, 1793 and 1795. Let us hope that the preachers may also apply the moral at home. New Poland sometimes shows that she is the legitimate issue of old Poland, by displaying the old Polish failings.

The word " compensations " was, fortunately, not sounded as a dominating note during the discussions of 1919. But we may run upon the idea not unfrequently in the writings of foreign publicists, and in the speeches of foreign statesmen. There is, for example, a strong belief on the Continent that Great Britain came through the war with less suffering and more profit than her allies. Her part in the victory is deliberately undervalued, her contribution in men's lives mis-stated, her colonial and commercial gains absurdly overvalued.

I have seen in French and Italian newspapers astonishing statements concerning the freedom of Britain from all taxation, and the universal prosperity in her cities. Hence the deduction that, to compensate for this alleged gain on her part, her allies must be allowed to repudiate their debts to her—and not only so, but be given leave to seek further territorial compensations from the vanquished enemy, on one excuse and another. The French claim to the whole Rhineland, the Italian claim to deprive the Jugo-Slavs of their Dalmatian seaports, have both been supported on occasion by the plea that nations that have suffered greatly must not come off less well from the settlement than an ally who has gained much and suffered nothing. That such "compensations" imply the forcible enslaving of unwilling aliens is passed over as a necessary consequence of victory, and as the right of the conqueror. Looking to another quarter, I should not be indisposed to recognize the trace of some theory of "compensations" in the details of the cutting short of the borders of Hungary for the benefit of the three powers of the "Little Entente." It certainly looks as if concessions to one of the newly-created national kingdoms had been carefully balanced by concessions to the other two.

But, as I said before, the word "compensations" has not been heard so frequently during the last few years as the two phrases which I have set down as representing the third and the fourth theories of boundary-building, which were all too popular in the eighteenth and the nineteenth centuries. I mean the phrases "natural frontiers" and "strategical necessity"; both of these were unhappily prominent in the discussions of 1919. Now, as to "natural frontiers" it seems at first sight quite plausible to lay down the rule that state boundaries ought to follow marked lines of geographical demarcation, and to argue that each of two neighbouring nations will be benefited by an agreement to draw their frontier along a great natural obstacle, a lofty watershed of mountains, a very broad river, or a chain of lakes and marshes. But there are three fatal objections to the general application of this attractive theory. The first is that there are many broad regions in Europe and elsewhere, where commanding natural boundaries do not exist—as, for example, between France and Belgium, Poland and Germany, or Poland and Russia. This, of course, might be put aside as a mere formal objection. The defender of the theory might say, "we cannot use them where they do not exist, but at least let us use them where they do exist." In reply I must urge that even where such marked physical features are to be found, it may prove unwise or immoral to use them. For, to begin with, two rival powers develop the most divergent views as to what *are* their "natural boundaries"? All through the nineteenth century French political geographers hankered after the idea that the Rhine is the obvious natural limit of France eastward, as it was in Julius Cæsar's Gaul. But to Germans it was equally obvious that watersheds are more correct "natural boundaries" than rivers, and therefore that the Vosges and the Ardennes are the proper westward frontier of Germany. Many German geographers went a step further, and claimed that the whole plainland of Holland and Flanders was only a westward extension of the great level flat of Northern Germany, and ought to be incorporated in the same political unit. Less familiar but equally virulent disputes existed between Serbian and Bulgarian and Greek, in the Balkan Peninsula. Bulgarians maintained that because the inner lands of Thrace were distinctly Bulgarian, it was their bounden duty to extend themselves to the obvious geographical limit of those lands—the sea coast—although there was absolutely no Bulgarian population along the water's edge, but only Greeks and Turks. Another example is the claim of Italy to the line of the Brenner Pass and the crest of the main chain of the Alps, because there lies the watershed between the rivers which flow south to the Po and the Adriatic, and those which flow north to the Danube. It is, I think, one of the most unhappy incidents in the whole of the Treaty-making of 1919 that this claim was conceded, with the result that 300,000 German-speaking Tyrolese on the Upper Adige and the Eisach have been turned against their will into Italian subjects, so that a "Tyrolia irredenta" has been created, quite as large as the "Italia irredenta" whose existence was such a legitimate grievance

to Italy during the days of the Hapsburg Empire. To-day
on "geographical first principles" the valley of Andreas
Hofer, the great Tyrolese patriot, the home of all Tyrolese
national sentiment, has become Italian soil! And this
enslaving of 300,000 German-speaking Tyrolese has been
allowed by the other allied powers, despite of their professed
adherence to the principle of "self-determination," which
was carefully and honourably applied in other regions of
Europe, such as Sleswig, Upper Silesia, or the regencies of
Allenstein and Marienwerder, where the population was
allowed every facility for choosing its own nationality.

Against the whole principle of "natural boundaries" it
may, perhaps, be sufficient to quote one crucial instance
where the strict use of it would obviously produce results
to which even the most insane advocate of this mischievous
theory could hardly give his approval. I allude, of course,
to that interesting anomaly Switzerland, which, on the theory
of "natural frontiers," ought most certainly to be divided
up between France, Italy, and Germany. For no one can
dispute that Canton Ticino, along the river of that same name,
is south of the watershed of the Alps, and belongs to the
basin of the Po, and therefore to Italy. While Cantons
Vaud, Valais and Geneva are equally obvious as the upper
reaches of that essentially French river the Rhone, which
descending from them runs for hundreds of miles through
the heart of Southern France. And the remaining larger
half of Switzerland, to the north and east, being drained by
rivers falling into the Rhine (or in one small corner into the
Inn) should I suppose be allotted to Germany and the
new Austrian Republic. When we add that Canton Ticino
speaks Italian and was in the Middle Ages part of the Duchy
of Milan, that Geneva, Vaud and Valais speak French and
belonged to the kingdom of Burgundy, and that Zurich,
Basle, Lucerne, Schaffhausen and all Northern Switzerland
speak German and were part of the essentially German Duchy
of Suabia, it must be obvious that in the eyes of the geographical purist, the real believer in "natural boundaries,"
Switzerland ought to be cut up to-morrow, trisected, and
handed over piecemeal to its proper owners. Yet I think

that even the most insane and fanatical exponent of the
" natural boundaries " theory would shrink from proposing
this infamy. If so, and if we once admit that the theory
cannot always be applied, I fail to see why its principles
should have any more validity if applied to the German-
speaking parts of Tyrol, to the Balkan Peninsula, the Jugo-Slav
regions adjacent to Trieste and Fiume, or the Rhineland.
The talk about natural boundaries is often a mask for
chauvinism and land-hunger.

The case is still worse with the fourth theory of boundaries,
that which employs the phrase " strategic necessity." There
is a close resemblance between this and the theory of " natural
frontiers." The only difference between them is that in the one
case chauvinism or land-hunger has concealed itself under the
cloak of inevitable geography, while in the other it casts
aside the cloak, and emerges naked and unashamed, and
simply sets forth the will of the stronger to take what is
convenient for him from a vanquished enemy. For it is
invariably the victor who talks of strategic necessity, and
pretends to dread the future revenge of the vanquished.
So did Napoleon in his day, so did the German General Staff
in 1871, when they insisted on adding Metz, a great fortress
but an absolutely French city, for whose annexation no decent
historical or racial excuse could be given, to the already
earmarked Alsace, for whose reunion with Germany much
more plausible justification could be made. But the most
striking exposition of this immoral theory that I have ever
seen is contained in Italian contemporary pamphlets and
speeches, of which I have come upon many, which set forth
quite openly the claim that the 700,000 Jugo-Slavs of Dalmatia
ought to be annexed to Italy, because the eastern side of that
peninsula is singularly destitute of ports and there is practically
none from Venice to Brindisi—while Dalmatia has countless
harbours which might in a possible future war between Italy
and the newly-established Jugo-Slav state, be dangerous lairs
of submarines, and bases for raiding squadrons.

The plea of " strategic necessity," always a mark of
chauvinism and greed, has become even more unconvincing
than of old since the late war. For recent military experience

has shown that so far are strategical lines, as drawn by the military geographer, from being the only positions that can be held, that almost any line, drawn across the map in despite of natural obstacles, can be held by a good army that knows its job, and has plenty of barbed wire and big guns. The most impossible lines, which seemed to defy all military rules, have been repeatedly held against the most formidable attacks—such were our own Ypres salient, held for years, the German salient at St. Mihiel, east of Verdun, or the line along the Piave on which the Italians stopped the Austrian advance after their disaster at Caporetto—which said disaster incidentally proved that a line of the most formidable strategic excellence, such as all specialists would approve, cannot necessarily be held under all conditions. The moral factor in strategy is more important than any geography, and much prized lines of defence studded with strong fortresses may prove broken reeds in the moment of need, like Namur or Antwerp, or useless to affect the general trend of a war like the great group of Russian strongholds round Warsaw, in 1915. They have often in past years been mere army-traps to ruin their holders, like Magdeburg in 1806, or Metz in 1870, or Plevna in 1877. Wherefore I hold that more than ever to-day "strategical necessity" should be marked down as an immoral plea, the cloak of unscrupulous lust for annexation.

But to come to the last lap of my argument—the critic may perhaps observe that if we have stigmatized boundaries by "compensation," and "natural frontiers," and "strategical" boundaries as one and all immoral and objectionable, we are driven back on to the sole principle of the will of the inhabitants of a district, what President Wilson called "self-differentiation," as our guiding principle. And this principle, the critic will say, and with perfect truth, is hard to apply in some cases, and absolutely incapable of application in others. This must be frankly conceded if we wish to be honest. Though in Western Europe there are few regions where it is impossible to draw a just and satisfactory frontier, the same is not the case in Eastern Europe, or many parts of Western Asia. There are terrible problems for an "honest broker" on all the frontiers of Poland, in what was once Hungary, in the Baltic lands, most of all perhaps in the Balkan Peninsula and in Transcaucasia. We find regions like the Banat, or Macedonia, or South Thrace, in which it may be said that no race has the complete numerical superiority which entitles it to decide on the fate of a district, in which it lives mixed up with not one but perhaps two, or even three, alien nationalities. And we find regions, such as some parts of Eastern Galicia, and of Upper Silesia, and of Sleswig, where the balance of races is so nice that we ask ourselves whether the vote of 51 per cent. of the people must absolutely and entirely override that of 49 per cent. Or, again, we may find tracts where national feeling is so doubtful or undeveloped that it would seem that the people themselves hardly know what they want, as in many parts of the Ukraine, and in the not far distant White Russia. Often districts with a local majority of one race are cut off by considerable intervening tracts, of alien blood and sympathy, from the nearest large patch of their own nationality ; this is very much the case in Transylvania, in some parts of Macedonia, and on the borders of Poland and of East Prussia.

Now it is clear that no sane drawer of state-boundaries could sanction the creation of a permanent political settlement which should make the map of Eastern Europe resemble an enlarged edition of the county of Cromarty on the map of Scotland, by which national states should be divided into several isolated *enclaves* or patches, not cohering, but separated from each other by long distances. What is the remedy ? We cannot in the twentieth century call for a new Senacherib or Nebuchadnezzar, who should deport all small outlying groups of population, and replant them in districts more geographically convenient. Something of the sort might conceivably be done on a small scale, by bargain and consent between the two states concerned, each undertaking to find land for its kinsmen on the acres from which aliens have been removed. Even so, every deported farmer would grumble that he had lost by the exchange—for such is human nature. But on a large scale, where old national traditions are concerned, and the people who are to be transferred possess a

history and a national consciousness, this can hardly be done—
it seems to sin against fundamental human rights. Though
to be sure there have been cases seen quite lately where racial
minorities, left behind after a change of sovereignty, have
been seen to migrate in order to "follow the old flag," as
happened more or less with the Turkish minority in Thessaly,
after that region had been made over to Greece in 1878, and
with many ardently Francophil Alsatians in 1871, after the
annexation of Alsace to Germany. The converse, by the
way, seems to be happening in Alsace now, since many irre-
concilable German settlers in that country are retiring to their
place of origin. But such movements cannot be relied upon
to settle our difficulty ; more often the local tie is too strong,
and the persons affected stay behind—and grumble not
unnaturally.

The best solution that can be suggested for such problems
is a not wholly satisfactory one. This is the grant of liberal
local privileges to alien *enclaves* of population, which must
yet be made to understand that they have no racial autonomy
as against the nation to which they have had to be assigned
because it encircles them on all sides. I mean such privileges
as the concession of the official use of their own language,
alongside with that of the language of the state, and full
protection for their schools, churches and other cultural
necessities. These are the kind of rights which we have
granted to the Dutch of Cape Colony, to use a familiar instance.

The difficulty is that the administration of such privileges
in practical detail generally leads to friction. The state
is normally accused of being unsympathetic and arbitrary ;
the privileged minority is accused of being captious, provocative, and irrationally suspicious. And generally there
is considerable truth in each of the countercharges. The
case becomes especially difficult when there exists at a short
distance from the discontented *enclave* of population, a national
state to which this outlying patch belongs by culture and
sympathy. Then the malcontents always receive moral
aid and support from outside against their own Government,
as the Alsatians till the Great War used to receive from
France, or the Italians of Trieste from Italy, or the Greeks

in Turkey from Greece. It is hard to see a complete remedy for this ; a state entrusted with the Government of alien minorities should possess an almost superhuman capacity for patience and justice, which (while men are men) it is difficult to expect.

There is one larger and more heroic solution for such a problem, the ideal which may be seen in Switzerland, and to a certain extent in the Dominion of Canada and the Union of South Africa—that is in the organization into a composite federal state of the whole group of diverse races, whose close juxtaposition and geographical interpenetration causes the difficulty. For, of course, the lot of people dwelling in one of these racial "pockets" or *enclaves* would be quite different if the state with which they are incorporated is not a wholly alien one, but a composite unit, in which their own outlying countrymen, a few score miles away, form part of the governing body.

Take, for example, the Balkan Peninsula—the most puzzling perhaps of all the problems before us. The wisest heads in that quarter of the world have already thought of this solution ; the idea was at the bottom of that "Balkanic League," of which M. Venizelos was long the prophet and exponent. Local minorities, he taught, might learn to tolerate their position, if the supreme governing power was one in which their co-nationals elsewhere, who were local *majorities* in their own corner, had an important part. The idea of the League was undoubtedly a good way out of the difficulty— a very good idea indeed in 1913. But is this solution possible to-day, in the case of peoples who during the Great War have been engaged in bitter strife with each other ? In 1915–18 the Bulgarians, in alliance with Austria, the hereditary enemy of Serbia, and Turkey, the hereditary enemy of Greece, committed atrocities on a very large scale among the Greek and Serbian populations which had fallen for a time under their sway. Indeed we are not doing them injustice if we say that they actually attempted to exterminate the Greek and Serbian elements in Macedonia by fire and sword. Can it be expected that within any short period of years the injured nationalities, who have now come to their own, owing

to the general victory of the Allies, will consent to take
Bulgarians into complete and equal partnership, and give
them their aliquot share in the organization and administration
of a general Balkan League ? It is interesting to see that
the Bulgarians have now begun to talk on this topic, and to
place all blame for their own crimes and misdoings on their
dethroned monarch Ferdinand and his political satellites.
But the question is now not what Bulgarians may think,
but what are the views of the Serbian and Greek peoples.
They would be more than human if they were to see much
attraction in the idea of being partially governed by the
representatives of a nation which is not only an old enemy,
but has during the last few years displayed the extreme of
chauvinism and barbarity. It is probable that the happy
idea of the Balkan League must remain an aspiration for the
future, when hatreds have had time to cool, rather than a
practicable scheme to be applied in the immediate present.
It is a case of "wait and see."

The idea of federalization applied in this corner of Eastern
Europe may lead us up to the idea of its application in other
regions. There are clear opportunities for its use among
the minor states on the Baltic—Finland, Esthonia, Latvya,
Lithuania—or again in the minor states beyond Caucasus,
Georgia and her lesser neighbours, when once they shall
have got loose from the Bolshevik domination. Yet in each
case there seem to be local jealousies and suspicions hindering
what seems the best road to safety and survival—perhaps
the only road, in view of dangers from without to states
none of which are by themselves of any great strength.

But the moral seems to be that if localism and particularism
be so dangerous to minor states, the only remedy lies in
extending the idea of federalism so widely, that it ceases
to be a mere attempt to combine close neighbours in an
unwilling union, and becomes something much larger. I
allude, of course, to the great scheme on which so much is
being spoken and written at present—the idea to which in
its widest form the name of the "League of Nations" has
been given. So many writers and speakers have given so
many different shapes to that attractive ideal, that he would

be a bold man who would venture a definite pronouncement upon any shape that it ought to take. Critics have pointed out the practical difficulties that must attend its inception, its organization and its practical working. The difficulties are obvious. On what principle would the seats in the governing council of the world be allotted ? Can states with an evil record like Germany, Bulgaria, or Mexico be admitted at once to take their part therein ? What would be the organization and composition of the international armed force which must be the ultimate executor of the mandates of the omnipotent central board ? Granting that such a force is created, adequate and competent to discharge the purpose for which it is raised, what are to be the methods of punishment for disobedient and vanquished dissidents ?

One may suggest dozens of such questions, all plausible and hitting on real difficulties and dangers. The discussion of them might be interminable—as recent experience in the United States of America seems to show. Yet I am optimist enough to believe that " where there is a will there is a way," and that no small part of the problem is solved when we find that all over the world there is a general and reasoned approbation of the main ideal of the " League of Nations." Plausible as are the criticisms that are put forth against it, the important thing is to note that they *are* criticisms not blank denials of the ideal. Few or none among the critics dare to repudiate the whole scheme ; they carp at details, because they dare not deny the moral justice or reason of the ideal itself. And this is a great gain : the aspiration being once set travelling round the world, time is its ally. We must be patient, and allow the propaganda to make its own way, without hurrying it on, or allowing ourselves to be discouraged by temporary checks and hindrances. For my own part, I believe that as the world realizes more and more what the horrors of the next great war would be, every one, save a Bolshevik, must see that such a war ought never to be allowed to come about. It may seem, perhaps, a truism or a piece of banal optimism to say, in these troublous times, that if an ideal is the right one, it will conquer in the end. But believing in that ideal as I do, I am content to leave the problem to be pondered over by each individual in his own heart. I do no more than repeat the words of Gamaliel of old. The ancient Jewish teacher said, when the first Christian doctrine was laid before him, " If this counsel be of *men* it will perish ; but if it be of God, beware lest ye be found fighting against God."

IX

THE TUDORS AND THE CURRENCY, 1526–60

It used, till February 18, 1920, to be the special boast and glory of the English currency that for more than a thousand years it has maintained its original weight and purity in a far higher degree than any of its neighbours. Until Mr. Austin Chamberlain in a moment of panic debased our silver money by a 50 per cent. alloy of base metal, only one severe shock has been given to the credit of the English coinage for about a thousand years. Save in this one single case, the currency has been spared by even the worst, the weakest, and the most unfortunate of our rulers. In the clash of the Norman Conquest, in the evil days of King John, in the long thriftless administration of Henry III, in the anarchy of the Wars of the Roses, in the sharpest stress of the Great Rebellion, no ruler of England ever laid hands on the coin of the realm to alloy its purity. It is true that in the attrition of the ages the first of English coins, the venerable silver penny, has sunk to about one-third of its original weight, though it retained its original quality. Offa, its first creator, struck it to the standard of 22 grains ; King George's silver Maundy penny of 1920 weighs 7¼ grains. But this shrinkage had been due not to deliberate dishonesty in any series of kings or ministers, but to the variations of the ratio between gold and silver in the last five centuries, since the day when Edward III first added gold money to the currency of the realm. When Edward III, or Henry IV, or Edward IV, from time to time reduced the size of their silver pieces, they did it to bring under-valued silver money into its proper relation to their gold coins, not in order to fill their own pockets. For from the year 1344 to the year 1816 England was cursed with a bimetallic system of currency, and felt acutely every variation in the ratio of the red and the white metal. Whenever silver rose in value the Government set things right for the moment, by reducing the weight of the silver money. In the course of time another crisis arose, and then came a further reduction. This process only ceased with the final introduction of a single gold standard in the days of our own grandfathers. In no single period, save in the years 1543–51, was this cutting down of the weight of silver in the penny or the shilling a dishonest and deliberately immoral act on the part of the Government.

Foreign currencies were not so fortunate. In no other country of Europe has the original coin-standard shrunk so little as in England. In the year 800 the English penny of King Offa and the denarius of Charles the Great, current in France, Germany, and Italy, were the same in all respects ; for Offa's coin was a deliberate copy of that of Charles, so that the word denarius, the proper name of the Frankish coin, was always used as the Latin equivalent of our own penny. Hence comes the d. printed at the head of our pence-column in the reckonings of to-day. The English penny, as we have already said, has decreased to one-third of its former self in the last thousand years. But the fall of the denarius of the continent has been far more humiliating. The Carlovingian denarius was the parent of the French *denier*, the German *pfennig*, the Italian *danaro*. Now, the *denier* in France had by the end of the eighteenth century shrunk into one-twelfth of the *sou*, which was itself one-twentieth of the *livre*, a coin practically equivalent to the modern franc. A denier of Louis XV was therefore only worth about one-seventieth of a denarius of Charlemagne. Similarly, in Germany on the eve of the Great War of 1914, the *pfennig* was one-hundredth part of the silver mark, a coin of about 85 grains. It started at about 22 grains of silver ; but would in 1914 (if so small a piece could have been struck) have been of about the weight of ·85 of one grain. All other European money standards show similar results.

It may seem absurd to link together in a common condemnation, as the only two debasers of the English silver currency, Henry VIII and Mr. Austin Chamberlain. The *svelte* and austere figure of the modern statesman does not contrast more strongly with the Tudor king's sinister grossness than do their mentality and their morality. Nevertheless it remains true that the only two occasions when the English coinage was deliberately mishandled and abused, grew abominable and became unsightly, were in the reign of Henry VIII and in the Chancellorship of Mr. Austin Chamberlain. It is with the offences of the former that we have to treat in this paper. When that prince ascended the throne, the English coinage was in an eminently satisfactory condition. With all his faults Henry VII had been a thrifty and economical administrator, the kingdom was unusually prosperous under his rule, and the growth of monetary transactions is shown by the fact that—first of all English sovereigns—he was able to coin large gold and silver money. The shilling, previously mere money of account, was by Henry of Richmond produced as a fine piece weighing 144 grains, and bearing on its obverse the King's head, the first true portrait ever seen on English money. Similarly the double-rial, or 20s.-piece, which was soon afterwards to be called the " sovereign," appeared in the year 1489. Thus Henry VII simplified all calculations by giving to his nation the tangible pieces of money which corresponded to the names in use. How hard it must have been to count up large sums of money into pounds and shillings, when the coins in hand were angels of 6s. 8d., and groats of 4d. with their fractions, we find it difficult to realize. To break with tradition and give a tangible shape to the old names was an unqualified boon. If we ask the causes of Henry's innovation, we must content ourselves with a general answer that the growth of monetary transactions, to the prejudice of payments in kind, must continually have been increasing : that although *prices* had remained practically stationary for an unprecedentedly long period, yet the *quantity* of business was growing, and that therefore people who were continually expending shillings felt the inconvenience of having to pay everything in groats ; *e.g.* if anyone had to pay a 5s. bill, how much more time

and trouble would he take in counting out 15 groats than
5 shillings ! Similarly, in dealing with a large sum of pounds,
there was enormous convenience in counting out 100 sovereigns
rather than 300 angels.

It is well worth our while to detect in Henry VII's coinage the working of the artistic spirit of the Renaissance as
well as that of the growth of trade. Ever since Edward III
the aspect of English money had remained the same ; the
conventional full-faced king's head, with its wooden mediæval
smile, was repeated for king after king without variation :
Edward III might be an old and bearded man, Richard II
a young boy, but the same stereotyped head was repeated
from the coin of the former on to that of the latter. Similarly, the noble still retained its king standing with drawn
sword in his tub-like little sailing boat, the " ship " of which
the Flemings (making a pun which holds good in our language
as well as in theirs) said that it should be exchanged for a
sheep, since England's naval power was declining while its
wool trade was ever growing larger. Henry broke with these
time-honoured conventionalities ; he placed on the shilling
an excellent portrait of himself with a side-face, quite unlike
the mediæval full-face, and showing the awakening of England
to real, as opposed to conventional, art. So, too, on his sovereign appeared a full-length figure of himself seated in state
on his royal throne beneath his royal canopy—a handsome
type, showing more traces of mediævalism than the portrait
head on the shilling, but wanting the attribute of stiffness
which it would have shown a hundred years earlier.

Henry died in 1509, leaving behind him a treasure which
contemporary chroniclers estimated at three or even four
millions sterling, but which Bacon calculates at only £1,800,000.
This last, however, was an enormous sum enough, when we
consider the value of money at that date. It was not to
remain much longer laid up in the cellars of Richmond
Palace. On the side of political economy hoarding may
be bad, but from the point of view of the English nation
the use which Henry VIII made of his father's treasure was
far more disastrous than the most exaggerated form of hoarding could have been.

England had now for nearly sixty years remained aloof from the confusion of Continental politics. First the Wars of the Roses, then the wise policy of non-intervention pursued by Henry VII, had kept her from being sucked into the whirlpool. Both, Edward IV, indeed, and Henry himself, had appeared with armies on French soil, but their invasions were momentary and episodic; they brought money to England rather than spent it, for each of them allowed himself to be bribed into a prompt departure, and made no real attempt to enforce the old claims to the French crown which had cost so much blood and treasure during the Hundred Years' War. The period of non-intervention was now at an end, and with it was to depart the long spell of internal prosperity which England had enjoyed in the fifteenth century.

Few historical facts are more extraordinary than the stationary condition of English life during the period which was now drawing to a close. From the Black Death to the beginning of Henry VIII's interference in foreign politics the price of living appears, if we may trust Thorold Rogers's figures, to have remained almost unchanged. The part of the nation which worked and saved was steadily maintaining its prosperity. Not even the great French war—a war, indeed, fought on French ground and to a great extent with French money—could stop the growth of England. The long struggle of York and Lancaster seems to us who look back on it to have been a period of horror—yet " nobody seemed one penny the worse," save the barons and their retainers, who made their way to some convenient heath or hill-side, and there slaughtered each other by the thousand. The nation sat at its ease in plenty and contentment, and though the rival factions slew each other before its judgment seat, cared for none of these things, like Gallio of old. I need hardly repeat the well-known fact that the struggle was waged with less general rapine and ravaging than any mediæval civil war of which we have knowledge. Except the harrying of the towns along the line of the Great North Road by Queen Margaret's northern moss-troopers in the winter of 1460–1, there is hardly an instance of wanton

destruction of life or property that can be quoted.[1] The
middle and lower classes refused to take sides in the quarrel,
and submitted to each victorious party in turn, so that
the storm practically passed over their heads. The years
1455–85 were a time of growing wealth, expanding commerce,
increased civilization. When tried by that excellent test
of prosperity, the amount of church-building which they
show, compared with the generation before and the generation after, they account for an astonishing number of the
large, well-lighted, perpendicular churches which are the
glory of Cotswold and East Anglia. The struggle, indeed,
had no visible influence for evil on the country's prosperity ;
perhaps it may even have worked indirectly for good ; the
carnage of Towton and Barnet must have had a considerable
effect in thinning that superfluous mass of " unemployed "
—the discharged professional mercenaries bred by the long
French War, whose descendants were a hundred years later to
become the " sturdy and valiant beggars " of the reigns of
Henry VIII and Edward VI.

Our digression has, perhaps, extended too far ; let us
return to the sixteenth century. Henry VIII was no sooner
established on the throne than he set to work to throw away
his father's accumulated wealth, in the pursuit of that intan-
gible and chimerical prize, the Balance of Power. To endeavour to establish any abiding status in a Europe whose
direction was in the hands of such dishonest politicians as
Louis XII and Maximilian of Austria, or Francis I and Charles
V, was a pursuit as hopeless as the brain of man ever conceived. If Henry had owned the philosopher's stone, and
possessed the patience of Job, he could not have been successful. The trimmer may find a pleasure in making his power
felt as he swings from side to side, but he will never earn
either honest attachment or respect. All through the thirty
years' duel of Francis and Charles, the power of England
was courted by the party which for the moment felt itself
weaker ; but when the balance began to incline the other

[1] I can only remember the Earl of Devon's sack of Exeter and the
Earl of Wilts' plunder of Hungerford in 1459.

way, Henry would find himself deserted by his friend of the
moment, who felt that he had been supported merely because
the balance of power required that he should not be reduced
to too low a condition. England would then ally herself
with her enemy of yesterday, and the whole process repeated
itself again.

In this endless alternation of wars Henry was enabled
to spend two such hoards as had never before been in the
hands of an English king—his father's savings and the plunder
of the monasteries. When once Henry VII's accumulations
were gone, and the long course of foreign wars entered upon,
it became a mere matter of time to calculate in how many
years Henry would be driven to desperate expedients to
recruit his exchequer. From 1515 to 1523 he lived from
hand to mouth on the proceeds of forced loans and benevolences. In the parliament of the latter year Wolsey calculated
that to provide for the French war then in progress, it would
be necessary to raise £800,000, by taking the fifth of every
man's goods and land, to be paid in four years—a demand
of unparalleled magnitude, as the king had already got two
shillings in the pound by way of loan. Instead of his 20
per cent. tax, the Cardinal obtained only a grant of 5 per
cent. for two years, and Henry's financial difficulties continued to increase. The régime of benevolences commenced
again, and the king was glad to get money in any manner
devisable. In 1526 the coinage was for the first time in his
reign made the subject of his experiments, though on a
small scale compared to the gain which he afterwards made
of it.

On July 25 in that year a writ was issued : " To Thomas,
Cardinal Archbishop of York, Legate *a Latere* of the See
Apostolic, Primate of England, and Chancellor of the same,"
commanding him to carry into effect the king's desire for
reducing his money, "and to determine its rate, value, fineness, lay, standard and print, as should by him and . the
Council be thought requisite." This lowering of the standard
—unlike all the later experiments of Henry VIII—was not
a deliberate attempt to debase the coinage of the realm for
the king's benefit. It was only one of a hundred vain endea-

vours to remedy a change in the ratio between gold and
silver, by lessening the sterling contents of the coins of the
metal which was at the moment appreciating. The causes
given for the present lowering of the gold currency were
the usual ones : there was an efflux of gold money from
England, because, as the commissioners alleged, the English
coins were so much better in quality than those of foreign
princes "that they were taken abroad and melted in France
and Flanders, the price of gold therein being rated so high
that the money of the realm was transported thither by
merchants, as well denizens as aliens." "Now the king had
made requisition to several foreign princes for the reformation
of their coins without effect. Also, he had commanded
statutes against the export of money to be put in execution,
yet nevertheless it was still secretly exported. Therefore,
that gold and coin might remain and be plenteously brought
into the kingdom, His Majesty deemed it necessary to make
all money current within the realm to be of like price as it
was valued at in foreign countries." The way His Majesty
set to work on this laudable design was by proclaiming that
in future the sovereign should be worth 22s. 6d., the half-
sovereign 11s. 3d., and the angel 7s. 6d.—instead of 20s.,
10s., and 6s. 8d. respectively ; whereby every holder of coin
found himself 12 per cent. richer, but every creditor,
though receiving the same *nominal* amount, would receive
only eight-ninths as much bullion. It is hardly necessary
to remind ourselves that Henry was in the debtor class, not
in the creditor class, at the time. Leaving his father's and
his own early pieces to circulate at the very inconvenient
rate newly affixed to them, Henry set to work to coin gold
and silver at the 12 per cent. reduction : a "George
noble " to pass for 6s. 8d., though it contained gold to the
value of 5s. 11½d. alone of the old standard ; a gold crown,
nominally 5s., but at the old value equal to 4s. 5⅓d. ; and
silver shillings, which would equal 10⅔d.

It is only fair to concede in Henry's justification that
the difficulty of exchange which he pleaded as his excuse
did really exist. Hall and Holinshed remind us that in
the English coinage six angels, which weighed exactly an

ounce, were exchangable for 40s., or 12 ounces of silver coin. But in Flanders, Zealand, and Brabant the Government would give silver coin to the weight of forty-four shillings, or 14⅔ ounces of silver bullion, for the amount of gold contained in six English angels. It was therefore profitable to take English gold abroad, sell it for silver bullion, and bring that bullion back into England to be coined at the mint. Henry's fault lay in trying to be a bimetallist, to make both his gold and his silver coins worth their exact amount; he could not see that the relative value of the two was continually changing, and that, unless he was prepared to alter their weight and fineness every few months, the equilibrium of gold and silver could not be kept up. There were several devices which he could have used with better effect from his own point of view :—

(1) He might have left the silver coins at their old size and purity, and enhanced the nominal value of his gold coins, or "cried them up," as the phrase then was.

(2) He might have left the names of his gold coins the same, but have put less gold into each, while leaving the silver unchanged.

(3) He might have left the gold unchanged, but put more grains of silver into each of his shillings and groats. But all these would have been mere palliatives. It would have been too much to expect that Henry would take the only real remedial step—viz. to forbid all contracts in silver, refuse it when tendered for any sum over £1 or £2, and decline, if necessary, to coin it at the mint when presented in inconvenient quantities.

As a matter of fact, by shifting the weight both of gold and silver, he established a momentary equilibrium in the exchange of gold and silver with Flanders, but committed himself to further difficulties in the near future.

Henry further showed his ignorance of economical principles by "forbidding any person to raise the price of any wares and merchandise under colour of the money being enhanced." This practically meant that every one should take 12½ per cent. less for that which he had to sell than he would have taken in 1525.

Wolsey, having charge of the coinage of which we have been speaking, caused such of the groats as were struck at York to be stamped, by way of mint mark, with his cardinal's hat, a fact which was remembered against him when the articles of 1529 were exhibited. These charged him as follows : " The said Lord Cardinal of his further pompous and presumptuous mind hath enterprised to join and imprint the Cardinal's hat under Your Majesty's arms in your coin of groats at your city of York, which like deed hath not as yet been seen to have been done by any subject within your realm before this time." This, however, even Henry's judges could not venture to wrest into an offence against any existing law, as it was proved that many of those who had previously been responsible for local mints had stamped their family badges, and notably the bishops of Durham their episcopal crosier, on the coins issued in their districts.

Henry's depreciated coinage was followed by an immediate rise in the price of most staple commodities, in spite of his absurd ordinance to the contrary. The quarter of wheat averaged 6s. 5¾d. in the six years previous to the recoinage ; in the six years after it ran to the unprecedentedly high average of 8s. 10d. The great impetus which cattle breeding was receiving at the time prevented the price of oxen and sheep ascending at anything like the same rate. By the reacting of the same cause, the price of labour remained stationary, for the increased cattle breeding was driving many agricultural labourers off the land, and thus the increase of supply of labour quite counterbalanced the decrease in the value of money, which (had the labour remained the same) must have led to something like a 12 per cent. rise in wages.

Henry's first tampering with the coinage was not for some time renewed. By one expedient and another he made ends meet, till the great epoch of the plundering of the monasteries arrived. Then for a time he found himself as wealthy, and even far more wealthy, than he had been when, twenty-seven years before, his father's treasure-chamber was opened to him. From 1536 to 1542 his prodigal waste was supplied, and the heaped-up treasures of centuries passed through his hands, in quantities that would have glutted the maw of any sovereign but himself. But by 1542 all was exhausted, and the king again began to incur large debts. There was no such resource as the confiscation of monastic property now open to him, and six years of wilful waste had made him more reckless and headstrong than ever. In 1543 his parliament relieved him of the payment of the loans which he had made in the previous year, but this was of little account to Henry. He hated economy; his old debts were no sooner cleared off than he proceeded to plunge into further expenditure, and in the same year he resumed his experiments with the currency.

The measures of 1543 differ in kind from any other dealings with the money of the realm that had been essayed by Henry's predecessors. Hitherto all the successive reductions of the coinage had been carried out with an honest if ignorant desire to save the realm from difficulties of foreign exchange, by establishing a working ratio between gold and silver. The recoinage of 1527 had been of this kind; the weight of the currency had been tampered with but not its purity. Now, however, the king made a deliberate attempt to cheat his creditors by the issue of base money. Both gold and silver were attacked; the sovereigns and nobles were left comparatively untouched; the alloy in gold money was only increased by 2 dwt. in the pound. But in silver pieces the proportion of alloy was suddenly raised from one-thirteenth to one-fifth in each coin. Instead of being 11 ounces 2 dwt. fine, the new money contained in each pound-weight 10 ounces of silver and 2 ounces of alloy.

Nor was this all; the pound of gold, which since 1527 had been coined into £20 of money, was now to be coined into £28, and similarly the pound of silver into 48s. instead of 45s.

If Henry had confined this operation to the gold there would have been comparatively little harm in it. The debasement of the standard was not very great, and the purity of it was still greater than that of many of the current gold coins of Europe. But the debasing of the silver was a fatal expedient, when gold and silver were alike legal tender to

any amount. The gold was now $\frac{23}{24}$ fine, *i.e.* one grain of
gold was valued at 1·252 pence. The silver, being only
five-sixths fine, one grain of silver was thus valued at ·12
of a penny, or almost exactly one-tenth of the value of gold.[1]
But all over Europe at the time gold was worth more than
ten times its weight of silver : in France in 1540 the proportion was 1 to 11·82, in the Low Countries 10·62, in Germany 11·38. The fact was that the influx of silver from
America was just beginning to make itself felt, silver was
growing appreciably cheaper than it had been of old, and
the fact was beginning to register itself in all the continental
currencies.

The immediate consequence of issuing a coinage in which
too little silver bought a golden sovereign was of course
that gold began to pour out of England. The English merchant found himself obliged to pay his bills abroad with
the comparatively fine gold, since the over-valued silver
was refused by his continental correspondent, to whom it
was only worth ten-twelfths of its nominal value. Of course,
the export of gold was privy and secret ; English kings
always frowned on the sending over-seas of the noble metal,
and laid all sorts of pains and penalties on the exporter,
when he was unfortunate enough to be caught. Nevertheless, the gold went : for no government can ever be so
Argus-eyed as to detect and prevent the merchant's well-
laid plans for shipping off the commodity.

The chief result, therefore, of Henry's debased silver
coinage of 1543 was that the current gold money of the realm
began silently and imperceptibly to vanish away over-seas,
and to be more replaced in ordinary use by over-valued
shillings and groats with their one-fifth of alloy. Meanwhile,
however, by using this fatal device, the king had paid off
debts with only five-sixths of the weight of silver that he
would have required had the coinage been pure.

Yet did not this content him ; hardly had a year elapsed
when, in desperation, the now hardened criminal threw all
prudence to the winds. 1545 was a year of misfortune for

---

[1] The alloy being left out of account in each case.

England ; not only had she suffered the defeat of Ancrum Moor on the Scotch frontier, but the French were pressing on her with a vigour unknown before. For the first time since the reign of Richard II, England was seriously threatened with a foreign invasion. A French fleet had mustered at Havre, which far exceeded any force that Henry could bring against it ; there were 60,000 men on board the French vessels, and Francis meant mischief. Henry was at his wits' end ; he raised 120,000 men and distributed them in four armies, three on the south and east coasts, one in Northumberland. In addition he got together every ship that could be utilized for warlike purposes, from Hull to the Land's End. The danger was really pressing, and the expense enormous. After alarming all England for months the French came down ; they fought an indecisive naval battle in the Solent, they landed small forces in the Isle of Wight, in Sussex, and in Kent ; then sickness broke out in their crowded ships, and they returned to Havre without doing further damage. England was safe, but Henry's finances were at the lowest ebb that he had yet known. The pay and equipment of his army and navy had cost him enormous sums ; there were no resources to discharge them. Then all moderation was thrown aside, and the coinage treated in a reckless manner. Instead of $\frac{23}{24}$ fine, the sovereign was reduced to $\frac{22}{24}$, and £30, not £28, were coined from the pound of gold. The weight of the silver remained the same as in 1543, but no less than half of copper alloy was mixed with the good metal. By this change a grain of gold was now evaluated at 1·353 pence, while a grain of silver became worth ·2 of a penny. Instead, therefore, of gold standing in the already too low proportion of 10 to 1 to silver, it was now placed at the absurd relation of 6·765 to 1. This too was in face of a slight but steady tendency of silver to grow more and more plentiful and cheap. Instead of ebbing slowly away, gold disappeared wholesale. But Henry had not yet filled up the full measure of his iniquities. In 1546 he was still unable to pay his way, and in sheer desperation the gold was brought down to $\frac{20}{24}$ fine, the silver to one-third fine, there being actually in the new shilling twice as much copper as silver. Hence the grain of gold was now worth 1·5 pence, that of silver ·3 of a penny, *i.e.* gold was only valued at five times its value in silver. The economical state of England was now desperate ; the greatest wrench that English social life had ever known, the dissolution of the monasteries, a change which threw a quarter of English property into new hands, had fallen into the same period as that other complication caused by the substitution of cattle farming for the cultivation of corn. While society was trying to settle down on its new basis, the king threw in the incalculable evils of a fearfully debased currency.

One would have thought that few men in England in those fearful times would have had leisure to joke at their own wretchedness. Nevertheless, tradition has preserved to us several jests connected with King Henry's base money. To understand them it is necessary to remember that the copper which formed the larger part of the so-called silver coins soon showed itself, when they had received a little rubbing in passing from hand to hand. Moreover, the King's head was represented full face on this base money, so that the wear first affected the most prominent part of the face, the nose, where the copper soon became visible.

"Sir John Rainsford," says Camden, "meeting Comptroller Brooke, who passed as having advised these later debasements to the King, threatened to break his head ; for that he had made his sovereign lord King Henry, the most beautiful of princes, to have a red and coppery nose."

Again, we find epigrams written on the shillings or testoons :— [1]

> Testons begone to Oxenford, God be your speed,
> To study in Brasen Nose College, there to proceed !

---

[1] A synonym for the coin, borrowed from the French *teston*, the name of the large piece which resembled our shilling in size and bore the king's head as chief type.

In another place :—

> These testons look red : how like you the same ?
> 'Tis a token of grace : they blush for shame.

When Henry died, in 1547, the currency had lapsed into a curious state owing to these last changes ; the gold had migrated overseas, save a very small proportion, which was treated as a mere commodity, and was continually changing in nominal value when expressed in terms of the silver. Of course, no one would give a sovereign of $\frac{20}{24}$ fine for twenty shillings of $\frac{1}{3}$ fine. For, if expressed in terms of the old unadulterated coinage of the years before 1526, the former was still worth 14s. 2d., and the latter worth no more than 5s. 6⅝d. When Strype tells us that he had seen " 21s. in testoons given for an old angel, to gild withal," we see that the rate was very reasonable. Twenty-one shillings of 120 grains each, at $\frac{1}{3}$ fine equal 840 grains of pure silver. An old angel contained 80 grains of gold, and the buyer of the angel was, therefore, getting his gold coin at the ratio of 10·5 to 1, which was cheaper than he had any right to expect, unless, indeed, some of his twenty-one testoons were those of the issues of 1543 or 1545, and therefore of better silver than the current piece of 1546–50. A similar note may be made on another price of this time. The pound of raw silver was selling, we are told, at £3 12s. in 1548, whereas before the coinage of 1526 it had been worth only £2. Now, considering that £3 12s. in testoons contained only £1 4s. of pure silver, it is obvious that the purchasing power of coined money was still very much above the intrinsic value of the good metal in it, even when we take into consideration the fact that silver bullion had been falling since 1523 to some slight but appreciable extent, owing to the influx from the American mines.

Henry died on January 28, 1547, and was succeeded by his young son, Edward VI. The ring of self-seeking courtiers who clustered round the boy-king determined from the first to conjure with the rod of their old master. But they were conscious of the unpopularity which his tampering with the coinage had produced, and tried to do furtively what

Henry had been wont to do with a brazen front and unmoved effrontery. Their first device was to go on for more than a year using the old king's coin-dies to strike as much as they dared of the debased gold and silver under the cover of his name. Hence there are hardly any known coins of Edward's first two years—in both metals they are extremely rare ; on the other hand, there is a large bulk of coins bearing the name of Henry VIII, which, from the mint marks and some changes in the portrait-figure on the obverse, can be attributed to the first twelvemonth of the reign of his son.

The earlier coinage of Edward VI, whether struck with his own name or his father's, is of the same metal both in gold and silver as that of the concluding years of Henry VIII. But in 1549 joyful rumours were set abroad by the government ; the coinage was to be purified and the new money was just about to appear. It came, and it *was* more pure than that which had been circulating since 1546—but it was very much lighter. The new sovereign was 22 carats fine out of 24, as against Henry's last issues at 20 carats. But it only weighed 170 grains as against 192, *i.e.* it contained 156 grains of pure gold as against 160. The silver testoon was not, like the sovereign, actually less valuable than its predecessor, but was a half-and-half coin of silver and alloy ; but as it was only two-thirds the size of the last testoon of King Henry, it contained exactly the same number of grains of pure silver, *viz.* 40.

The public disappointment found voice in the sermons of Bishop Latimer. "We have now," said he, "a pretty little shilling, indeed a very pretty one ! I have but one, I think, in my purse, and that I had almost put away yesterday for an old groat,[1] and for such, I believe, some will take them. The fineness of its silver I cannot see, but thereon is printed a fine sentence : 'Timor domini fons vitæ.' I would God that this sentence were always printed in the heart of the king in choosing his officers."

---

[1] An old groat weighed 48 grains only, and the new shilling 80, so the good Bishop of Worcester was using some exaggeration in pretending to mistake one for the other.

The boon of a diminished coinage was soon supplemented by Somerset and his friends; the later money of Henry VIII was suddenly "cried down." It was said that "the late king having set current among his subjects testons of great baseness, his present Majesty perceiving that such coins were by reason of their baseness counterfeited both at home and abroad, had caused other better coins to be made. Now, it appeared that persons were using the old coins and their counterfeits in buying up victuals and merchandise, giving they cared not what for the same, so that they might get rid of the coin. The king, therefore, being minded to call in and recoin all such base money, could not bear the expense of receiving it back at the price at which it was issued. Every old teston, therefore, was, after August 31, to be current for 9*d.* only."

For this mean repudiation England had to thank Somerset : his baser successor, Northumberland, treated the country still more cruelly ; in 1550 he issued a further edict reducing the old testoon from 9*d.* to 6*d.* only, as preparatory to the introduction of a better coinage. What was worse, he issued coin baser by a trifle than even that of Henry VIII. There were £80,000 of royal debts still outstanding ; to pay this off Northumberland coined silver to that value, whereof only a quarter—3 ounces in the lb.—was of good metal, while 9 ounces were copper. This was the basest money England ever knew ; no great quantity, it is true, but the manner it was foisted on the royal creditors just before the great recoinage was especially disgusting.

In 1551–52 something was at last taken in hand. A large issue of shillings, sixpences, and also of silver crowns and half-crowns (the first of those high denominations ever issued in England) were set in circulation. They contained 11 ounces 1 dwt. fine out of the 12 ounces, or practically the old standard which was current before 1527. In weight they were half-way between Latimer's "pretty little teston" and the old shilling, being made 60 to the pound, not 72 as the last base money had been, nor 45 as the old shilling of Henry VII. At the same time the sovereign was raised from the weight of 170 grains to 174¼ of 22 carats fine—*i.e.*

it contained about the same 160 grains of pure gold as had the last sovereign of Henry VIII, and was appreciably better than those of the years 1549-51.

Thus we see an honest standard of coinage once more reintroduced, and gold now standing to silver in the ratio of 1 to 11·05, which very fairly coincided with the average of continental ratios of the day, and was well calculated to suit the country's needs.

There was, however, one most important step still necessary to redeem the credit of the English coinage and restore the currency to a healthy condition. It was absolutely necessary to call in two millions of base money which had been issued since 1543, and to exchange it for good money. This, however, was not done : Northumberland did not dare to face the enormous expense which the buying back of the base money, even at a great reduction on its facial value, would bring about. The new silver and gold began to issue from the mint in a fairly copious stream, but scarcely had they got into private hands when they seemed to disappear as if by magic. The fact was that they were mostly hoarded by the first receivers, who were doubtful if the shifty Northumberland might not slip back into the paths of bankruptcy, but partly exported for foreign trade. For the merchants who had dealings abroad found that the new money was eagerly taken by Antwerp and Amsterdam, which had been so loth to handle the debased issues of 1543-51. Thus Gresham's law, not yet the public property of financial experts, worked its inevitable process. The bad money drove out the good. The new coinage was hoarded or exported ; the old money alone was seen in the markets and haunts of men. The copious stream of fine pieces poured out in 1551-3 seemed to vanish just as it touched the trading world. Prices did not fall appreciably, for " de non existentibus et de non apparentibus eadem est lex," and the public, seeing only the baser sort of coins, persisted in fixing its values by them.

Meanwhile Edward died, and was succeeded by his sister Mary. That princess declared her intention of restoring the " good old times," in the matter of the coinage as well

as in spiritual things. She placed on her groats the motto
" Veritas Temporis Filia."   But her promises were not destined
to be fulfilled. Her reactionary spirit changed the aspect
of the coin back to a copy of the currency of Henry VII,
and caused a large coinage of groats, a denomination which
had sunk out of sight somewhat since the rise of the shilling
and sixpence. Similarly, she restored the old types of the
noble and angel, the sovereign in the ship, and the figure
of St. Michael treading down the dragon. But Mary's pro-
testations that she was about to redeem the national credit
were mere words. The all-important measure of buying
back from the public the base moneys of 1543–51 was not
taken. In her second and third years famine and scarcity
caused a commercial crisis ; when this passed away she
involved herself in her husband's continental wars. There
was never time or money forthcoming for the redemption
of the base currency. It was to no purpose, therefore,
that all her own not very copious issues were of good
metal ; like those of 1551-3, they were exported or
hoarded.

It was Elizabeth who was destined to do away with the
base money which had cursed England for seventeen years.
Her measures were drastic but efficient. An estimate was
made of the bulk of depreciated coinage still outstanding
in the hands of the public. Every one has heard of the quaint
device which is said to have been adopted. Discreet persons
were sent on a fixed day to all the butchers' shops of London,
who, under colour of settling a wager as to the proportion
of the good, bad, and indifferent money in actual circulation,
were to persuade the butchers to allow them to count over
and divide into categories one day's take of their shop-tills.
On the rough evidence supplied by this enumeration the
Council are said to have founded their estimate of the proportion of base money in use. They then issued a proclamation calling in such moneys, but only allowing for each
piece its real value in silver, not the arbitrary allowance
of 6d. per testoon made when Northumberland " cried down "
the base money in the reign of King Edward. The bulk
of the circulating medium, the coins struck between 1545

and 1549, were ordered to pass and be taken at the mint for 4¾d.—a loss of 1¼d. to each holder of a testoon. The worst pieces of all—the £80,000 of money nine-twelfths base with which Northumberland had cheated the royal creditors— came down to 2¼d., a loss of 3¾d. to the last unfortunate possessor.

This, however, being done, Elizabeth set to work to call in all her father's and brother's base money, giving in exchange her own neat shillings and sixpences of the coinage of 1560–1. These were of the old standard, never seen since 1527, but in weight exactly similar to the last and best of Edward's pieces, the coinage of 1551–3. Glad to get rid of their base money at any price, the people readily gave in their currency to the exchangers whom Elizabeth sent into every market town. In a year the business was complete. The queen received 631,950 pounds troy of base metal of all sorts and sizes and alloys, some of it being the ten-twelfths pure coins of 1543, some the half-pure coins of 1545, some the one-third pure money of 1546–9, and a very small proportion of the basest issue of all—that of 1550. This mass of metal was received for £638,113 16s. 6d., that being the value of it by the last reduction. When it was refined, 244,416 pounds troy were found to be pure silver, and 397,534 pounds alloy. To the surprise of the queen, who had expected to make a loss by the transaction, it was found that there had been given in much more of the less alloyed sort of money —the issue of 1543—than had been expected. This compensating for the baseness of later metal, the mass of refined silver was coined down into £783,000.[1] Thus the queen got £150,000 more than she had expected. But the cost of coinage had to be taken into consideration, and deducting this the actual profit was reduced to between £15,000 and

[1] 244,416 lb. at 60 shillings to the lb., would of course make only £733,248 of pure silver ; but the alloy at 11 dwt. per lb. accounts for the fact that £783,000 was coined out of the above-named weight. Professor Thorold Rogers at this point gets hopelessly mixed between pounds troy and pounds sterling, and fails to see exactly what Elizabeth did.

£18,000. It is apparently unjust to blame Elizabeth for making profit out of her subjects in this point; she had honestly expected to find the quantity of the worst money more than it was, and had so miscalculated to her own advantage. She expected to lose £50,000 by the transaction, but actually she made £15,000.

Thus the great debasement was remedied; but its effects were not so easily dissipated. The prices of almost every product and manufacture had doubled or trebled in the twenty years. If we take wheat, the two decennial periods, 1500–10 and 1510–20, show 5s. 5d. and 6s. 8d. a quarter as its average price; but the value in the period 1540–50 went up to 10s. 8d., and in that of 1550–60 to 15s. 3¾d. Similarly the price of oxen went up from 22s. or 23s. to 75s. or 78s.; that of sheep, in spite of the fact that they had been largely bred in the period, from 2s. 4d. or 2s. 5d. to 5s. or even 6s. It would be useless to point out further examples. What made this rise so important, was the fact that wages had not risen in anything like the same ratio. The unskilled labourer received about 4d. a day in 1520; in 1560 his pay had only risen to 7d., or had not quite doubled, while the price of food had nearly trebled. This of course came from the fact that labour was abundant, owing to the wholesale evictions which followed the appropriation of monastic lands and the enclosing of commons for sheep-farming. Moreover the practical evil of the debased currency had fallen on the class least able to bear it. "The richer sort, understanding the thing beforehand, did put all good money away, and passed off the base money on to their servants and hired men, so that when the pieces were cried down it was the poor who suffered, since in their hands for the most part the base money lay." There is no doubt that prices were destined to rise in the sixteenth century: the influx of the precious metals from America settled that. But if the process had worked by itself, it would have been slow and imperceptible. What Henry VIII did was to raise prices suddenly by his depreciations, and thereby to give a shock to the whole of English society. He aggravated suddenly and artificially a change which might have taken place without any great loss and discomfort to the nation.

When Elizabeth's reformation of the currency took place, the effect of the American discoveries was making itself felt very distinctly. Both gold and silver, and especially the latter, were so far more plentiful all over Europe than they had been in the days before 1540, that no relapse of prices took place in consequence of the recoinage. No one profited, as had been hoped, from a universal cheapening of the articles of consumption, whose prices had been driven upward in the days when the debased testoons formed the sole visible currency of England. The advantage to the nation which really ensued was that foreign commerce was more easily conducted, and that internal payments grew once more fixed and honest. The whole of the inhabitants of the realm were no longer forced to spend their time in the degrading employment of trying to put off their basest pieces on each other. Commerce and trade adjusted themselves, and the only permanent sufferers were the more unskilled labourers, whose wages had not risen commensurately to the general increase in the price of articles of consumption, and the landholders who depended on old fixed customary rents. For rents in the early years of Elizabeth had hardly risen appreciably above their rate in the early years of her father. Hence, the main result of the great debasement of 1543–51 may be said to have been the handicapping of the agricultural classes of England, both great folks and small ; while the manufacturing and trading classes came out of the troublous times little injured, and therefore proportionately more important in the national strength than they had ever been before.

So by 1561 the last of the debased Tudor money disappeared from view. The small amount of it which escaped recoinage survives only in the cabinets of museums and collectors. It is deplorable-looking stuff—its colour varies from pale copper, through dull leaden shades to rusty red. The surface has often flaked off in parts, when the component metals seem to have been roughly mixed. But horrid as is its appearance, it is not much more repulsive than Mr. Austin Chamberlain's great coinage of 1920–21. In the earliest issue of this stuff there was some alloy—bad nickel, it is said, from old military stores—which turned brown, green or orange in spots—producing a fine "ring-streaked and speckled" effect. Occasionally the white surface of a florin has turned to various shades of light brown, so that the coin might be mistaken for a penny. The later emissions of 1921 are not so much spotted as uniformly pale lemon yellow, but have an unpleasant way of shedding some of their surface—we have seen specimens in which one of the shields on the reverse of a florin, the date, or part of the king's head, have come off, leaving a shallow pit behind. It is sad to reflect that the issue of this stuff had no justification whatever. When the Coinage Bill of 1920 was passed in a panic, silver stood at 88 pence per ounce. It only remained at that prohibitive price for a few weeks, and has now for two years stood close in the neighbourhood of 35 pence per ounce. The old standard of purity might have been preserved without any loss to the revenue—indeed bullion purchased at 35s. and coined at the pre-war rate would give a profit of over 40 per cent. to the Crown. Let us hope that some spiritual successor of Queen Elizabeth may arise ere long, to sweep the unsightly mass of the money of 1920–21 into merited oblivion.

We cannot say that its circulation has had any appreciable economic effect—the abandonment of bimetallism in the British monetary system after 1816 has made the intrinsic value of subsidiary silver coins of no great importance. But the ugliness and bad workmanship of the new debased coinage are a public scandal. And we should not like to say that its issue has not had some bad moral effect also. The pieces are obviously base tokens, not good silver, and there is a temptation to throw away recklessly stuff that looks like the trash that it is. We have seen it stated that Charles James Fox, in his gambling fits, was a much more reckless punter with club-tokens of ivory or metal, than when he was fingering golden guineas of pleasant hue and convincing weight. We fancy that this is a common human failing—one is extravagant with currency that looks worthless. And wastefulness is of all things the most besetting sin of 1922—not only with

governments and profiteers, but with the man in the street.
Wherefore let the coinage of these last two deplorable years
be withdrawn as soon as possible, to prevent us from flinging
it away in an instinctive desire to rid ourselves of such repulsive
tokens.

X

THE MODERN HISTORIAN AND HIS DIFFICULTIES

There are two common mental attitudes which the writer and teacher of history meets in his mingling with the world. In their extreme forms they fill him with about the same measure of humorous despair.

The first is that of the ordinary practical man, who has run against some topic in which history is involved—probably a political problem of to-day : Why is Danzig a German and not a Polish town ? Why does Corsica belong to France and Sardinia to Italy ?—or some such other anomaly. He comes to his friend the historian to ask him to solve the difficulty in two minutes. He is vaguely under the impression that there must exist somewhere (or at least, that there *ought* to exist somewhere) a general repertory of historical information, which will answer his query in three pages—perhaps even in three lines. His point of view is that history is a bundle of facts which can be packed into an encyclopædia, and that every one can discover what he wants to know by turning up the right word in some universal dictionary. This is a pleasant and confiding attitude of mind, which assumes that all facts are ascertainable, and that they have only to be caught and bottled by competent historical experts for the benefit of the general public. It comes with a shock to this sort of inquirer to be told that the short question that he has asked has no universally accepted answer. He makes some simple inquiry such as " What was the effect of the rise of Christianity on the Roman Empire ? " or " What was the origin of the English Parliament ? " And the historian tells him in reply that he cannot give him any answer which is universally accepted, but can only present him with a series of doubts, or a number of rival hypotheses, each supported by a plausible array of arguments. Probably the historian will try to persuade his friend to read half a dozen controversial volumes, after which he will have some notion of the meaning of the question that he has asked. The practical man of the world will most certainly refuse to take this trouble, and will go away with a poor opinion of historians, as men destitute of certainty, and unable even to agree among themselves. He would like to regard history as a string of facts, and cannot see why the deductions from these facts should vary according to the temperament and point of view of the writer who manipulates them. Historical facts, however, cannot be boiled down into a syrup equally grateful and satisfactory to all consumers. The decoction which one man will find to be exactly the nourishment required for the maintenance of his spiritual and political equilibrium, will be declared by another man to be rank poison. The historian must be prepared to find himself denounced from one side or the other as a purveyor of mischievous mental provender—perhaps he may achieve the honour of being equally blamed from both sides, because he has struck some middle line of thought acceptable to neither. It is almost inconceivable that any history of the Protestant Reformation, or the French Revolution, or the Modern German Empire should fail to irritate and anger half the readers before whom it is placed. If such a book could possibly be written, inoffensive to all parties, it could only be written by shirking the moral problems involved, and reserving the author's comment on them— indeed, it would tend to be an arid waste of hard facts, with no guidance given for the comprehension of their meaning.

History, in short, is not what the " practical man " would like to find, a record of names, dates, and events ; it is the interpretation of these things from the point of view of the historian. And since the political, moral, and national stand- points of historians always have differed, and will always continue to differ, it is impossible to produce " standard histories," as they have been called, on any period, topic, institution, or individual which will satisfy all readers— unless, indeed, the subject-matter has become so remote, and so entirely out of touch with modern problems, that it has ceased to provoke any division of opinion. One may perhaps construct a standard history of the ancient Egypt of the Pharaohs, or of Roman military tactics, or of mediæval witchcraft, or of Alexander the Great. But can anyone conceive a standard history of the Jews or the Jesuits, of the Balkan Peninsula in the Middle Ages, or of Napoleon or Bismarck, which should be equally acceptable to a Jew, a Roman Catholic, a Protestant, a Greek, a Serb, a Bulgarian, a Turk, a Frenchman, and a German ? A celebrated historian once declared that " history is only ancient politics " ; and there is so much truth in the statement that I am sometimes inclined to think that as politics cannot exist without controversy, so history cannot exist without it either. Or at least we may say that if there is any large section of history on which no controversy ever takes place, then that must be a dead and not a live section of history.

The " man in the street " comes to us with a historical query : it is unfortunate, but only too often we must give him, not the certain and definite answer that he is expecting, but a thesis or a piece of propaganda which may honestly set out our own views of the truth, but which we acknowledge that other people may regard as inaccurate, false, and mischievous. For history is not an objective thing, a list of events ; it is the historian's way of envisaging and correlating these events. And two historians of different politics or nationality may string the events together in very various patterns and produce two pieces of work which the unlearned can hardly perceive to be constructed out of the same materials. Who, on a first reading, would guess that Thiers' and Lanfrey's accounts of the career of Napoleon were constructed from the same set of original documents ?

We must tell the " man in the street," therefore, that history is a way of looking at facts ; that the way depends on the bias of the individual historian ; that, in order to arrive at an opinion of his own on any problem, he ought in fairness, and in reverence for truth, to read the works of controversialists on both sides. He will reply that he has no time for lengthy historical studies, and will probably ask for the name of the author who sets forth best the views of the party, nation, or religious sect to which he himself belongs. And so history-writing has become, much though we may regret it, the most important line of political, national, or religious propaganda.

So much for the dealings of the writer of history with the common practical layman. There is, however, another mental attitude, of a very different sort, against which he will certainly run during the course of his work. And it will cause him an even greater trouble than the complaints of the disappointed and disillusioned layman. This is the mentality of the historical specialist, the man who has made some corner of history his own, who thinks that he has acquired a certain monopoly in it, and that he possesses "patent rights," with which no other author must meddle, over this particular century, or institution, or great individual. In history, as in every other science, the jealous and narrow-minded specialist is a common type. The difficulty of dealing with this person is that he is fully convinced that the whole course of world-history turns round his own particular little preserve. To him all Roman history may be a story which mainly hinges on the *Proconsulare Imperium*, or all English history may depend on the growth of the Manor, or all German history on the statutes of the Hanseatic League. I once knew a learned ecclesiastical historian who made the obscure tribe of Jerahmeel, mentioned twice in the Old Testament, the originators of all Jewish nationality. He did not make converts, but he conducted much controversy, and thought very poorly of all those who rejected his theory.

The professional historical specialist is too often like the man in the proverb, who cannot see the wood because all his attention is concentrated on his own particular tree. If you trust him with the compiling of a general history, you will find that every other period and event has assumed an ancillary position around the ten or twenty years in which he himself is interested. As to histories written by other people, he will assure the world in perfect honesty that they are all wrong in perspective, because they do not show that the period or personage of his predilection forms the central point round which all the rest of history revolves. And every one else who ventures to touch on his own pet subject will undoubtedly appear to him an irreverent intruder into a region reserved for himself. No other historian can possibly get the right view of that subject—be it the Athenian Archonship, or the Council of Trent, or the character of Stephen Dushan—because the rash adventurer comes to conclusions of his own, which differ in greater or less detail from the orthodox creed formulated by the one competent and omniscient authority.

In short, after coming into collision with the true specialist, the workaday historian goes away feeling almost as depressed, and doubtful of his own right to exist, as he was when the "common practical man" dismissed him as useless and incompetent.

Need he, therefore, despair ? Must he make up his mind that history should mean either on the one hand the collection of dry annals without a connecting link of philosophic thought, or on the other a series of minute monographs, in which each researcher remains inside his own little fence, resents the appearance of any other researcher within it, and cares very little for all the rest of history which lies outside his sacred paddock ?

It would be deplorable if any student came to this conclusion. As historical research stands to-day, there is a most honourable place waiting for the codifier and the philosopher. Indeed, they were never so much wanted as at the present moment. The characteristic of historical study during the last thirty years, in every country of Europe, is that there has been a very rapid and copious collection of new facts from unprinted sources and archæological discovery, but that the arrangement of these facts in orderly, logical, and philosophic symmetry has been sadly neglected. The day of great histories seems almost over—monographs, biographies, economic or constitutional studies, diplomatic papers or statistical tables, or records of excavations and inscriptions, rain in upon us in profusion. But it seems to be no man's business to arrange this mass of new material in perspective, or to determine the relative importance of each item—or at least, no competent man's business. For unfortunately there is a class of people who "rush in where angels fear to tread," and try to generalize on history without having any detailed knowledge of it. We all have met the man who after reading half a dozen popular manuals is prepared to lay down the scheme of the whole universe, ignoring all difficulties because he does not know of their existence. This is the type which the French call the "*vulgarisateur*," the man who offers to make history, science, or art easily accessible to the multitude, by leaving out all their problems and uncertainties. It was a common genus enough in the eighteenth century, commoner in the nineteenth, but appears to have reached its extreme development in the twentieth, when literary men of all calibres seem inclined to generalize on the history of England, France, or the whole Universe, merely on the justification of a fluent pen. To attack such subjects with no wide knowledge of languages, no power or leisure to read original authorities, no foundation of detailed studies, can only result in producing "the second-rate at second-hand."

It is, I think, the existence of the *vulgarisateur*, and the fear of being taken for one of that dreadful class, which deters many competent historians at present from writing large-scale histories in the old style. They feel a real horror of the possibility that when they are trying to follow in the steps of Gibbon or Ranke, they may be accused of being the spiritual comrades of the universal sciolist.

Yet there never was a time when the historical codifier and philosopher was so much wanted. The greater the mass of undigested and chaotic facts that is being thrown up by the excavators in the field of historic research, the greater is the need for the patient man who will be content to spend long years in sifting out the heap of material, of all shapes and values, in order to collect all the more important fragments. Thus only can the fabric of history be rebuilt from year to year, each new discovery being fitted into the ever-changing mosaic.

The modern student, as Lord Acton once remarked, is in considerable danger of being overwhelmed by the vast bulk of new and unsorted historical material which is shot in upon him by the researcher. This, indeed, happened to that admirable man himself; for while trying to read every volume that appeared in every language on the subject which he had chosen for his *magnum opus*—the evolution of the idea of Liberty—he forgot his advancing years, and was surprised by death while he was still wrestling with new books, before he had written even one volume as the result of his many decades of study. Not even the youngest of us can hope to be one day omniscient,—and then to start writing. The only practical ambition is to collate and set forth the sum of knowledge as it exists in one's own day. The discoveries of the future will be for the next generation to work upon. All that the writer of to-day can hope to accomplish, is to bring history up to date, so far as in him lies, by the honest and laborious piecing together of all the new information available. It will not be an easy task; some of the new matter will have to be read only to be rejected as worthless or unimportant, more of it will have to be subjected to ruthless criticism. But there will be a large residuum of new facts which must be worked into the general fabric of history. It will be no dishonour to the great historians of older days if their books have, with all reverence, to be laid aside, or sent up to the more inaccessible shelves of our library. It would be absurd to accept in 1921 a book which was an admirable summary of its topic in 1861. This is as true in History as in Medicine or Chemistry: we are dealing with a progressive science, not with an infallible Bible.

It is, no doubt, a disheartening thought to remember that twenty or thirty years hence—perhaps even at an earlier date —our own books on history must go to the same limbo of forgotten things as the books of our revered predecessors. There is no finality in History, any more than there is in Natural Science. A new recension of knowledge is required by the new generation; and our works, which we cherished so much, will disappear to the top shelf of the Public Library —if not to the cellar. We must think ourselves happy if they appear to our grandchildren rather as glimpses of the obvious than as expositions of exploded heresies. Nevertheless, we claim that we have not been without our use: every generation must codify and collate its own stock of knowledge; and the codifiers, if their work has been honest, have served well the men of their own time. To the man of the future they can only say *Morituri te salutamus*—our work must perish; but it had to be done.

XI

THE EARTHLY PARADISE

It is a noteworthy fact that in almost all the religions of the ancient world, the human soul, though it may be defined as immortal and disembodied, seldom entirely quits this earth. Before the birth of Geography, men imagined the world to be large enough to contain, not only the land of the living, but also the land of the dead, and even the habitations of the gods themselves. The Greek divinities dwelt on an Olympus which was originally earthly and local ; so did the Indian gods on their Mount Meru ; so, too, the deities of the North abode in an Asgard, which men conceived as a fixed point exactly in the middle of the face of the earth. And if a terrestrial dwelling could be found for the gods, much more could a habitation be discovered for the disembodied spirits of men. Soul-lands, then, whether figured as under-worlds or Isles of the Blessed (to use familiar names), are of almost universal acceptance. With the former class we are not here concerned ; but to the latter, when a place on the surface of the earth is assigned to them, we may apply the name " Earthly Paradise." These, then, form one branch of our subject ; along with them must be ranged the Christian Paradise, which was identified with the Biblical Eden—and also the deathless lands, not destined for souls, but for living men, with which we sometimes meet in mediæval legends.

The regions which belong to the first of these classes are invariably placed in the West. Of this fact the most plausible explanation is, that all the ancient nations, when imagining the journey of the departed soul, had in their minds the journey of the sun, the one god who dies daily, yet who has not really perished, but is only withdrawn from human sight. Nearly every tribe had some knowledge of a sea towards the West, with whose limits they were, in the early part of their history, quite unacquainted. Accordingly the soul-land was usually conceived as lying across the unexplored Western waters. The Egyptian abode of the dead was an exception to this rule, for not sea but desert forms the impassable western boundary of the Nile Valley. But none the less the Egyptian soul-land was placed in the West, though the spirit of the departed had to cross the desert, the " dark land of Apap," before arriving at the home of Osiris, the hidden sun.

There are two ways in which the setting of the sun into the west may strike the mind of the beholder. On the one hand, the sight of the end of a fine summer day, when the whole horizon is a sheet of vivid colour and the sea is divided by a golden path, calls up ideas of a land of glory where the sun-god rests after the labours of the day. On the other hand, after a day of mist and tempest, when the sun has seemed to wrestle with the black clouds, and finally sinks, swallowed up by them, into a dark and stormy sea, the sight of his end suggests only gloomy thoughts. So we get the double idea of the West,—as the bright Elysian plain or the garden of the Hesperides ; and, on the other hand, as the dim shadowy land where the disembodied souls spend an aimless and hopeless existence.

Both these ideas appear in the Homeric poems. Although in the *Iliad* the " dark home of Hades " is certainly below the earth, yet in the *Odyssey* when Ulysses visits the shades, he does not descend, but meets them on the misty shore of the land of the dead. Its situation, in accordance with all Aryan ideas, is in the West, or perhaps North-west. Although in the Homeric poems the gloomy view of the after-life—which allots a colourless and unhappy existence to the souls of the greatest heroes, Achilles, Ajax, and their fellows, as much as to the souls of the common herd—is generally found, yet the more cheerful aspect of the West is shown in at least one passage, where Proteus prophesies to Menelaus that his last end will be to come to " the Elysian plain and the ends of the earth, where abides the fair-haired Rhadamanthus ; where life is easy for mortals ; where is no snow nor storm nor rain, but always the ocean sends up the cooling breath of the west wind,"—a description well known as copied by Lucretius and Tennyson.

In Hesiod we first find this Western land mentioned by the

name which afterwards became its proper title, Μακάρων νῆσοι. Speaking of the heroes of the Theban and Trojan wars, he makes Zeus bear them away after death, " to have their life and their abode apart from men, so that they dwell undisturbed in the Islands of the Blessed, by the deep-flowing ocean, where the fruitful earth brings forth her harvests thrice a year."

A similar picture is found in the Olympian Odes of Pindar, who speaks of the Island of the Blessed, round which the ocean breezes blow—where earth and water alike blaze with golden flowers, and the just dwell wreathed with garlands beneath the gentle sway of Rhadamanthus.

After Pindar it is unnecessary to mention the numerous allusions to this Western land which are found in the Greek poets. It seems, however, to be different from Leuké, which would appear to have been a sort of private Earthly Paradise for the hero Achilles. Before the extent of the Euxine was known, he was supposed to inhabit an island in its extreme west, where he was united to Helen, and was accustomed to drive his chariot along the smooth promontory called Achilleôs Dromos.

When the Euxine was explored, the idea vanished, or rather shrank into the worship of Achilles as ruler of the sea at the colony of Olbia, the Greek colony nearest to the legendary position of Leuké.

After a time there came the materializing age of ancient history—that in which all the old legendary spots were fitted with places in the real lands of the Western Mediterranean, when Phæacia became Corcyra, and Sicily the dwelling of the Cyclops. At this time the Isles of the Blessed were placed outside the Straits of Gibraltar. But some centuries later, about 100 B.C., actual islands of pleasant aspect were discovered in that direction. Hence these, which we now call the Cape de Verde Islands, got the name of Fortunatæ Insulæ : and though no one asserted that they were inhabited by the souls of the just, yet the old wonders of the isles of the blessed were related of them ; and we read of their perpetual spring, and the three harvests a year which they produced. The accounts of these islands in sober geographers, which survived into the middle ages, were certainly one of the reasons which induced the exploration of the Western sea.

Unlike the Greeks, the Romans succeeded to the rule of a world which had been explored ; and except in a few allusions in the poets and in Pliny, manifestly borrowed from the Greek, we do not find the islands of the blessed in their old sense mentioned till a very late date. Strange to say, however, among the very last of the Roman authors, as if we were coming on the shadow which the approaching middle ages cast before them, we find the old Western spirit-land of the *Odyssey* reappearing. In Claudian we meet with the following passage : " There is a land, where the farthest end of Gaul stretches out into the ocean, where Ulysses is said to have invoked the silent folk with libations of blood. Here, even now, the pitiful wailing of the souls is heard as they flit past, and the peasants see pale shapes, the forms of the dead, taking their way from earth."

This allusion is amplified by the longer passage on the same subject found in the Byzantine writer Procopius, who flourished under Justinian in the sixth century :—

" Opposite the north-western coast of Gaul," he writes, " there is a large island called Brittia ; it is divided into two parts by a wall stretching north and south. East of the wall is a pleasant land which is occupied by the Britons, Angles, and Frisians. What the land to the west is like, no one knows, for its air is deadly to breathe, and any one who passes the wall instantly expires. Now on the extreme northwest coast of Gaul," he continues, " there dwell certain fishermen, subject to the Franks, but excused from all tribute on account of the strange duty which they perform.

" Every night one of these fishermen, in rotation, is roused from sleep by a gentle tapping at his door, and a low voice calls him to come down to the beach. There lie dark vessels, to all appearance empty, but deep in the water, as if weighed down by a heavy burden. Pushing off, the fishermen arrive at the coast of Brittia in one night, though it is on ordinary occasions six days' journey from Gaul. During the voyage they hear the sound of voices in the boat, but no intelligible words, only a subdued whispering. Arrived at the strange coast, they hear the names called over, and different voices answering to them, while they feel the boat gradually growing lighter ; at last the roll-call ceases, and they are wafted back to their country with the same miraculous speed with which they had left."

Such is the last trace of the old soul-land which we meet in

classical literature.   In the shrinkage of the known world
which followed the fall of the Western empire it has got localized
in Britain—and apparently in Wales or Cornwall!

In its next appearance the Earthly Paradise is entirely
changed, and in Christian hands has ceased to be the habitation of departed spirits, and has shifted altogether its position
on the earth.   So greatly is its character altered, that many
authorities would derive the mediæval legends dealing with it,
not from any pagan source, but entirely from the literal
interpretations of the Bible which obtained in the middle ages.
It hardly seems to be due to the principle enunciated at the
beginning ; and only in its wider developments is it influenced
by the old Greek or Keltic beliefs.   The true and orthodox
terrestrial Paradise of the middle ages lay, not across the
mysterious Western ocean, but in the equally mysterious lands
of the sun-rising.   It was universally identified with the
Garden of Eden, in which Adam and Eve had been placed ;
and it was therefore impossible to seek it in any other quarter
than the East.   Now in mediæval times the limits of the known
world were shrunken far within the boundaries known to the
later Roman geographers, Ptolemy, Strabo, and their fellows.
In the twelfth or thirteenth century the Western world knew
almost exactly as much, or rather as little, of Asia as Herodotus
had known 1,600 years before.   The very stories which the
father of history related of Indians and gold-producing ants, of
griffins and Arimaspi, had returned to their old localities in
Central Asia, though in Roman days they had for some time
continually receded further and further into the unknown
North-east.   Now again, as in the fifth century before Christ,
men believed that beyond an India of no great extent, there
lay no more inhabited lands, but only desert and sea,   But
unlike the ancients, the mediævals placed in the furthest part
of this region the Earthly Paradise, either as an oasis in an
expanse of rocks and sands, or as an island in an unnavigable
ocean.   Sometimes we read of it as inaccessible by reason of
lands of mist and darkness, or insurmountable precipices ;
sometimes it is tempestuous seas or rivers which bar the way.
But beyond them, if a man could but penetrate, he would find
the Eden where our first father had dwelt, where rise the four

mysterious rivers, and where grows every tree that is pleasant to the sight or good for food.

"There," says Neckam, "is a beautiful land where whole tracts are overgrown with the noble vine ; there are clear springs, and groves watered with pleasant streams. Glorious is the fruit which enriches its gardens, and no sterile tree can grow in its soil. Never do storms come near it, nor violent winds, but there always blows a gentle breeze. Thither never came the waters of the all-destroying Flood."

"In that Paradise," says in a more prosaic strain the author of the Polychronicon, "is everything that is congruent to life. It hath salubrity and wholesomeness, for it enjoyeth an equal temperance, feeling neither coldness nor heat, insomuch that nothing that has life may in any wise die within it. In testimony whereof, Enoch and Elias wait yet therein, having the bodies with which they left this life still uncorrupt. Moreover, that place has all pleasantness, for it is the store-house of all that is fair, where no tree ever loseth its leaves, and no flower withereth. There is mirth and sweetness from the fruit and trees that grow there, for every tree that is therein is sweet to eat and fair to see. And there is security, for no harm may come near it, nor even did the water of the great Flood come nigh."

Thus far all the authorities coincide ; but there were certain points in the earthly Paradise which gave rise to dire controversies. Various authors give various situations for it. In some it is a great island lying south and east of " Inde the Great," apparently occupying the place of Ceylon. Thus it appears in the "Hereford Mappa Mundi" as a circular island enclosed by a wall, lying just opposite to the mouth of the Ganges. But a little later, when Ceylon was more or less known, it receded to a continental position somewhere in China. Still later, when thirteenth-century Europe had heard of Cathay and the Great Khan, the insular theory was revived ; and as lying south of China and east of India, we must identify the final position of Eden with Sumatra, Java, or some of the islands in that part of the world.

Here lay Paradise in the early fifteenth century, and from this spot it vanished into nothingness, when in the end of that century the voyages of the Portuguese and Spaniards revealed both East and West, and banished from the world numbers of the old myths which had survived for so many ages. Vasco de Gama, Columbus and Magellan destroyed not only the impass-

ability of the Cape of Storms, the unlimited breadth of the
Atlantic, and the unorthodoxy of a belief in the antipodes, but
also the beautiful old idea of the Earthly Paradise. Men
might still sail to seek Ophir, or the North-west Passage, or
El Dorado, but no room was left on earth for the terrestrial
Eden. If ever we find it mentioned in books of the sixteenth
century, it is because an author is discussing where *was* the
Paradise of Genesis, not where *is* the beautiful land in which
the fourteenth century believed.

In the vague and misty ideas which were entertained in the
middle ages about Eastern geography, a little disagreement
about the exact *position* of Paradise was not likely to cause
very hot disputes. But it was otherwise concerning the shape
of that locality : here the wise geographers and chroniclers
had their own inner consciousness to draw on, and three sets of
views were put forth, whose supporters argued angrily against
each other's suppositions. Now no one doubted that the
terrestrial Paradise was not touched by the Flood (for, said
they, if it had been, we should have been told of it), and that it
was quite or almost inaccessible to man. The oldest way of
explaining these two facts was by making Paradise a pillar-
shaped mountain, with a table-land on its summit, but with
steep and inaccessible sides. So great was its height, that we
are assured that it all but touched the orbit of the moon.
This being the case, we can easily understand that it was
undisturbed by the Flood ; for although the waters rose forty
fathoms above the highest hills, the summit of the mountain of
Paradise was forty fathoms above the highest limit of the
Deluge. Adding these eighty fathoms to the highest mountain
known to a twelfth-century chronicler, we can obtain an idea
of the distance from the earth at which the moon was supposed
to revolve, for Paradise *very nearly* touches the moon's orbit.
Allowing 20,000 feet altogether as a fair margin, we cannot but
think that the twelfth century was a little weak in its astronomy ; indeed we may be deeply thankful that its calculations are not exactly true—for who can tell what dreadful
results might not follow if the moon came into collision with
Mount Everest, or any other elevation rising a little above the
height which was allowed to Paradise ?

The same school of geographers who held this view on the moon-orbit, maintained that the world was not a globe, but a mass of land, of various heights in different places, which rests upon the face of a limitless ocean.   They argued that Scripture speaks of " the waters under the earth," and that this would be an incorrect description if the ocean merely formed part of the surface of a terrestrial globe.   The earth must, therefore, be a body placed upon the level face of the circumfluent ocean. Moreover, so small did they imagine the world to be, that they objected to the globe-theory that the mountains of the world, and more especially the mountain of Paradise, would prevent the earth from being a perfect figure.   So Neckam writes :—

> "Ausi sunt veteres terram censere rotundam,
> Quamvis emineat montibus illa suis.
> Quamvis deliciis ornatus apex Paradisi
> Lunarem tangit vertice pæne globum."

It was the same school who deduced from Ezekiel v. 5 the fact that a circle drawn from the centre of Jerusalem, with the radius to the extreme west of Spain, would exactly embrace the whole land of the world ; for was it not written, " This is Jerusalem : I have set it in the *midst* of the nations round about " ; and " God is King of old, working salvation in the *middle* of the earth " ?   So map-making was simplified or complicated (opinions may differ on the subject) by making all the earth centre round Judea, to the sad distortion of out-lying peninsulas like Norway or India.

The second school of geographers were prepared to admit that the world was round, and maintained that Paradise was no lofty mountain, but a spacious country, "not less in size than Egypt or India " ; for, said they, if Adam had not sinned it would have had to contain the whole human race, and must therefore be of no mean size.   Again, the idea that Paradise was the highest point of earth was displeasing to them.

"We must not think," says Higden, "as do some men of small intellect and little experience, that Paradise is far away from all habit-able lands, and reaches up to the orbit of the moon—for neither reason nor nature allows this belief.   Neither air nor water could support the weight of such a burden.   Moreover, the element of fire, as all wise

men agree, fills a space between our lower air and the orbit of the
moon. The summit, then, of Paradise would be in the region of fire,.
where no vegetable can possibly exist, nor human life. How, then,
can Adam or the tree of life have been there ? And again, if the place
were so high, its summit would continually be getting between us and
the moon, and causing eclipses, especially in Eastern lands. No one,
however, has ever seen or heard of such an eclipse. Besides this, four
rivers rise in Paradise, which flow through well-known countries ;
therefore it must be contiguous to our habitable world, or the rivers
could never reach us. The rational view of Paradise is, that it is a
large fair region in the extreme East, only separated from the homes of
men by that fiery wall, the sword of the cherubim, of which we read in
Genesis."

So much for the views of home-staying sages on the terrestrial Eden. Let us now turn to the testimony of a traveller.
Inventive as was the unscrupulous author of *Sir John Mande-
ville's Travels*—who veiled his real identity under the name of
that apocryphal knight—there seems no reason to doubt that
he had some personal acquaintance with the East. Thus he
attained some knowledge both of India and of Cathay, and
therefore localized it in neither, but to the south-east, "hard by
the land of Prester John." He is gracious enough to confess that
he never went there himself, both because of the distance and of
his own unworthiness, but gives us some accounts drawn from
conversations with those who had striven to approach it :—

"Paradys," he had learnt, "is enclosed all about with a wall, of
which men know not the matter. For it is covered all over with mosse
as it seemeth, and is not of the natur of stone. And that wall stretcheth
from the south to the north, and hath but one entry, that is closed with
fire burning, so that men may not enter. And ye should understand
that no man may by any means approach to that Paradys. For by
land no man may go for the wild beasts that are in the deserts, and for
the high mountains and huge rocks, and for the dark places that be
there right many. And by the rivers may no man go, for that the
water runneth rudely and sharpely, because that it cometh down
outrageously from the high places above. And it runneth in so great
waves that no ship may not row nor sail against it ; and the water
roareth so, and maketh so huge noise and so great tempest, that no
man may hear other in the ship, though he cry with all the might he
have, in the highest voice that he may. Many great lords have essayed
with great will many times for to pass by that river toward Paradys,
with full great companies ; but they might not speed in their voyage :

and many died for weariness of rowing against the strong waves; and many became blind, and many deaf, for the dashing and noise of the water; and some were perished and lost within the waves,—so that no mortalle man may approach to that place without special grace of God: therefore of Paradys can I say you no more."

Among these great lords whom the pseudo-Mandeville mentions, was, according to Paludanus, no less a person than Alexander the Great himself. Indeed we are told that his Eastern conquests were especially undertaken for the purpose of attaining to the Earthly Paradise. When he had reached India, and was nearing his goal, some of his soldiers captured a venerable old man in a ravine, and were about to conduct him to their king, when he said, "Go and announce to Alexander that it is in vain that he seeks Paradise; all his efforts will be fruitless, for the way of Paradise is humility, a way of which he knows nothing." And in truth Alexander could pursue his purpose no longer from that day, because of the mutiny of his soldiers, who would go no further from their native land.

We have found only one account of a man who was actually asserted to have entered the terrestrial Paradise. This is the tale of the Norwegian Eirek.[1] This Saga of Eirek, however, hardly purports to be an actual itinerary, and was allowed even in the middle ages to be more of a religious novel than a sober narrative. Eirek, we are told, made a vow to find the Earthly Paradise, and having obtained information as to its locality from the Byzantine Emperor, diligently sought for it to the east of India. At last, after passing through a gloomy forest, he came upon a narrow strait separating him from a very beautiful land. From his instructions he recognized that these were Paradise and the river Pison, and determined to cross the water, though the only mode of access to the distant shore was a narrow stone bridge, which was completely blocked up by a dragon of portentous size. The Norseman drew his sword and deliberately walked into the monster's mouth, which, to his surprise, did not close on him, but vanished. Thus he passed without obstacle to the further shore, where he found the usual characteristics of the Earthly Paradise—

[1] See Baring-Gould's *Curious Myths of the Middle Ages.*

undying flowers, marvellous fruits, clear rivulets, but no living being.

At last he came upon a sort of tower suspended in mid-air, to which access could be had by climbing a slender ladder. On ascending to this tower Eirek found a dinner thoughtfully prepared for him in one of its chambers, of which he partook, and soon fell asleep. In his sleep he saw in a vision his guardian angel, who promised him a safe return to Norway, but added that, at the end of ten years, he would be carried away from the earth never to return again. Eirek retraced his steps over the bridge, and through the simulacrum of the dragon, which was apparently nothing more than a show to appal the faint-hearted. After long travelling he came back to his native town of Drontheim, and told his story, to the great edification of all true Christian folk. Ten years after, as he went to prayer one morning, he was caught up and carried away by God's Spirit, and was never again seen of men.

The saga of Eirek is evidently in great part allegorical : we seem to recognize the narrow strait of death which separates the Christian pilgrim from Paradise ; and in the dragon, death itself, terrible to the coward, but which, when resolutely faced by the brave man, turns out to be an empty horror with no power to harm.

There are yet two more points connected with the terrestrial Eden which must be mentioned before we pass on to the consideration of the Western deathless land, in which there was also belief in mediæval times. Firstly, as to the rivers of Paradise mentioned in Genesis, the geographers universally identified the Pison with the Ganges, and the Gihon with the Nile ; but how to bring the sources of these two rivers into juxtaposition with those of the Tigris and Euphrates was indeed a hard task. Those who maintained that Paradise was an island, generally explained the matter by alleging, that although the Ganges might *seem* to rise in North India, the Tigris in Armenia, and so on, yet really the first appearances of these rivers were not their sources. The real sources were in Paradise, from whence the water was conveyed in a mysterious kind of submarine and subterranean canal to the places where the rivers apparently take their rise.

Those who made Paradise continental had not quite such a hard task in their explanation. They made out that the Ganges, Euphrates, and Tigris actually flowed down from Paradise, over whose boundary they fell in a cataract, which finally divided into three streams. Moreover, they added that the roar of this cataract was so tremendous, that those who approached too near were usually rendered deaf for the rest of their life, and that the children of a tribe of savages who dwelt not far off, were even born deaf, from their ancestors having lived for generations near the cataract. The last thing which we must mention concerning the Earthly Paradise is, that there was a difference of opinion as to whether the famous Phœnix lived *in* Paradise, or merely close to it. The former view was not so generally held as the latter. It was, however, supported by some who brought forward the passage of Claudian, who speaks of the dwelling of the Phœnix as the " green grove surrounded by circumfluent ocean, beyond the Indians, close to the sunrising." This might easily be identified with Paradise. The majority, however, placed the home of the Phœnix close to but not within the terrestrial Eden. So we read that Alexander the Great, though he could never reach the earthly Paradise, did come upon the Phœnix in the most easterly point of his expedition, within the same grove where were the talking trees of the sun. So, too, Neckam places the bird in Panchæa in India ; and in other authors it is found in its old Herodotean position in Arabia, where it appears in the " Hereford Mappa Mundi."

So much for the Eastern Paradise, the ancient seat of our first parents. We must now endeavour to give some ideas of a more hazy and mysterious land, the Western region of unending spring and perpetual youth, which Morris represents his seafarers as seeking in his poem " The Earthly Paradise." Although the voice of ecclesiastical tradition pronounced that in the East, and there alone, was the happy land to be sought, there was nevertheless a mass of legends which insisted on placing it in the West. A very large number of these stories are derived from Welsh or Irish sources, and it seems almost certain that they are not mere mediæval inventions, but survivals of the old Keltic mythology. Like most other nations, the Kelts had imagined for themselves a soul-land across the Western ocean : and when they were converted to Christianity, and forbidden to look either for a heaven on earth, or for a Paradise in the West, they did not entirely give up their old belief, but merely modified it to a form which did not clash with the new religion. The Western land might not be the earthly Paradise, but none the less it might exist. Such was the true origin of the Land of Avilion or Avalon, the Isle of Apples, to which King Arthur was borne away, and also of the long-sought Isle of St. Brandan. Moreover, the King Arthur of more sober history (I mean the authentic *dux bellorum*, not the legendary monarch of all Britain), is now asserted by many writers to have been a Keltic demi-god long before he became a Damnonian prince. Sad to say, the all-devouring Sun-myth-theory laid claim to him, as it has to most other heroes, and we were invited to recognize in him the sun sailing into the Western shades in his golden boat, or wrestling at his end with the dark clouds of evening. Arthur, then, to the votaries of this school was a god brought down by euhemerizing means to the form of a man, not a man raised by exaggerated traditions to an over-important place in history. Moreover, if we take this view, certain points in the Arthur of the romances seem well explained by it. Thus we can understand his mysterious and apparently superhuman birth, the strange legend which tells how he was not really King Uther's son, but was brought to Tintagel by the magic ship, and left on the shore a new-born babe in Merlin's hands. Thus we can see how he is claimed as brother by the Queen Morgan le Fay, who is certainly no mere human being. Thus it is only right that this mysterious sister should bear him away, after that last dim battle in the West, to some fair land beyond the sea, in the barge wherein Sir Bedivere placed him. He is no man merely departing " to heal him of his deadly wound," but a superhuman being returning to the place from which he came.

And as Arthur is held to be no mere Damnonian hero, so Avilion is no mere Glastonbury, as the materializing chronicler would make it. It is the old Keltic soul-land beyond the Western ocean. We may notice, in confirmation of this, that the mediæval chroniclers of Glastonbury, when they identify it

with Avilion, generally add that the Welsh call the place
Inysvitrin, the Isle of Glass.   Now in the Irish legends a hill or
island of glass is invariably mentioned as one of the marvellous
features of Fathinnis, the land of departed souls.   It is notice-
able that the Morgan le Fay, the lady of Avilion, has not from
a goddess become an evil spirit, as did Hörsel the goddess of
the German Venusberg ; she is neither angel nor fiend, but a
fairy, superhuman without being satanic.

After the Arthurian legend had become popular, Avilion
was made the resting place of other heroes.   Ogier the Dane
came thither, at the end of his life, to rest after all his toils in
the castle of Morgan le Fay.   So did the famous Paladins, and
even, as some say, the great Kaiser Charles himself.   In short,
it became a sort of Elysian Fields for all the heroes whom the
mediæval mind could admire, but at the same time could not
conceive as fulfilling the ideal of the Christian saint.   The
Christian heaven above was the fit place for the ecstatic
adoration of holy men and martyrs, but it was not suited for
the heroes of the romances ; for them there was imagined a
more earthly resting-place, a fairy-land where they might for
ever enjoy youth and quiet repose.

After Avilion, the most famous legendary Western land was
undoubtedly the Isle of St. Brandan.   Brandan is said to
have been an Irish monk, and abbot of Birr, at some time in
the seventh century.   He was induced to undertake his
marvellous voyage by a monk, who told him that he had
sailed from Ireland till he had at last come to Paradise, which
was an island full of joy and mirth, where the earth was as
bright as the sun, and everything was glorious, and the half-
year he had spent there had slipped by as a few moments.   On
his return to his abbey his garments were still fragrant with
the odours of Paradise.   Excited by this story, Brandan
embarked in a vessel with some of his monks.   We are told in
the oldest form of the legend that he sailed due east from
Ireland ; but as this must have necessarily brought him to
England, or some part of North-western Europe, we soon find
his voyage transferred to the West.   The marvels which he
met were extraordinary.   Among the first was the astounding spectacle of Judas Iscariot afloat upon an iceberg, who

explained to the saint that for one day in the year he was permitted to cool himself from the fires of hell, in consideration of
a single good deed which he had performed on earth.   Matthew
Arnold has versified this episode of the Brandan legend.   After
passing through a sea filled with icebergs and vexed with
storms, Brandan reached a more clement region, where he first
came on an island inhabited by sheep alone, which, in consequence of the luxuriance of the herbage, grew as large as oxen.
Soon after, the saint came to another island, where he found to
his surprise an abbey of twenty-four monks, who informed him
that in that isle was ever fair weather, and none of them had
ever been sick since they came thither.   Yet further on was a
third island, where was, in the words of the legend, " a fair
well, and a great tree full of boughs, and on every bough sat a
fair bird, and they sat so thick on the tree that no leaf of it
might be seen, the number of the birds being very great, and
they sang so merrily that it was a heavenly noise to hear.
Anon one of the birds flew from the tree to Brandan, and with
flickering of his wings made a full merry noise, like a fiddle,
that the saint never heard so joyful a melodie.   Then did the
holy man command the bird to tell him why they sat so thick
upon the tree."   The answer of the bird was surprising : he
explained that he and his companions were once angels—
namely, those of the heavenly host who in the time of Lucifer's
rebellion refused to assist either God or His enemies.   In
punishment for this they were doing penance in the form of
birds, but, after many years, were to be readmitted to their
lost estate.   Leaving the island of birds, the voyagers came to
another land, " the fairest country," we are told, " that any
man might see—which was so clear and so bright that it was
an heavenly sight to behold ; and all the trees were charged
with ripe fruit and herbes full of flowers,—in which land they
walked forty days and could not see the end thereof ; there
was alway day and never night, and the country was attem-
perate, neither too hot nor too cold."   At last, however,
Brandan and his companions came to a broad river, on the
banks of which stood a young man, apparently an angel, who
told him that this stream divided the world in twain, and that
no living man might cross it.   On the further bank they could

see the true Paradise, but might not approach it ; wherefore they retraced their steps, and set sail for Ireland. They reached their country in safety, but were surprised to hear that they had been absent, not a few months, but seven long years.

Such is the legend of St. Brandan, and the existence of these marvellous isles to which he had attained was firmly believed for centuries. Sometimes men declared that they were not far from the west of Ireland, and could be seen in clear weather ; but whenever an expedition was fitted out to reach them, they somehow seemed to disappear. More frequently the islands were described as lying beyond the Canaries. There lay, as the Portuguese declared, the island which had been sometimes lighted upon by accident, but which when sought could never be found. Its existence was regarded as so certain that we are told of one adventurer who received a formal grant of it "when it should be found." And when the Portuguese Crown ceded to Spain its rights over the Canaries, the island of St. Brandan was specially included, being described as " the island which has not yet been found." In 1526, 1570, and again in 1605, expeditions set sail from the Canaries to discover this land ; but all met with uniform failure. Still the belief died hard, and did not become extinct for many years after the third of these unsuccessful voyages. Any one who has the curiosity to look over the old atlases of the seventeenth century, will find as late as 1630, the Isle of Brandan delineated as an island of no great size, lying west of Ireland and north-west of the Canaries ; it is even said that in one map published as late as the beginning of the eighteenth century, this fabulous land is still indicated.

There is yet remaining one more belief which ought to be mentioned in this place—that of the Fountain of Youth. The original locality, it is true, was in the East as is shown in the fabulous letter of Prester John to the Byzantine Emperor Manuel ; indeed the Pseudo-Mandeville says that he found it himself in Ceylon, only it was not true that one draught of it gave perpetual youth—this was only acquired by a regular course of several years' drinking. He had only time to try it for two days, found it pleasant to the taste, and thought he felt all the better for it, but experienced no occult effect. However, in the fourteenth century the fountain migrated to the most western of the Canaries. It was not even destroyed by the discovery of America, but was only relegated to one of the Bahamas in the West Indies. Finally, it receded to the mainland of North America, and was sought by Soto in Florida. There, as was to be expected, it was not to be found, and it became obsolete long before the day of the final disappearance of St. Brandan's Isle. Two more beliefs which attributed wonders to the West may be passed over as not bearing any relation to the Earthly Paradise, though proceeding probably from similar sources in the old Keltic mythology. These were St. Patrick's Purgatory, a sort of subterranean soul-land, modified by Christianity into an entrance to the region of purification by suffering; and the island in a lake of Ulster in which no one could die. There, as we read, when the inhabitants reached extreme old age and became nothing but a burden to themselves, they had to be carried to the mainland before their spirit could depart. This is no doubt another perverted form of the old belief in the deathless land of the West.

In conclusion, there is one more view which we venture, with all deference, to suggest. Surely the mediæval folk were much the happier for all these ideas. Our own map of the world is dreadfully deficient in romance: it is really very hard to feel an eager interest in the exploration of Central Africa, or the discovery of the South Pole. If some traveller does delete the last white patch in the map of the Congo Free State, or push up some ice-crack to an open Antarctic Sea, we do not expect to gain any great good from it, or to hear any particularly startling news about these regions. It will be the difficulty of the task, not its results, that will direct attention to them. The discovery of a few more tribes of thoroughly uninteresting negroes, or a few more ice-blocked bays, has nothing in it to stir the heart of the world. We look for no marvels to be unveiled, no great problems that are to be solved. The naturalist may indeed be gladdened by the knowledge of a new species of Arctic gull, or a few varieties of tropical plants; the collector of folk-lore

may rejoice over some new and original negro funeral ceremonies ; the merchant may find a new market for his cottons,
—but these things will not prove very interesting to the mass
of mankind.

Now in the middle ages everything was exactly the reverse
of this. The greater part of the world's surface was still
unknown. There was hardly anything on which the adventurous traveller might not come. He might reach populous
lands and cities, rich far beyond the ideas of the European
world ; he might, on the other hand, come to the land of the
griffin and the flying serpent, or, as Shakespeare puts it in
Othello, to

> "antres vast and deserts idle,
> Rough quarries, rocks and hills whose heads touch heaven,"

and to

> "The Cannibals that each other eat,
> The Anthropophagi, and men whose heads
> Do grow beneath their shoulders."

There was a glorious uncertainty in these voyages of discovery :
one man would find the passage to India round the Cape of
Good Hope, or kingdoms like Mexico or Peru ; another would
follow after equally uncertain rumours, and meet nothing but
disaster, or even never be heard of again. Discovery could
not possibly manage to be uninteresting in those days ; and
as if there were not enough real marvels to be found, the
legends were continually holding out fabulous ones for the
adventurous to seek. Now of all the legends, it can hardly be
disputed that the legends of the Earthly Paradise were the
most attractive. Men might not desire at once to leave their
present life for the search after the beautiful land of endless
rest without death ; but still it was a comfortable feeling to
know that such a land *did* exist. If a man's life went hopelessly wrong, if he was in despair and felt that the world was
out of joint, there was still this refuge left for him ; it only
needed a little more perseverance and courage than that of
the last voyager who had *almost* reached the happy land, and
then there would be for ever a quiet and blissful repose in
some Avilion of the Western sea. We do not say that the

men of the fourteenth or fifteenth century were happier than
we of the twentieth ; but certainly it *was* something not to be
bound down by the prosaic bonds of that knowledge which
forbids us to dream that we may

" Some day be at rest,
And follow the shining sinking sun down into the shining West."

The world grows terribly small, and as it shrinks the glory
of romance and adventure dies away.

THE END.

CPSIA information can be obtained
at www.ICGtesting.com
Printed in the USA
LVHW081933020420
652027LV00013B/363

9 781346 356716